FUN
FAMILY
VACATIONS
in the
SOUTHEAST

Kent & Sharron Hannon

PEACHTREE PUBLISHERS
Atlanta

For Shane and Blake

Published by
PEACHTREE PUBLISHERS, LTD.
494 Armour Circle, NE
Atlanta, Georgia 30324

Manufactured in the United States of America

Cover design by Jennifer Ellison
Book design by Candace J. Magee
Composition by Kathryn D. Mothershed

Photographs:

p. 11   Panama City Beach, FL / courtesy Panama City Chamber of Commerce
p. 47   Downtown Atlanta, GA
p. 79   Colonial Williamsburg's Historic Area Forge, VA / courtesy Colonial Williamsburg Foundation
p. 107   Great Smoky Mountains National Park, NC
p. 133   Amelia Island Plantation, Amelia Island, FL / © Lynne Frazer
p. 179   Big Thunder Mountain Railroad, Magic Kingdom, Orlando, FL © 1990 The Walt Disney Company
p. 239   The Hydra-maniac, Wet 'n Wild, Orlando, FL

Library of Congress Cataloging in Publication Data

Hannon, Kent.
   Fun family vacations in the Southeast / Kent and Sharron Hannon.
     p. cm.
   Includes index.
   ISBN 1-56145-050-2 (trade paper)
    1. Southern States—Description and travel—1981- —Guide-books.
  2. Family recreation—Southern States—Guide-books.   I. Hannon,
Sharron. II. Title.
F207.3.H35 1991
917.504'63—dc20

C O N T E N T S

INTRODUCTION

The origins of this book date back to the 1950s when our parents were in charge of planning family vacations and we were just the kids in the back seat. Interstates hadn't been invented, automobiles weren't equipped with air conditioning and then, as now, family vacations didn't always go smoothly. Ours included.

Sharron grew up in Boston in the pre-Disney World days when, if you wanted to visit the Magic Kingdom, you had to go to Disneyland. Undaunted by the rigors of traveling cross-country with three kids in a station wagon, Sharron's parents set out for California. What they hadn't counted on was Sharron's younger brother being car-sick off and on for 6,000 miles.

Kent is from the Midwest and his family vacations weren't exactly idyllic either. He remembers fog-shrouded drives through the mountains of North Carolina, with his mother hiding her eyes for fear his father was going to drive off the edge of the Blue Ridge Parkway. As a kid, he saw a lot of "See Rock City!" signs, but never the real thing. And he sympathizes with Sharron's younger brother, because he used to get car-sick too.

Evidently, the good times outweighed the bad because we still reminisce about those childhood vacations and they haven't discouraged us from traveling with our own kids. Our son, Shane, was an infant when he took his first airplane ride from New York to Atlanta, and just 3 years old when he took his first overnight train trip.

We lived in the middle of Manhattan back then. Kent was a writer at *Sports Illustrated* magazine and Sharron was a freelancer at work on a book about childbirth. In 1979, shortly after the birth of our daughter, Blake, we moved to Georgia, where we've lived ever since.

Before moving to the Southeast, we had traveled there on vacations and business. But the areas we were most familiar with were Orlando, Hilton Head, Atlanta—and Jekyll Island, Ga., where we spent our honeymoon. What we've discovered after living in the Southeast for 12 years is that we're smack in the middle of the nation's No. 1 travel destination.

But don't take our word for it. As we go to press, the most recent statistics released by the U.S. Travel Data Center in Washington, D.C., show that the Southeast topped all other regions in 1989, accounting for 23 percent of domestic vacation travel. The raw data shows that Americans made more than 200 million "vacation person trips" in '89, with a vacation person trip being equivalent to someone taking at least a 100-mile trip for vacation purposes. The Southeast was No. 1 in that category in both 1988 and '89, and the '89 stats represent a whopping 30 percent gain over '88.

Why are so many Americans choosing to vacation in the Southeast?

Climate, for starters. When snow flies in the Midwest and Northeast, people who live up there can come down here and frolic in the sun. By March, we've got warm weather almost everywhere—and it lasts throughout a very long fall.

Beauty is another factor. The Southeast has gorgeous beaches along both the Atlantic and Gulf coasts, plus the breathtaking peaks and valleys of the Appalachian Mountains, which stretch through the interior of the region.

Given these natural blessings, it's no surprise that tourism is an increasingly important part of every Southeastern state's economy. This means that the welcome mat is out, and that you'll find new attractions, accommodations and restaurants popping up everywhere.

Two factors make the Southeast a particularly good place to travel with kids: it's easy to get here and the prevailing atmosphere is casual and family-oriented. With the exception of a few elegant restaurants here and there, you'll find that kids are not only tolerated but welcomed most anywhere adults are.

We know from perusing bookstores that there are a number of guidebooks about the Southeast, but we couldn't find one that focused on family travel. On the other hand, there are books about family travel, but they don't provide much coverage of the Southeast (perhaps due to the fact that the authors are from other parts of the country).

What we've written is the kind of travel book we were looking for but couldn't find. Our aim is to provide useful information for adults traveling with kids, and we've organized that information by activity instead of geography. We think it makes more sense to decide what kind of vacation you want to take first (e.g. beaches, resorts, theme parks), and then decide where you want to take it.

We've been very selective about the places we've chosen to write about. Since there's no way to offer comprehensive coverage of the Southeast without sacrificing detail—something we weren't willing to do—we didn't include every possible thing you can see and do here. Instead, we picked what we consider to be some of the best destinations and activities for family vacations and we've covered them very thoroughly. Our feeling is that if you pick up a travel book and see a two-paragraph entry on a resort like Callaway Gardens or a page or two on Walt Disney World, you're missing out on a lot of vital information.

What you'll find in this book are what might be called "consumer-tested vacations." In the two years before we sat down to write, we made whirlwind tours throughout the Southeast, kids in tow. We returned to some of our favorite places and researched others for the first time. For example, we revisited Disney World for the umpteenth time in the summer of 1989, returned to see MGM Studios and Typhoon Lagoon in the spring of 1990, then made a third trip to Orlando in the summer of '90 after Universal Studios opened.

It's a tough job but somebody's gotta do it!

Before going to press, we checked and double-checked our entries to make sure everything was up-to-date, but we can't guarantee that a restaurant won't close or a hotel property won't change hands. Please let us know if you find anything significantly different than the way we've described it.

Here's to all your family vacations. Hope you enjoy them as much as we do ours.

TRAVELING WITH KIDS

We love family vacations because they allow us to escape our day-to-day routine and have fun together. As our children grow older and become more involved in their own activities, vacations provide our best opportunity for quality "family time."

We also look on vacations as a learning experience. And we're not just talking about the history/geography lessons that you pick up by visiting various places. The subtler lessons taught on family vacations are at least as important: patience, flexibility and how to learn to enjoy new experiences.

We've written this book with the hope that it will help your family plan some great vacations. Our focus is the Southeast because statistics say it's the most popular vacation region in the U.S.—and from personal experience, we know why. We've written about places where our family has had some great times, and have tried to provide you with enough information so you can decide whether your family would enjoy a similar trip.

This is not so much a "how to travel with kids" book as it is a "where to travel with kids" book. If you need the former, try *How to Take Great Trips with Your Kids* by Sanford and Joan Portnoy or *Travel with Children* by Maureen Wheeler.

We've kept our general travel advice to a minimum, though you will find some tips on getting to your destination in this first chapter. Mainly, we concentrate on the things to do in a given area so you can think about how you'd spend your vacation there. And we go into detail about where to stay, supplying information about accommodations in a variety of price ranges and noting those which offer special family rates and kids' activities programs. We also tell you about places to eat where you can enjoy a good meal and not feel out of place because you've brought the kids along. Finally, we tell you about the best times to visit various areas, an important point to be mindful of in terms of weather, economics and seasonal activities.

When you travel with kids, a key element is planning. Which doesn't mean you need to devise a complicated schedule and stick to it religiously, but rather that you should prioritize things you want to do and work out when you want to do them. It's a good idea not to pack your days so full that you come back from vacation needing another one. Figure that with kids along you probably can't do as much in one day as you could on an all-adult outing.

And speaking of adults, we recommend that you bring some others along with you—at least on occasion. By traveling with friends or relatives, you can mix and match the kid-adult combos so that everyone gets time together and time on his or her own. And though it may take some extra work on the logistics, it's fun to travel as a group. For single parents, it's often salvation.

HOW TO GET THERE

This is a decision generally dictated by time, money, destination and personal preference. But when children are along, they're another factor to weigh.

By Plane

The best thing about air travel with children is that you get where you're going much faster than by car or train. The major problem with flying is that kids are expected to sit quietly in their seats—and if they don't, you may encounter disapproval, if not downright hostility, from your fellow passengers. So be prepared. Some suggestions:

Boarding—Many airlines will let you preboard with children, so you can get settled without the crush of other passengers. But if your child is very active, you may prefer to wait till the last minute. In either case, make a trip to the restroom before getting on the plane.

Seating—Bulkhead seating (at the front of the coach section) offers more floor space than other coach seats. There's often enough room for kids to stand and stretch, sit cross-legged on the floor, or even stretch out and sleep there. Unfortunately, the armrests on these seats don't retract— a drawback if a young child wants to lie in your lap.

Meals/snacks—Many airlines offer children's menus of the burgers-hot dogs-spaghetti variety. Some provide jars of baby food and toddler meals of cereal and fruit. Make arrangements for these when you book your reservation, then check back a few days before your flight to make sure the order made it into the computer. Regardless of whether a meal is offered on the flight, bring your own snacks (your kids may get hungry before the food arrives). And don't forget gum to help with ear-popping.

Juice boxes are another good item to bring along. If they're tipped over they don't spill much, and sucking on the little straws also helps relieve cabin pressure. If you're traveling with a non-nursing baby, be sure to have a bottle or pacifier handy at takeoff and landing.

Cockpit visits—Many airlines allow these, but you have to make arrangements before you're in the air. Some visits take place on the ground.

Fares—As we go to press, children under the age of 2 are allowed to ride free on airlines, provided they sit on their parent's lap. But the National Transportation Safety Board has petitioned the Federal Aviation Administration (FAA) to require that infants be secured in safety seats. If the FAA resists, Congress may pass legislation to mandate their use. What's not clear is who will be responsible for providing the seats. Chances are that in the future parents traveling with infants will need to bring their own car seat and pay an additional fare.

Most airlines currently offer reduced fares for children ages 2-12. And occasionally a kids-fly-free program will pop up. A travel agent can check on the best rates and latest deals and save you lots of time on the phone doing your own comparison shopping. Even if you generally like to make your own travel arrangements, we recommend purchasing airline tickets through an agent. There's no charge for the service.

By Train

Traveling by train can be an entertaining way to get where you're going—particularly if your children have never ridden a train before. A big advantage that trains have over cars and planes is that kids don't have to spend the whole trip sitting in their seats: they're free to move around and explore. Long-distance trains generally have dining cars, lounge cars where you can play board and card games, and sleeping cars.

The popularity of Amtrak, the national passenger railroad, has increased significantly over the last decade as improvements were made in accommodations and service. The railroad now runs nearly at capacity and actually turns away prospective passengers. So it's imperative to book reservations well in advance of your trip.

Amtrak offers several routes through the Southeast which will take you to or near destinations we cover in this book. The routes are outlined in *Appendix 2*. The possibility of a new line from Chicago or Detroit

> **TRAVEL TIP**
>
> ✈ Atlanta-based Delta Air Lines has made a special effort to focus marketing and services on families, even billing itself as the "Official Airline for Kids." On every flight, youngsters ages 2-12 get a cardboard Mickey Mouse visor and a copy of *Fantastic Flyer* magazine, with stories, puzzles and contests. They also receive an enrollment card for the Fantastic Flyer program which Delta launched in 1988, a year after becoming the official airline of Disneyland and Walt Disney World. Members of the Fantastic Flyer Club get goodies in the mail throughout the year.

through Atlanta to Jacksonville, Fla., is being studied but is several years away at best.

Amtrak also offers some escorted tour packages to locations in the Southeast, but these are generally more geared to adult interests.

How do you reach areas not directly served by trains? In some cases, with Amtrak Thruway bus service, which offers coordinated connecting schedules, guaranteed connections, through ticketing and fares, and direct service to and from the Amtrak rail station to selected locations. While we don't recommend long-distance bus travel with children, these relatively short hops aren't too bad.

If you'll need a car where you're going, you have two options: 1) take your own along on the auto-train (which runs between Washington, D.C., and Florida) or 2) rent a car at your destination. Hertz rental cars can be reserved at the same time you make Amtrak train reservations.

Here are some things to consider in planning a train trip with kids:

Luggage—Generally, each passenger is allowed to check up to three pieces of luggage and carry on two pieces. Be sure you have all the clothing, snacks and activity items you'll need en route in your carry-ons, since you won't be able to get to checked bags.

Clothing—Trains tend to be cool, so children will probably be most comfortable in something that covers their arms and legs. Sweatsuits (with a short-sleeved t-shirt underneath) are great because they're comfortable enough to sleep in and are easy to slip on and off. Have shorts handy once you reach a warm-weather destination.

Snacks—While food (ranging from sandwiches to full-service dining) is always available, you may want to carry some snacks with you to save money.

Sleeping—One potential hassle of long-distance train travel is trying to get some sleep. While kids are generally intrigued with the berths in a sleeping car, younger ones may be uneasy about the train's motion and may worry they'll fall out of bed. Sharing a berth may reassure the child but isn't too likely to produce much rest for the parent. If money is a concern, you may decide to save the extra expense of the sleeping car and just try to sleep in the coach car (pillows are provided and seats often have fold-out leg rests).

By Car

This is our family's favorite way to travel for the simple reason that it allows us to follow our own schedule. Having logged many, many miles on the road with our kids, we think we've figured out a few things about how to make car trips as pleasant as possible for all concerned.

The main question, of course, is how to keep the kids occupied so they don't start complaining or picking on each other as soon as you leave the driveway. We have friends who travel in a van equipped with VCR and Nintendo, and our kids think that's definitely the way to go. Our thinking on the matter is that vacations are a time to get away from it all—not take it all with you.

> **TRAVEL TIP**
>
> Don't leave crayons on the back ledge of a car with the sun beating in (as we did once). You'll end up with a waxy mess.

Still, you've got to provide some form of entertainment to help pass long hours on the road, so here are some suggestions:

Cassette tapes—Check bookstores and mail order catalogs for story and activity tapes. You can also order direct from a small company called Family Travel Tapes (9920 A-1 Parkway East, Suite 125, Birmingham, AL 35206, 205-836-0638). They've produced two 40-minute tapes and have a third in the works. A source for rental tapes of full-length books—including children's classics—is Books on Tape (PO Box 7900, Newport Beach, CA 92658, 800-626-3333).

Cassette players—Once our oldest reached his teen years, we decided a sanity-saver was to invest in small cassette players for each child—with headphones. Now they each listen to their own tapes and the adults can actually have a conversation at the same time. We bring an ample supply of batteries, plus the gizmo that plugs into the car's cigarette lighter so one of the cassette players can operate without them (available at Radio Shack).

Travel games—Milton Bradley markets a line of travel games which are small, plastic versions of such favorites as Hangman, Memory and Win, Lose or Draw. Radio Shack also has some pocket-sized LCD and battery-operated games that work well for travel. But we think the best things going are the "invisible ink" activity books—inexpensive, no mess and they're geared to different ages.

Atlases—Kids like to find where they are and where they're going. For this purpose, atlases are better than maps, which get torn and are impossible to refold. You can also make up geography games (guessing state capitals, naming states in regions) and use the atlas to check answers.

Comfort is another important factor in keeping a car full of happy campers. Some recommendations:

❏ Bring pillows. Kids are far more likely to nap in the car if they have one. We also bring a couple of extra small pillows for the adults—one for the navigator to use for 40 winks and one for the driver to tuck behind a tired neck or back.

❏ Get sun screens for the windows. Otherwise you'll hear moans that "the sun is in my eyes/I'm too hot." Screens come in two varieties: retractable shades or tinted plastic shields that attach to windows via suction cups.

❏ Have drinks and snacks accessible. Juice boxes or ice water in a thermos are better choices than cans of sugary, caffeine-laden sodas. And apples or boxes of raisins beat bags of salty chips. (Now all you have to do is convince your kids.)

❏ Make periodic stops. Don't go more than a few hours without taking a stretch break. Keep an eye out for roadside rest areas on the interstates. You'll find picnic tables, restrooms and grassy areas where kids can run. Or stop at a fast-food place with a playground and give them 15 minutes to blow off steam.

❏ Avoid jamming the car so full that no one can move. This is easier said than done, especially if—like us—you drive a compact car. But give some real thought to what can be kept in the trunk versus what must go in the back seat.

❏ Keep backseat clutter under control. Purchase over-the-seat organizers with pockets and use them to stash stuff. (A mail order source for these and other useful car-travel items is Lillian Vernon, Virginia Beach, VA 23479-0002, 804-430-1500.) In addition, let each child carry a small bag or backpack and be responsible for keeping his or her junk in it, not all over the car. And don't forget litter bags for trash.

T R A V E L   T I P

Trip routing is one of the benefits of membership in the American Automobile Association (AAA). Their national travel department is in contact with state highway departments for updates on construction delays and other potential traffic bottlenecks, which they can help you avoid. Check your phone book for a nearby chapter or contact their headquarters at 8111 Gatehouse Rd., Falls Church, VA 22047 (703-222-6000).

WHERE TO STAY

In the other chapters in this book we go into details about where to stay at various destinations. But here is some general information to keep in mind when making your selections.

First of all, the good news is that many chains are now marketing to families, not just business travelers. What this means is that it's getting more and more common to find kids-stay-free deals. Some chains (Days Inn and Sheraton, for example) also include free meals for kids during certain seasons or at selected sites.

How do you find out about these offers? Check the ads in the Sunday travel section of big-city newspapers (if you don't live in a big city, go to the library). Or contact chains directly for information. Note that we've listed 800-numbers in the appendix, rather than repeating them throughout the book.

In addition to bargains, you can also find special activities for kids. For instance, in 1989 Hyatt Hotels and Resorts inaugurated

> **TRAVEL TIP**
>
> Many chains are now marketing to families, not just business travelers.

a kids' program called Camp Hyatt at many of its properties. For a fee, children 15 and under can participate in supervised camp activities—which range from sand-castle building to museum tours, depending on the location. At some Holiday Inns you'll find Holidome indoor recreation centers with ping-pong tables, mini golf, video games and so forth. Kids love 'em.

Another boon for family travelers is the growth of the all-suite motel/hotel business. First introduced in the Sixties, this concept has really taken off in the past few years and now several chains are getting into the act.

What we like about suites is that they give the adults some measure of privacy, a treasured commodity when traveling with kids. Plus, they generally have at least a mini-refrigerator and microwave, if not a full-scale kitchen, so you can save some money by eating in.

Some details on two of the largest all-suite chains:

Embassy Suites Hotels—Each suite in these high-rise hotels has a bedroom (with choice of king-sized bed or two double beds) and a living room with a sofa bed. Rollaways are also available in some locations, but since these rooms are fairly compact, you'll find it's a tight squeeze to fit one in. Cribs are available at all locations and they're free. The fact that there's only one bathroom is something of a drawback, but at least there are two TVs. Other features include a mini-refrigerator, microwave, coffeemaker and wet bar. Kids 12 and under stay free. Best deal about Embassy Suites: the free cooked-to-order breakfast buffet served each morning in the lobby atrium. Most properties also have an on-site restaurant.

Residence Inn by Marriott—These are two-story units with a residential neighborhood feel. Two floor plans are offered: studios and "penthouse" suites. The studio has a sleeping and living area, but no doors or partitions separate the two and the sofa does not pull out to a bed. The penthouse has a queen-sized bed in an upstairs loft and a bed that pulls out of the wall below. In the penthouse, you also get two bathrooms and two TVs. Both layouts have fully equipped kitchens, right down to the microwave with free popcorn. A complimentary continental breakfast is offered in a reception area near the registration desk, and cribs are free at all locations. No on-site restaurant.

You'll find a range in prices as well as amenities in all-suite properties. At the economy end of the line are the new Days Suites (an addition to the Days Inns chain) and Comfort Suites (from Quality Corp., which also owns Quality Inns, Quality Suites and Comfort Inns).

Speaking of prices, we do not list specifics with properties described in this book for two reasons. One, they change frequently and would soon be out of date. Two, the regular price listing (known as the "rack rate") doesn't take into account special packages and discounts. For example, many big-city hotels offer a bargain weekend rate to fill rooms that business travelers have vacated. By planning accordingly, you can get deluxe accommodations at a reasonable price.

But what if your main concern is to sleep cheap, especially when traveling on the way to your destination? Be aware that the budget motel industry has segmented recently into a couple of tiers. The very cheapest places offer minimal services and few amenities. Rooms will be small and you'll probably find only a shower (no tub). If kids don't stay free, the additional charge per person could put the rate at or higher than what you'd pay for a nicer economy chain nearby.

> **TRAVEL TIP**
>
> If you're going to need a crib, be sure to ask for one when you make your hotel/motel reservation—don't wait until you arrive at the registration desk. Availability is usually limited.

Among the chains we recommend for value and amenities are:

Hampton Inns—This is the budget arm of Holiday Inns, with close to 300 locations, primarily in the Southeast. Kids 18 and under stay free when sharing a room with one or both parents. Cribs are also free. A complimentary continental breakfast that includes cereal is offered in the lobby or a reception area, and there's a free in-room movie channel plus a pay-per-view selection.

La Quinta Inns—This Texas-based chain has gotten high marks for value from both consumer and industry publications. All 200 locations (many in the Southeast) are approved by the American Automobile Association. Kids 18 and under stay free when sharing their parents' room. Cribs are free, but there is a charge for roll-away beds.

WHERE TO EAT

There are three general categories of restaurants: fine dining, casual and fast-food. In general, fine dining is not something you do with kids. Some upscale establishments tolerate children, but only if they're well-dressed and well-mannered. And worrying about proper behavior all through a meal is not much fun for parents or kids.

Nevertheless, we haven't eliminated this category from our book. Especially at resort and city destinations, we've noted some restaurants that we highly recommend. But make arrangements for the kids so you can enjoy a peaceful, adults-only meal. Many hotels offer or can recommend babysitting services. Others have on-site evening programs for kids, which usually include dinner and a movie or other entertainment. They'll have fun and you'll get a needed break.

Most of the restaurants we discuss in this book fall into the casual dining category—a popular and fast-growing segment of the industry. We make specific recommendations in the various chapters, but there are also several chains that we think are a good bet wherever the location. Among these are:

Chili's—Rapidly spreading in Georgia, Florida and other Southeastern locations, this Dallas-based chain is a favorite of ours. The decor is colorful, the service friendly and the menu ranges from a garlicy shrimp Caesar salad to good-sized burgers of all descriptions. Plus soups, nachos and, of course, chili.

Red Lobster—These family-oriented seafood restaurants are extraordinarily popular because the food is good and there's plenty of it. The children's menu (age 10 and under) offers more variety than most and is printed with clever games to keep them busy until the first course arrives. To avoid waiting in line for a table, eat early or late.

Morrison's Cafeterias—You'll find these at malls throughout the Southeast and they're a good place for a reasonably quick, reasonably priced meal (provided you don't load up on desserts and extras). The menu is home-style Southern and you'll find several selections of entrées and vegetables. Children's plates are available.

Shoney's—If you want to tank up with a big breakfast before starting a long day of sightseeing, you won't find more food at a better price than at Shoney's breakfast bar, which is available every day of the week. And since it's buffet-style, you can eat and run.

There's no need to say much about fast-food restaurants since they're usually a mainstay of American family life whether at home or on the road. But we'll note for the record that our kids are nuts about Wendy's Superbar and it's a change from the usual burger/chicken choices.

BEACHES

Myrtle Beach

Hilton Head

Jekyll Island

Gulf Shores

Atlantic Ocean

Emerald
Coast

Panama City
Beach

Gulf of Mexico

GULF SHORES ✪ EMERALD COAST ✪ PANAMA CITY BEACH

✪ HILTON HEAD

✪ JEKYLL ISLAND

✪ MYRTLE BEACH

BEACHES

As you might expect in a book about vacations in the Southeast, there are lots of references to beaches in these pages. We cover Miami Beach in the CITIES chapter and St. Augustine Beach in HISTORY PLACES. Two of our featured resorts—Amelia Island and Kiawah Island—are located on the Atlantic Ocean. A third, South Seas Plantation, is on the Gulf of Mexico and a fourth, Marriott Bay Point Resort, is just a stone's throw from the Gulf.

The beach areas covered in this chapter are places where the primary drawing card is sand and surf, and the main activities are beach-related: swimming, sailing, shelling, sunbathing and watersports. Which is not to say you won't be tempted by the activities and attractions we've listed in the "Things to Do" and "Shopping/Nearby Fun" sections—a list which goes on and on. We've also included some sightseeing trips to forts, botanical gardens and zoos. But if you prefer to just relax by the ocean, that's permitted.

Shelling is a good family beach activity, and most public libraries have books which can be xeroxed before you leave home in order to help kids identify what they collect. One rule to pass along to your kids: Never take shells with live animals inside. To bring out the natural color and luster of the empty shells you collect, rub them with mineral oil or baby oil. And to make sure your shells make it home intact, pack them in tissue paper or newspaper and bring along a plastic bag or bucket to hold the precious booty.

Sand castling is another interesting and relaxing way for families to spend time together at the beach. The most important factor in making good sand structures is to use wet sand which clings together when rolled in your hand. If you're planning something extravagant, inquire where and when high tide hits so your grand creation won't get washed away before you're finished having fun with it. For sculpting tools, you can use shovels, ordinary kitchen utensils, popsicle sticks and, of course, fingers and hands. Buckets, cups and jars can serve as molds.

Don't forget sunglasses or accessories such as frisbees or beach towels/umbrellas. And bring plenty of suntan lotion. Coat yourself and your kids with it whenever you're out in the sun, and cover little ones with t-shirts if they're in and out of the water a lot. Nothing ruins a beach vacation quicker than a bad sunburn. Travelers checks, you can replace. But losing a layer of skin really stings.

Three of the Southeast beaches covered in this chapter are located on the Atlantic Ocean along a 150-mile stretch of shore: Myrtle Beach, S.C., Hilton Head, S.C., and Jekyll Island, Ga. We're also fond of another 150-mile stretch along the Gulf of Mexico which includes Gulf Shores, Ala., and three contiguous locations in Florida: Ft. Walton Beach, Destin and Panama City Beach.

Regardless of which beach you decide to visit, you and your family have an important decision to make regarding lodging. Do we stay "on the beach"? Do we pay extra for an "ocean view"? Or do we save money and stay a few blocks away? Whatever you decide, make sure you stipulate that when you're making reservations. And upon arrival, make sure you're getting what you're paying for.

This decision-making process is complicated by the fact that some resorts—the Caravelle in Myrtle Beach, for example—are such vast properties that even though they bill themselves as an "oceanfront resort," parts of the resort are oceanside and other parts may be one or two blocks away. Which is not to say the Caravelle isn't a good place to stay; it is, and many of its units, including those in the new all-suites tower, provide guests with an ocean view. But of its nine different towers and condominium complexes, only three—Carolina Dunes, St. Clements and the original Caravelle Resort (built in 1962)—are actually on the beach.

SHELLING TIPS

❑ Never take shells with live animals inside.

❑ To bring out the natural color and luster of the empty shells you collect, rub them with mineral oil or baby oil.

❑ To make sure your shells make it home intact, pack them in tissue paper or newspaper and bring along a plastic bag or bucket to hold the precious booty.

SANDCASTLING TIPS

❑ Use wet sand which clings together when rolled in your hand.

❑ Inquire where and when high tide hits so your grand creation won't get washed away before you're finished having fun with it.

That brings up another lodging question you need to answer before you make reservations: Are you a high-rise hotel/condo family or low-rise motel/villa dwellers? We're the latter—mainly because we favor easier in-out access. Bottom line: Write for brochures, visit your travel agent or call and ask questions before making a decision about where to stay. If you're interested in renting a private home, condo or villa, call the Chamber of Commerce and ask for information.

If you have avid golfers in your family, you are aware that this hobby has gotten to be extremely expensive. So if you can help it, never pay the regular greens fee at a golf course—unless you're independently wealthy. Here's why: To play 18 holes on Sea Pines' Harbour Town course at Hilton Head, the average person off the street has to pay roughly $130. But if you're on a vacation package deal at Sea Pines, you can play one round at Harbour Town for nothing and subsequent rounds for a surcharge in the $20 or $40 range, depending on the time of year.

As you'll note from reading this chapter, we haven't picked quiet, out-of-the-way beaches where the principal activities are sunning, reading, napping and eating. You can do all of those things at the beaches we've recommended, but those aren't the main reasons you'd go there. These are places where you can have a good time both on the beach and off and we like them not only because our kids do, but because they bring out the kid in us.

TRAVEL TIP

When friends ask us about essential differences between beach experiences on the Atlantic versus the Gulf, we usually sum it up by saying, "The Gulf has beautiful water, and the kind of fluffy, white sand that feels great between your toes. The Atlantic has better surf, and sand that's packed so hard you can ride bikes on the beach."

For the benefit of those parents who are allergic to neon, go-kart fumes and day-glow sunscreen, we've listed a few out-of-the-way beaches, state parks and protected recreation areas where you can just relax and enjoy nature to its fullest. If you check the "Where to Stay" section of this chapter, you'll also find occasional lodging entries which are not at the beach.

A word of caution about beach-area restaurants: Some close around the end of October and don't reopen for two or three months. So always call before showing up at the front door.

GULF SHORES ▲ EMERALD COAST PANAMA CITY BEACH

Gulf Shores, Ala., is located near the southernmost tip of the state on a finger of land that juts out into the Gulf of Mexico. Across the border in Florida are two beachfront communities—Destin and Fort Walton Beach—which are part of the area known as the Emerald Coast, owing to the gorgeous Gulf Coast water you find there. Together with Panama City Beach, which claims to have the "World's Most Beautiful Beaches," these four areas encompass 150 miles of Gulf Coast shoreline. Stop almost anywhere, and you'll find crystal-clear water and gorgeous white sand beaches.

ABOUT THE AREA

The stretch of coastline from Gulf Shores to Panama City Beach is sometimes loosely referred to as the "Redneck Riviera." If you haven't been there, you might assume from that unflattering nickname that this area is just one continuous beer blast and wet t-shirt contest. We can assure you that isn't the case. Youthful exuberance does exist here, but to find it you generally have to go to public beaches at spring break or to college nightclubs on Saturday night.

We grouped these four beaches together because they're practically contiguous and you can drive from one end to the other in, say, three hours, depending on traffic—and how many times you slow up to marvel at that emerald-colored water. And just wait till you get in it; you'll feel like you're in the Caribbean. We stayed at both ends—the Perdido Beach Hilton in Gulf Shores and the Marriott Bay Point Resort in Panama City Beach—and you can't go wrong at either. But the next time we go, we're moving our headquarters to either Fort Walton Beach or Destin because they're in the middle; that way, we'll be within easy reach of every amusement, activity and outing listed in this section.

If the area has a drawback, it's the heavy traffic which sometimes clogs the main beachfront arteries—Highway 182 in Gulf Shores, U.S. 98 in Fort Walton Beach and Destin, and U.S. 98 Alt. in Panama City Beach. For the most part, these thoroughfares are loaded to the gills with hotels, motels, condos, restaurants, souvenir stands, amusement parks, t-shirt shops, beach boutiques and bars. But if you select the right place to stay and it has a private beach, you can sample as much or as little of the glitz as you like. In fact, you should be able to enjoy your stay here as much as you would at a more tranquil location such as Hilton Head.

THINGS TO DO

Gulf Shores

The entire family will enjoy themselves at **Waterville, USA** (see the "Best of the Rest" section in the WATERPARKS chapter).

Zooland is a 15-acre park with lions and tigers and bears— oh, my!— plus alligators, zebras, wolves and coyotes. There's also a petting zoo and mini golf (Hwy. 59, just north of Waterville, 205-968-5731).

All four of **Gulf Shores' golf courses** are open to the public, and if you're a low-handicapper you'll want to try the Arnold Palmer-designed Cotton Creek Club (County Rd. 4, east of Hwy. 59, 205-968-7766 or 800-327-2657). But the other three courses are nice, too: Gulf Shores Golf Club (Hwy. 59, one mile north of the beach, 205-968-7366), Gulf State Park Resort (Hwy. 182, 205-968-2366) and Lakeview Golf Club (Rte. 20 south of Foley, 205-943-8000). We also recommend Perdido Bay Country Club, which is just across the Florida state line (Beach Hwy. past Innerarity Point, 904-492-1223).

Pirates Island Miniature Golf is located next door to the Alabama Gulf Coast Welcome Center (Hwy. 59 just north of the Intracoastal Waterway, 205-968-8397).

You can rent bikes at **Gulf State Park** (205-948-7275), which covers more than 6,000 acres of Pleasure Island. Island Recreation Services (205-948-7334) rents bikes, mopeds and an assortment of water sports equipment, including sailboats. Gulf State Park has tennis courts, too.

Gulf State Park is also a good place to fish. There's an 825-foot pier and you can rent flat-bottom boats to use on a 500-acre freshwater lake. Deep-sea fishing enthusiasts can sign onboard the Marina Queen (205-981-8499) and there are dozens of charter boats to choose from in nearby Orange Beach. May to November is the time when great sports fish— tuna, wahoo and sailfish are striking, and it's not unusual to land a blue marlin in the 500-700 lb. range. For a brochure, call 205-981-8000. For information on Alabama fishing licenses, call 205-261-3260.

Fort Walton Beach

The Indian Temple Mound Museum and Park uses dioramas and a variety of exhibits to portray the 10,000-year history of the American Indian, including seven pre-Colombian cultures. An ancient temple has been recreated in a modern shelter on an authentic temple site (on U.S. 98, downtown, 904-243-6521).

Popular **golf courses** include Shalimar Pointe Golf and Country Club (on Choctawhatchee Bay in Shalimar, 904-651-1416), the Fort Walton Beach Municipal Golf Club (off Lewis Turner Blvd. across from the fairgrounds, 904-862-3314), Hidden Creek (3070 PGA Blvd., Holly By The Sea, in Navarre, 904-939-4604) and Tiger Point Golf & Country Club (3455 Santa Rosa Dr., in Gulf Breeze, 904-932-1333).

Tennis lovers will find 12 courts at the Fort Walton Beach Tennis Center and 12 more at various locations throughout the city; for information call the Parks & Recreation Dept. (904-243-3119). Shalimar Point also has six clay courts which are open to the public (904-651-8872).

To rent **watersports** equipment, visit PBS Watersports (1320 Hwy. 98E, 904-244-2933). Hobie cats can be rented at The Hobie Shop (12705 W. Hwy. 98, 904-234-0023).

Destin

Big Kahuna is one of those oddball, one-stop fun emporiums. It features waterpark rides, a 56-hole mini golf extravaganza and a 4,000-seat amphitheater for live music concerts—all three of which require separate admissions (U.S. 98, 904-837-4061).

Museum of the Sea and Indian has, as the name implies, extensive marine and Native American exhibits. You'll find two ponds with alligators, ducks and game birds (eight miles east on Beach Hwy./Old U.S. 98, 904-837-6625).

The most beautiful stretch of public beach occurs five miles east of town at **Crystal Beach Wayside Park.** Protected for five miles on either side by undeveloped, state-owned property, the park includes picnic tables, changing rooms, restrooms and lifeguards in the summer.

Destin is known as **"The World's Luckiest Fishing Village"** and you can enjoy a half-day, full-day or overnight fishing trip by calling Charter Boat Barbi-Anne (904-837-6059/837-2930) or Charter Boat Doc Holiday (904-837-0005).

Popular **golf courses** include: Indian Golf Bayou and Country Club (Airport Rd., 904-837-6191), Seascape Resort Club (100 Seascape Dr., 904-837-9181), Santa Rosa Beach Resort (Rte. 1 in Santa Rosa, 904-267-2229) and the Sandestin Beach Resort, where 27 of the 45 holes are open to the public (5500 U.S. Hwy. 98E, 904-267-8155). If you can't find time for golf during the day, check out the Island Golf Center, which has two nine-hole layouts lighted for night play, 36 holes of mini golf and nine holes of pitch and putt (U.S. 98 on Okaloosa Island, 904-244-1612).

The Destin Racquet Club has 10 tennis courts (Airport Rd., 904-837-8548).

Panama City Beach

Miracle Strip is a nine-acre amusement park with more than 60 rides and attractions, including a roller coaster with a 2,000-foot run and a nice collection of small-fry favorites. Miracle Strip's sister property, **Ship-**

wreck Island, is a waterpark. For more information on it, see the "Best of the Rest" section in the WATERPARKS chapter. Both parks are located at 12000 W. Hwy. 98-A (Miracle Strip: 904-234-5810, Shipwreck Island: 904-234-0368).

Gulf World is a scaled-down version of Sea World. Bottle-nosed dolphins, sea lions and parrots entertain daily. Other marine animals playing supporting roles include penguins, alligators and sharks—which you can get uncomfortably close to, thanks to a special walk-through channel in their tank (15412 W. Hwy. 98A, 904-234-5271).

St. Andrews State Recreation Area, at the eastern end of the Panama City beach area, is a gorgeous spot for swimming and there's a protected area behind the jetty that's perfect for small children. You can also snorkel, picnic or go for a hike. The snorkeling is particularly breathtaking here because in 1977 the Department of Natural Resources sank a 441-foot ship in 70 feet of water. Other wrecks you can dive on include: a 105-foot tugboat sunk in 103 feet of water and a 465-foot British tanker which was torpedoed by a German U-boat and sank in 1942. It settled in 192 feet of water, but its bow section rises some 60 feet off the ocean floor. You can also dive on a ship that once belonged to Antarctic explorer Admiral Byrd, and beginners can warm up with a dive on a tugboat which sank in 25 feet of water less than a mile from the shore. For more information, call 904-235-3390.

If you're not staying at a hotel or resort which has a fishing pier, try the 1,642-foot **city pier** which is eight miles west of the city on U.S. 98. There's a nominal charge, but fishing from the nearby county pier (three miles to the east on U.S. 98) is free. To charter a fishing boat, contact Capt. Anderson's pier (904-234-3435 or 800-874-2415).

Popular **golf courses** include: Holiday Golf and Racquet Club (100 Fairway Blvd., 904-234-1800), The Hombre (120 Coyote Pass/U.S. Hwy. 98, 904-234-3673) and Signal Hill Golf Course (9615 N. Thomas Dr., 904-234-3218).

WHERE TO STAY

Gulf Shores

We stayed at the Perdido Beach Hilton, a luxurious, Mediterranean-style hotel which is divided into two towers, eight and nine stories high. Every room has a balcony and a view of the beach. Facilities include a heated indoor-outdoor swimming pool and four lighted tennis courts. The kids' activities program, Perdido Pals, runs six days a week from 9 a.m.-3 p.m. and 6-11 p.m. The program was free in 1990, its first year of operation, but the hotel is thinking of switching to daily and weekly fees (Hwy. 182 E., in Orange Beach, 205-981-9811).

The Gulf Shores Holiday Inn is a four-story hotel on a private beach. Facilities include a swimming pool and a wading pool, two lighted tennis courts and a game room. Kids 12 and under stay free (Hwy. 182 E., 205-968-6191).

The Quality Inn Beachside has a newer six-story wing to go with its original three-story wings. Families will enjoy the indoor and outdoor pools, shopping arcade, game room and playground. Kids 18 and under stay free (931 W. Beach Blvd., 205-948-6874).

A less-expensive alternative is the Gulf State Park Resort and Convention Center. Spartan in appearance, this two-story, state-operated facility has a restaurant and lounge, lighted tennis courts, an 800-foot fishing pier, a stretch of private beach and an 18-hole golf course located nearby. You can also arrange to stay in modern cabins which overlook Lake Shelby, and there's a campground with 468 sites; some are lakeside. Kids 11 and under stay free (on Alabama 182, 205-948-GULF or 800-544-GULF).

Fort Walton Beach

The Ramada Beach Resort and the Holiday Inn are both located on U.S. 98E on the Gulf. The Ramada was the Regency Beach Resort for a short period of time, and its boxy, six-story design isn't as imaginative as some of Ramada's newer hotels. But your kids will like the eye-catching Polynesian waterfall that dominates the pool/sundeck area and there are loads of amenities: lighted tennis courts, indoor spa, game room and supervised kids' program. Kids 17 and under stay free (904-243-9161). The Holiday Inn is a seven-story hotel with three swimming pools and lighted tennis courts. Kids 12 and under stay free. There's also a two-floor luxury level with suite accommodations and complimentary continental breakfast and refreshments (at Santa Rosa Blvd., 904-243-9181).

The Bluewater Bay Resort, located 18 miles northeast of the beach in Niceville, Fla., is an 1,800-acre resort surrounded by thick forests, freshwater lakes and the blue waters of Choctawhatchee Bay. Accommodations include motel-style rooms, studios with efficiencies and villas. Some rooms have fireplaces and fully equipped kitchens. Facilities include three nine-hole golf courses, a tennis center with 21 courts (18 are lighted and more courts are sprinkled throughout the resort), plus three swimming pools and a playground. The kids' activities program operates Monday-Friday, Memorial Day-Labor Day, and it's free if you're on a package deal (Rte. 20E in Niceville, 904-897-3613 or 800-874-2128).

Destin

Sandestin Beach Resort is a 2,600-acre resort located eight miles east of Destin. It offers every conceivable kind of accommodations—bayside inn, Gulfside high-rise condominium units, waterside patio homes with huge decks, cottages and villas on lagoons or fairways—and all come equipped with kitchens or kitchenettes. Facilities include two 18-hole golf courses and 16 tennis courts in three different surfaces: hard, clay and even grass courts reminiscent of Wimbledon. The supervised kids' activities program operates six days a week, Memorial Day-Labor Day. There's also a youth sports camp with instruction in tennis, golf and swimming (5500 U.S. 98E/Emerald Coast Parkway, 904-267-8150 or 800-277-0800). Also located on the property is the Hilton Sandestin Beach, which features an indoor-outdoor swimming pool and wading pool. Rooms are equipped with a refrigerator and hot plate (5540 U.S. 98E, 904-267-9500).

This section of U.S. 98, east of Destin, is jammed with modern beachfront, high-rise hotels/condos, some of which have low-rise villas too. Two of the nicest are the Tops'l Beach & Racquet Club (5550 U.S. 98E, 904-267-9222 or 800-476-9222) and the Edgewater Beach Condominiums (5000 Hwy. 98E, 904-837-1550). Both are loaded with amenities. Closer to Destin is the Holiday Inn, a nine-story hotel with a Holidome indoor rec center and a supervised kids' activities program which operates six days a week, Memorial Day-Labor Day (1020 U.S. 98E, 904-837-6181).

If you prefer villas to high-rise condos, a smart choice is the Seascape Resort and Conference Center, where you'll find one- to three-bedroom units in one- to three-story buildings which line golf fairways, tennis courts and freshwater lakes. Facilities include five swimming pools, an 18-hole golf course, eight clay tennis courts (six are lighted), mini golf, playground and a supervised kids' activities program, which operates seven days a week from Memorial Day to Labor Day. One drawback: U.S. 98 separates the resort from its 1,500-foot private beach. But the elevated walkway over the highway makes it pretty accessible (100 Seascape Dr., 904-837-9181, 800-874-9106 or, in Florida, 800-342-2710).

For something on the smaller and less hectic side, there's Summer Breeze, a three-story, Victorian-style condominium complex with only 35 one-bedroom units. But each one sleeps six, owing to a sleeper sofa and bunk beds in the hall. Facilities include a small pool with a nice deck and a jacuzzi (3885 U.S. 98E, 904-837-4853).

Panama City Beach

We stayed at the Marriott Bay Point Resort (see the RESORTS chapter).

The Edgewater Beach Resort features high-rise condo units in a pair of six-story towers, a 12-story tower and Caribbean-style villas in two-story complexes. Facilities include a scenic par-3 golf course, 12 lighted tennis courts, 20 shuffleboard courts and a lagoon-shaped swimming pool so huge it's surrounded by 20,000 tropical plants (11212 W. U.S. 98 Alt., 904-235-4044 or 800-874-8686).

The Holiday Inn Beachside is a seven-story high-rise with two swimming pools, a whirlpool and game room. Some rooms have refrigerators and kitchens. Kids 12 and under stay free (12907 W. U.S. 98, 904-234-1111).

Want to step back in time? Located on County Road 30-A, midway between Fort Walton Beach and Panama City Beach, is the village of Seaside, an 80-acre vacation and residential resort which has won awards for its urban design and turn-of-the-century architecture. Guests stay in one- to five-bedroom cottages which are surrounded by white picket fences. And if you read that Seaside doesn't have air conditioning, don't believe it; it just seems that way because some guests rely on ceiling fans and Gulf breezes to stay cool. Facilities include a swimming pool and two playgrounds, plus tennis, croquet and badminton courts. Some visitors come just to stroll the flower-lined brick streets. But there's also an open-air market, three restaurants, a shopping area and children's story-telling hours at the Sundog Book Store (10 a.m., spring-summer, 904-231-5481). For information, contact: Seaside Community Development Corp., PO Box 4730, Seaside, FL 32459 (904-231-4224 or 800-635-0296).

WHERE TO EAT

Gulf Shores

Perdido Pass overlooks the Gulf of Mexico and is a good choice for lunch or dinner. The lunch menu includes croissant sandwiches and a seafood platter; the dinner menu features fresh seafood and meats cooked to order: mesquite grilled, broiled, sautéed, blackened or fried. Child's plates are available (Beach Hwy. 182 at the Alabama Point Bridge, 205-981-6312).

The Original Oyster House has an 87-item menu, a pet alligator and a view of the bayou. Need we say more? (Hwy. 59, 205-948-4522).

Zeke's offers diners a nice view of Cotton Bayou and the Zeke's Landing marina. The bill of fare is steak and seafood, but there's an oyster bar and you can also get prime rib (Hwy. 182 E. in Orange Beach, 205-981-4001).

We were in the mood for a romantic meal without the kids, so we ate at Voyagers, a stylish, dimly lit room in the Perdido Beach Hilton. Fresh seafood, prepared Creole-style, is one of the specialties of the house; we ordered filet of grouper with crabmeat and blackened shrimp on a bed of spinach. Both were delicious, as were the shrimp remoulade appetizer and the Caesar salad for two. Lamb, filet mignon and duck are also on the menu. If you can't make it for dinner, go for the champagne jazz brunch on Sunday (Hwy. 182 E. in Orange Beach, 205-981-9811). Another fine-dining choice is Hemingways, where the bill of fare is gourmet cajun (Orange Beach Marina, 205-981-9791).

Fort Walton Beach

Both the Seagull Restaurant and Liollio's are located on the Intra-coastal Waterway. The Seagull features broiled and sautéed seafood offerings: poached scallops, snapper amandine, plus lobster and steak (1201 E. U.S. 98, 904-243-3413). Liollio's is a little more casual and adds Greek spices to its seafood (14 Miracle Strip Pkwy., 904-243-5011).

The Landing specializes in prime rib and seafood and there's a salad bar and entertainment (225 Miracle Strip Pkwy. SW, 904-244-7134).

Destin

Overlooking Old Pass Lagoon, Louisiana Lagniappe's specializes in Cajun cuisine. The menu features fresh speckled trout, crawfish, shrimp and oysters. Daily specials include soft shell crabs, blackened redfish, char-grilled tuna and tournados topped with jumbo lump crabmeat, crawfish tails and bearnaise sauce. If you like, you can eat outside on the deck. Closed November-February (775 Gulfshore Dr., in Sandpiper Cove on Holiday Isle, 904-837-0881).

Both the Flamingo Cafe and Harbor Docks afford diners a view of the Destin Harbor, and both have decks so you can eat and drink outdoors. House specialties at the Flamingo Cafe include oysters bienville, pan-fried soft shell crayfish and veal magenta (414 U.S. 98E, 904-837-0961). Harbor Docks adds Thai specials, homemade egg rolls, and red beans and rice to the usual steak and seafood offerings (538 U.S. 98E, one mile east of the Destin Bridge, 904-837-2506).

You can take the kids with you for lunch on the pool deck at Elephant Walk, but make dinner in the main dining room an adults-only affair. Part of the fun here is the exotic Asian flavor of the architecture and the fact that the restaurant overlooks the Gulf of Mexico. Modeled after the plan-tation owner's home in the 1954 Elizabeth Taylor movie of the same name, Elephant Walk serves seafood, steaks, duck and daily chef specials (at the Sandestin Beach Resort, eight miles east of Destin on U.S. 98, 904-267-4800).

Panama City Beach

Captain Anderson's opened its doors in 1953 and, rumor has it, there's been a line to get in ever since. And no wonder. The restaurant overlooks the Grand Lagoon and some of the recipes come from the Greek

Island of Patmos, which was home to the father of the current owners, Johnny and Jimmy Patronis. The menu includes charbroiled steaks and chicken, but seafood is the specialty of this house. Choose from grilled bay shrimp, grouper stuffed with crabmeat and the "world's finest seafood platter." There's even a bakery on the premises. But be aware that this restaurant closes for two or three months, beginning in late fall (5551 N. Lagoon Dr., 904-234-2225).

The Treasure Ship is a larger-than-life replica of a 17th-century Spanish galleon which was patterned after Sir Francis Drake's flagship, the *Golden Hind*. The ship rises 135 feet off the ground and a variety of restaurants, lounges and bars occupy its four levels. Level three has an observation deck which offers views of the Grand Lagoon and there's a game room, too. Depending on which level you choose, the menu may feature light snacks, sandwiches or steak, seafood and lavish desserts. This is another restaurant which takes time off during the winter (3605 Thomas Dr., 904-234-8881).

The Boar's Head Restaurant & Tavern features live Maine lobster and baby back ribs in a rustic setting (17290 Front Beach Rd./W. Hwy. 98 Alt., 904-234-6628).

SHOPPING/NEARBY FUN

Gulf Shores

Riviera Centre, a 20-store outlet mall, is open seven days a week, 9 a.m.-9 p.m. except Sunday, 10-6 (2601 S. McKenzie St., Hwy. 59 S. in Foley, 205-943-8888).

If your kids are old enough to appreciate something besides the beach or you can arrange for someone to watch them, we recommend a day trip up to **Mobile Bay** where the USS *Alabama* is anchored. You can tour the World War II battleship every day of the year except Christmas, and getting to Mobile (and back) is half the fun.

From Gulf Shores, it's a 22-mile drive west on Highway 180 to **Fort Morgan,** which defended Mobile Bay from Union troops during the Civil War. It was during heavy shelling from Fort Morgan that Union naval commander David Farragut uttered those immortal words, "Damn the torpedoes! Full speed ahead!" From Fort Morgan, drive your car onto the Mobile Bay ferry for a 30-minute ride to Dauphin Island. Another Civil War landmark, **Fort Gaines,** is located on the island and open to the public. From there, you can take a causeway to the mainland.

The causeway connects to Highway 193, which leads you to **Bellingrath Gardens,** which bills itself as the "Azalea Capital of the World." In the spring, you'll see 250,000 plantings and 200 different species (205-973-2217). For a preview of Mobile's points of interest, stop at **Fort Conde**

(150 S. Royal St., 205-434-7304), which is a living museum of colonial America as well as the city's official visitor center.

Battleship Memorial Park is much more than just the *USS Alabama*. You'll see a B-52 bomber, a submarine, a P-51 Mustang and a Redstone rocket (open 8 a.m. to sunset, 205-433-2703).

Following your visit to Mobile, you should return to Gulf Shores via U.S. 98 on the eastern shore of Mobile Bay, completing your circular route by making stops at Fairhope and Foley. **Fairhope** is a haven for artists and craftsmen and if you're hungry, Dusty Rhoades features gourmet continental cooking (Hwy. 98 at Morphy Ave., 205-928-8637). If you're in Foley at meal time, stop at The Gift Horse Restaurant for an excellent buffet. Lunch is served daily; dinner Thursday-Saturday (Hwy. 98, 205-943-3663).

Fort Walton Beach

Santa Rosa Mall has 125 stores and is the area's only enclosed shopping center (300 Mary Esther Cut-off, one block north of U.S. 98 in Mary Esther, 904-244-2172). A good place for bargains is the **Manufacturer's Outlet Center** (123 Miracle Strip Pkwy. SW).

The Zoo is home to more than 500 birds, mammals and reptiles representing more than 80 species. The main attraction is Colossus, one of the world's largest gorillas in captivity. Hop on the Safari Line Limited, a replica of an 1863 train, and you can see more than 100 creatures as they roam freely through 30 acres of ponds, lakes and open plains. Located 19 miles west of Fort Walton Beach (5801 Gulf Breeze Pkwy., in Gulf Breeze, 904-923-2229).

Eglin Air Force Base encompasses 720 square miles, making it the largest U.S. Air Force base in the world. You can take a three-hour tour of the base which sometimes includes a demonstration of how military dogs are trained. Tour tickets are available at area chambers of commerce and at the **Air Force Armament Museum** located at the edge of the base. Surprisingly, more than half of the base is used for public recreation. Most of this land is referred to as the **Eglin Reservation,** and it offers some of the best fishing, camping, hunting and canoeing in Florida. Camping permits are free; if you like to fish or hunt, there's a small fee for those ages 15-65 (on Eglin Pkwy., 13 miles northeast of Fort Walton Beach, 904-651-5253).

Destin

The Market at Sandestin is a festival shopping center with a variety of specialty shops (5500 U.S. 98E/Emerald Coast Pkwy., 904-267-8150).

Drive east on U.S. 98 for 30 miles and you'll come to the **Grayton Beach State Recreation Area,** where you'll find uncrowded beaches, great fishing, nature trails and camping, plus swimming, snorkeling and scuba areas (on Rte. 30A near Santa Rosa Beach and Grayton Beach).

Located on Okaloosa Island, equidistant from both Destin and Fort Walton Beach, **Gulfarium** and **Water World** are big with kids. Gulfarium is yet another variation on the Sea World motif with the usual marine mammals carrying out their usual entertainment roles (on U.S. 98, 904-243-6521). Water World lives up to its name with seven water slides, an activity pool, plus all sorts of watersports equipment to use on Choctawhatchee Bay: jet-skis, jet-boats, sailboats, windsurfers. Go-karts too! (U.S. 98E, 904-243-9738).

Panama City Beach

When it comes to shopping, we recommend the **Manufacturer's Outlet Center,** which is home to 12 famous fashion manufacturers (105 23rd St, one mile west of Hwy. 231 in Panama City, 904-769-6532). For a lunch-time stroll without the kids, head downtown to the **Olde Towne Mini Mall** on Grace Avenue, where you'll find several interesting shops and restaurants.

Across the bay in Panama City is the **Junior Museum of Bay County,** where you'll find science, art and nature exhibits designed for children. The museum also features concerts, puppet shows and a pioneer village with a log cabin where kids can feed chickens and ducks. Admission is free, and classes of all kinds are offered throughout the summer (1731 Jenks Ave., 904-769-6128).

It's a cliché, but time does seem to stand still on **Shell Island,** a barrier island south of the beach. Seven and a half miles long and nearly a mile wide, the island is accessible only by boat and would be virtually deserted if it weren't for tourists. The boat rides which take you to the island are an attraction in themselves because you pass the port of Panama City on the way, as well as the wildlife on **Audubon Island.** And keep an eye on the water because you're almost certain to see dolphins swimming near your boat at some point. The *Ashley Gorman* takes visitors on four-hour narrated cruises (904-785-4878). Captain Anderson's Marina offers three-hour cruises (904-234-3435) and you can also take a glassbottom boat ride to the island (904-234-8944).

WHEN TO GO

Tourist season runs from early March through early October, but Emerald Coast weather is conducive to year-round vacationing. Average daily high temperatures range from around 90 (August) to the 80s (May-August, September-October), to the 70s (March-April), to the 60s (January-February, November-December). Temperatures are slightly lower in Gulf Shores, but the difference is scarcely noticeable.

A word of advice: Unless you're looking to relive your youth, spring break is not the best time to visit this area—particularly Panama City Beach. It's not that you couldn't have a good time, but why buck the traffic and the congestion on the beach? Summer is a better time, and late August is when many hotels offer special deals.

FOR MORE INFORMATION

Contact:

Alabama Gulf Coast Convention and Visitors Bureau
Gulf Shores Pkwy./Hwy. 59, Drawer 457, Gulf Shores, AL 36542
(205-968-7511)

Fort Walton Beach Chamber of Commerce
34 Miracle Strip Pkwy./U.S. 98, Fort Walton Beach, FL 32548
(904-244-8191)

Destin Chamber of Commerce
Holiday Inn, Suite D, 1021 U.S. 98E, Destin, FL 32541
(904-837-6241)

Panama City Beach Visitors and Convention Bureau
12015 W. U.S. 98 Alt., Panama City Beach, FL 32407
(904-234-6575)

Hilton Head Island

Hilton Head Island, S.C., is located on the Atlantic Ocean, 95 miles south of Charleston, S.C., and 35 miles north of Savannah, Ga. (take either exit 8 or exit 28 off I-95 and follow the signs). The island is 12 miles long, five miles wide and features 12 miles of hard-packed beach.

ABOUT THE AREA

Hilton Head is the largest barrier island south of Long Island, New York. It gets its name from English sea captain William Hilton, who was commissioned by a group of Barbados planters to find new land on which to plant sugar and indigo. Capt. Hilton arrived at what is now Hilton Head in 1663, but the island didn't become well-known until 1790, when planter William Elliott raised Hilton Head's first crop of long-stem Sea Island cotton. By 1860, 24 plantations growing cotton, indigo, sugar cane and rice were in operation, but landowners were forced to flee the island when Federal troops occupied it during the Civil War. Nearly 90 years of isolation followed, with the island's few residents subsisting on small farms and oystering. In the 1940s, the island was known for its timber operations, but by 1956 Charles Fraser had finalized an idea for a master-planned resort community which would become the model for countless others across the U.S. Fraser's efforts, which were aided by the construction of a bridge to the mainland, resulted in Sea Pines Plantation—one of eight major planned communities now in operation on the island. The other seven include Hilton Head Plantation, Long Cove Club, Palmetto Dunes Resort, Port Royal Plantation, Shipyard Plantation, Spanish Wells and Wexford Plantation. But of the eight, only Sea Pines, Palmetto Dunes, Port Royal and Shipyard are commercial resorts; the other four are private residential communities.

Hilton Head's permanent population is about 23,000, but more than one million tourists visit the island every year, spending roughly half a billion dollars. Ironically, financial troubles threatened the island's future as recently as 1987. The trouble started in 1983 after Fraser sold his interest in Sea Pines. Considered a visionary in the resort management field, Fraser's absence was felt immediately. By 1986, heavily indebted Sea Pines was forced into bankruptcy court and its two premier sporting events—the PGA Tour's MCI Heritage Classic golf tournament and the Family Circle Cup tennis tournament—were in jeopardy of being lost. A group of local businessmen came to the rescue of the golf and tennis tournaments, and Sea Pines residents banded together to buy many of the assets of the plantation and restore stability.

Unlike Amelia Island or Kiawah Island (see the RESORTS chapter), Hilton Head is no longer a quiet hideaway. True, this is the place that set standards for intelligent land use and respect for nature. But over the years, Hilton Head has become so popular—and as a result, so overbuilt—that it's much more hectic than it ought to be. Don't forget, a million people vacation here every year. But they come because the island is still beautiful, and because tranquility still reigns within the plantations. There's a ton of stuff to do here, and Hilton Head visitors are incredibly loyal. Many people return to this island year after year—and wouldn't dream of changing their vacation habits.

THINGS TO DO

All 12 miles of Hilton Head beach are open to the public, and there are **35 public beach entrances.** The two main public parking areas are located at Coligny Circle, near the Holiday Inn, and on Folly Field Road, off U.S. 278 near the Hilton Head Beach and Tennis Resort. Signs along U.S. 278 point you to Bradley, Burkes and Singleton beaches.

One of the many nice things about the beaches on this island is that the sand is so hard-packed you can ride bikes on it. To rent them, call The Beach Factory (803-686-6565), Harbour Town Bicycles (803-785-3546), Cycle Center Rentals (803-686-2288), Fish Creek Landing (803-785-2021), Peddling Pelican Bike Rentals (803-785-5470), Sea Pines Bicycle Rentals (803-671-5839) and Vacation Services Ltd. (803-842-5522).

And remember, you can use **Sea Pines** as a day resort without actually staying there. For $3, which the resort puts into road maintenance, you can eat at Sea Pines restaurants, shop at Harbour Town, play golf, ride horses or drive down to South Beach, where you can rent a variety of watersports equipment (Island Water Sports, 803-671-7007). Windsurfing Hilton Head is located at South Beach Marina (803-686-6996), and Shore Enterprises is another source of watersports equipment (803-785-3494).

Sailors and fishermen can rent or charter at **nine different marinas:** Broad Creek Marina (803-681-7335), Harbour Town Yacht Basin (at Sea Pines, 803-671-2704), Outdoor Resorts Yacht Basin (803-681-2350), Palmetto Bay Marina (803-785-3910), Schilling Boathouse (803-681-2628), Shelter Cove Harbour (at Palmetto Dunes, 803-842-7001), Skull Creek Marina (803-681-4234), South Beach Marina (at Sea Pines, 803-671-6640) and Windmill Harbour (803-681-9235). For fishing information, call the Harbour Town Fishing Office (803-671-4534). If you like crabbing, the tidal creeks or the beach at low tide are your best bets.

Every hotel and resort on Hilton Head has special youth activities or, in some cases, a full-scale summer recreation program for kids. At Sea

Pines, for example, the "Fun for Kids" program operates Monday-Friday, June 1-August 31. Kids ages 4-6 attend a morning session; ages 7-12 can go all day. Kite flying, pony rides and adventure cruises are among the many activities.

A dependable source of year-round fun is the **Island Recreation Center** (20 Wilborn Rd., in the Hilton Head schools complex), which serves more than 110,000 islanders and visitors a year. Of particular interest to families on vacation are the association's day camps, which include tennis lessons, trips to the beach and arts and crafts. The rec center also offers sports camps in basketball, boardsailing, golf, racquetball, sailing, soccer, tennis and volleyball. For more information, contact: Island Recreation Association, PO Box 22593, Hilton Head Island, SC 29925 (803-681-7273).

Younger children will enjoy "Pigs Tales," an original musical fairy tale which is presented at 5 p.m. at the Overlook Restaurant, March-August. Kids can order from a special children's menu during the show. Adults can enjoy Broadway dinner theater here too (at Port Royal Plantation, 803-681-4444).

Generally speaking, you won't find neon amusement centers on Hilton Head. But there are several nice **mini golf courses**—at Treasure Cove Adventure Golf (8 Marina Side Dr., 803-686-4001) or Legendary Golf (900 Hilton Pkwy., 803-686-3399, or 80 Pope Ave., 803-785-9214).

When it comes to **real golf courses,** Hilton Head is one of the prime locations in the world. The island has 25 courses, 15 of which are public. Sea Pines, Palmetto Dunes and Port Royal Plantation all have three courses and Hilton Head Plantation has two. The most famous course is Harbour Town (803-671-2446) at Sea Pines, which is the site of the Heritage Classic. The longest are Oyster Reef (6,961 yards, 803-681-7717) and the Country Club of Hilton Head (6,936 yards, 803-681-4653), both at Hilton Head Plantation. The shortest are Sea Marsh (6,372 yards, 803-671-2436) at Sea Pines and Callawassie (6,319 yards, 803-842-4955) at Callawassie Island. The toughest are Harbour Town and the George Fazio course (803-785-1130) at Palmetto Dunes. The most expensive, by far, is Harbour Town.

Hilton Head has more than 300 **tennis courts,** and eight of the 19 clubs on the island are public. The most famous is the Sea Pines Racquet Club (803-671-2494), which is host to the Family Circle Cup, a long-time event on the women's pro tennis tour. The Van Der Meer Tennis Center (803-785-8388) has the most courts (21 hard, 11 clay), but Sea Pines (24 clay, 5 hard) isn't far behind. The Hilton Head Island Beach and Tennis Resort (803-785-7566) has the least (10 hard) but all of its courts are lighted; it's also likely to be the least expensive. The most expensive will probably be Sea Pines and the Rod Laver Tennis Center (803-785-1152).

Expect reserved court time to range from less than $10 an hour to something approaching $20 an hour. Walk-on players will pay considerably less.

If your family likes **horseback riding,** there are several fully equipped stables in the Hilton Head area. For information, check with the Chamber of Commerce (see "For More Information").

Wildlife abounds on Hilton Head. More than 350 species of native American birds have been sighted since 1980; most noticeable are the snowy egret, the bright white American heron and the Louisiana blue heron. Those birds with the strange beaks which curve downward are white ibis. Alligators are so plentiful that the South Carolina Department of Wildlife and Marine Resources uses Hilton Head as a resource to repopulate state parks and wildlife preserves where alligator numbers have diminished. A word of caution: Gators should not be approached or fed; keep your distance and you'll be fine. Deer can be seen in the wild areas of Sea Pines at the south end of the island.

WHERE TO STAY

Hilton Head accommodations range from budget motels along U.S. 278 which rent for $30 a night to luxury villas which rent for hundreds of dollars a night. All told, visitors have more than 3,000 hotel/motel rooms and more than 6,000 villas from which to choose.

The island has four major resorts: Sea Pines, which occupies the "toe" of this shoe-shaped island; Port Royal Plantation, which occupies the "heel"; and Shipyard Plantation and Palmetto Dunes Resort, which are located in between.

Sea Pines features 5,000 wooded acres, a 605-acre forest preserve, plus five miles of beach and 15 miles of bike trails. Accommodations include both villas and private homes (803-785-3333 or 800-845-6131). The other three major resorts are different in that they have contracted with major hotel chains to build luxury resort hotels on their property.

The most expensive of these hotels are the Hyatt Regency Hilton Head (Palmetto Dunes Resort, 803-785-1234) and the Hotel Inter-Continental Hilton Head (Port Royal Plantation, 803-681-4000 or 800-327-0200). The Hyatt is also the largest hotel on the island, and the Inter-Continental is perhaps the most luxurious and formal. Slightly less expensive choices include: Mariner's Inn (Palmetto Dunes, 803-842-8000 or 800-845-8001) and Marriott's Hilton Head Resort (Shipyard Plantation, 803-842-2400).

But not all lodging is located within the resorts. A more affordable choice is the Holiday Inn Oceanfront, a five-story hotel with a nice expanse of beach between Sea Pines and Shipyard (1 S. Forest Beach Dr.,

803-785-5126). The Sea Crest Motel (1 N. Forest Beach Dr., 803-785-2121 or 800-845-7014), located just east of the Holiday Inn, is the best-looking of the reasonably priced motels. Another inexpensive family favorite is the Red Roof Inn (5 Regency Pkwy., 803-686-6808), which is just a short drive from the public beaches.

RV owners can headquarter at Outdoor Resorts of America Motorcoach Resort (803-785-7699) or Outdoor Resorts RV Resort and Yacht Club (803-681-3256 or 800-845-9560). Campers should contact Stoney Crest Plantation Campground (803-757-3249).

For more information on Hilton Head lodging, contact: Hilton Head Central Reservation Center, Box 5312, Hilton Head Island, SC 29938 (803-785-9050 or 800-845-7018).

WHERE TO EAT

Hilton Head is swimming with restaurants and most of the non-chain variety serve fresh seafood, which is definitely the meal of choice here. The best places for a family to sample the catch of the day are Hemingway's and Hudson's Seafood House on the Docks. Hemingway's is an oceanfront restaurant which serves trout almandine and pompano en papillote in a relaxed, Key West-type atmosphere (Hyatt Regency Hilton Head at Palmetto Dunes, 803-785-1234). Hudson's is a former seafood processing factory located between markers 13 and 14 on the Intracoastal Waterway—and the sunsets are remarkable (1 Hudson Rd., 803-681-2772). Hudson's also has a family-style annex, Hudson's Landing, which is adjacent to the main building.

Alexander's (Queens Folly Rd. at Palmetto Dunes, 803-785-4999) is a nice, in-between choice for families with kids who like to eat at nice restaurants. Specialties at this lagoon-side eatery include salmon Oscar, blackened grouper and rack of lamb, and you can order child's plates. CQ's, a former artist's studio located in Harbour Town at Sea Pines (803-671-2779), is another smart choice. Specialties include crepes and quiche (lunch) and for dinner, prime rib and seafood.

A popular spot for families is the Crazy Crab, which overlooks the Harbour Town marina. Adults can order seafood or steak, the kids' menu features burgers and afterward, everyone adjourns to the huge oak tree outside, where troubador Greg Russell sings, plays guitar and tells stories. He performs from 8 to 10 p.m., Memorial Day-Labor Day (803-671-9494).

For an adults-only dinner, we recommend The Barony, where the bill of fare is "upscale country French" and a jacket and tie are required (Hotel Inter-Continental at Port Royal Plantation, 803-681-4000). If money is no object, try Harbourmaster's (in Shelter Cove Marina, off U.S. 278,

803-785-3030). Jackets are required at this multi-tiered establishment, which serves chateaubriand and New England rack of lamb laced with a brandy demiglaze.

SHOPPING/NEARBY FUN

Hilton Head has no shortage of shopping areas. **The Mall at Shelter Cove,** the island's only enclosed shopping center, has more than 55 stores (24 Shelter Cove Ln., just north of the entrance to Palmetto Dunes, 803-686-3090). Next door is **The Plaza at Shelter Cove** (803-785-1106), and strip shopping centers are everywhere. **Coligny Plaza** has more than 60 stores (Coligny Circle, 803-842-6050), and **Pineland Mall Mill Shops** has more than 30 (Hwy. 278, at Matthews Dr., 803-785-7437). **The Village at Wexford** (Hwy. 278, next door to Wexford Plantation, 803-681-2545) and **Shops on the Parkway** (Hwy. 278, just north of Shipyard Plantation, 803-686-6233) are also popular with shoppers. If you're interested in outlet stores, keep your eyes peeled for the **Low Country Factory Village** on Highway 278 just before you get to the island. One of the most beautiful spots to browse for gifts, sip a cool drink and gaze at Calibogue Sound is **Harbour Town at Sea Pines.**

If the kids are secure for a few hours, Mom and Dad could take a do-it-yourself tour of nearby **Beaufort, S.C.** (pronounced "BEW-fort") or **Savannah, Ga.** Beaufort is a picturesque seaport town where both *The Big Chill* and *The Great Santini* were filmed. For information: Beaufort Chamber of Commerce, PO Box 910, Beaufort, SC 29901 (803-524-3163).

Savannah's riverfront area is a lot of fun, and we also enjoy roaming the bookstores and art galleries of America's largest urban Historic Landmark District. Savannah bills its St. Patrick's Day celebration as "second only to New York's" and no matter when you're going to be there, make dinner reservations several days ahead of time at the award-winning Elizabeth on 37th Street (105 E. 37th St., 912-236-5547), which is one of our favorites. For information, contact: Savannah Area Convention and Visitors Bureau, 301 W. Broad St., Savannah, GA 31499 (912-233-6651).

WHEN TO GO

July and August are Hilton Head's peak periods, but the resort's off-season business—November-March—continues to grow every year because the weather is still hospitable and the rates are about half what they are in the summer, as are the crowds.

The average high temperature on Hilton Head ranges from the 80s (May-September) to the 70s (April, October) to the 60s (January-March, November-December).

March is Springfest month at Hilton Head, and along with all the good food, wine tastings and other adult fun, there are on-going Kid-Fest activities, including kite-flying, sand sculpture and oyster-shucking contests.

April is a big month for spectator sports with the Family Circle tennis tournament at Sea Pines in the first week and the MCI golf tournament at Sea Pines in the second week.

FOR MORE INFORMATION

Contact:

Hilton Head Island Chamber of Commerce
PO Box 5647, Hilton Head Island, SC 29938
(803-785-3673)

Jekyll Island

Jekyll Island, Ga., is located on the Atlantic Ocean, six miles southeast of Brunswick, Ga., and 65 miles north of Jacksonville, Fla. (take exit 6 off I-95 and follow the signs). The island features 10 miles of wide, sandy beach, and a 240-acre historic district where the Goodyears, Morgans and Rockefellers once spent their winters.

ABOUT THE AREA

Jekyll Island is the best known of Georgia's "Golden Isles," which also include St. Simons Island, Sea Island and Little St. Simons Island. The island was named by General James Oglethorpe, whose English friend, Sir Joseph Jekyll, helped him establish the first permanent Georgia settlement at Savannah in 1733. Plantations flourished on the island for more than a century, but the Civil War ended that system, just as it did on Hilton Head. In 1886, the island's sole owner, John Eugene du Bignon, sold the island to a group of wealthy northeasterners who were looking for a winter retreat. The selling price was $125,000, and the new owners included men like financier J.P. Morgan and other kingpins of New York society—men who designed St. Patrick's Cathedral (James Renwick), constructed Madison Square Garden (David H. King, Jr.) and raised money for the erection of the Statue of Liberty (Joseph Pulitzer). These men were bound together with 50 others as members of the Jekyll Island Club. In 1900, it was said that club members accounted for one-sixth of the world's wealth. But with the advent of World War II, the club dissolved and a committee appointed by the governor of Georgia recommended that Jekyll Island be purchased and preserved as a state park.

Jekyll still retains the look of a state park. For the most part, the accommodations aren't splashy, t-shirt shops are scarce and there's no strip for vacationers to cruise. The ocean side of the island is strewn with motels, but there are several public bathhouses with restrooms, changing areas and showers. The other side of the island is flanked by the Intracoastal Waterway and salt marshes, and Jekyll's overall lack of pretension and commercialism is beautiful to behold. Chances are, it will never change because the state will allow no more than one-third of the island to be developed.

THINGS TO DO

The newest attraction on the island is the **Summer Waves** waterpark (see the "Best of the Rest" section in the WATERPARKS chapter). Next door is the **Ski Rixen Cable Water Skiing** establishment, where you can water ski on a 12-acre man-made lake—and you don't even need a boat. If you've tried the Knee Ski ride at Wet 'n Wild in Orlando, Fla. (see the WATERPARKS chapter), you know how this gizmo works. If you haven't, you have to see it to appreciate it.

The island has two lighted **miniature golf courses** (on Beachview Dr., 912-635-2648). There's a **bike rental** place there too, and you can tour virtually the entire island via the 20 miles of paved bike paths which start right there.

The **Jekyll Island Recreation Center** offers a summer day camp for boys and girls ages 4-12 with morning, afternoon or all-day activities, Monday-Friday. Those activities include beach games, treasure hunts, crabbing, bike/nature hikes, arts and crafts, rollerskating, mini golf and swimming in the rec center pool (at the recreation and fitness center on Beachview Dr., 912-635-2232). For a small fee, you can use the fitness center to work out. It features a full complement of Nautilus equipment, plus a whirlpool, steam room and sauna. Family rates are available.

If your kids are in day camp or with friends or relatives, you could take a 90-minute tour of the **"Millionaires' Village"** where some of the original Jekyll Island Club members used to live. The tour includes a look at William Rockefeller's cottage. Also of interest is Faith Chapel, where the stained-glass windows are signed by none other than Louis Comfort Tiffany.

One of the real pleasures of vacationing here during the summer are the Broadway musicals which are performed under the stars at the **Jekyll Island Amphitheater** (on Sable Rd., in the historic district).

The **Jekyll Island Marina** is a place where you can simply drop a fishing line into the water or charter a deep-sea fishing boat. The boat will take you east to the 40-mile reef, where you'll fish for grouper, red snapper, black sea bass and amberjack (912-635-2891).

Jekyll Island has 63 holes of **golf**. All three of the 18-hole courses— Oleander, Pine Lakes, Indian Mound—measure roughly 6,600 yards, and Indian Mound is the newest of the three. It was created by Joe Lee, who designed the famous Blue Monster course at Doral Resort and Country Club in Miami. For starting times at any of these courses, call 912-635-3464. Jekyll's nine-hole Oceanside course opened shortly after the turn of the century. This is where the millionaire members of the Jekyll Island Club played golf, and the course has been in continuous operation ever since. For starting times here, call 912-635-2170. Rates on all Jekyll Island courses include unlimited all-day play except during the spring peak season, and unlike a lot of resort courses, you don't have to rent electric carts (main clubhouse on Capt. Wylly Rd.).

The **Jekyll Island Tennis Center** is one of the most attractive facilities we've ever seen, mainly because wood-framed screens have been used in place of the usual metal fences—which enables the center to blend beautifully with the live oaks and pines that surround it. You'll find 13 clay courts here, seven of which are lighted for night play (on Capt. Wylly Rd. adjacent to the golf clubhouse parking lot, 404-635-3154). The J.P. Morgan Tennis Center has eight hard courts, five of which are lighted, plus one indoor court (on Riverview Dr. adjacent to the Jekyll Island Club, 912-635-2600, ext. 1060).

WHERE TO STAY

If you've longed to stay in a grand Victorian-style hotel where millionaires once romped and played—and where kids can do the same without sideways glances from management—there is such a place: the Jekyll Island Club Hotel, which was the center of social activities during the club era. Built in 1887 and restored in 1985 to the tune of $17 million, this distinctive, four-story structure has a cupola on top and 124 custom-decorated guest rooms and suites inside. Now a Radisson Resort, the hotel is located on Jekyll Creek, with a view of the wharf (371 Riverview Dr., 912-635-2600).

The remaining 10 motels are all oceanside. Less expensive choices—all of which are nice—include: Jekyll Inn, Villas By The Sea, Holiday Inn Resort and Comfort Inn Island Suites.

Formerly a Hilton property, the Jekyll Inn is the largest hotel on the island, with 200 guest rooms and 70 townhouse villas, some of which are equipped with kitchenettes. Children 12 and under stay free (975 N. Beachview Dr., 912-635-2531). Villas By The Sea features full kitchen facilities in every one- to three-bedroom villa, with private living rooms and separate bedrooms. Children 15 and under stay free (1175 N. Beachview Dr., 912-635-2521, 800-841-6262 or, in Georgia, 800-342-6872). The Holiday Inn has several features which make it a good choice for families: swimming pool, playground, bike rentals and two tennis courts. Children 18 and under stay free (200 S. Beachview Dr., 912-635-3311 or, in Georgia, 800-238-8000). We like the Comfort Inn Island Suites for many reasons: the suites are nice, and both the breakfast buffet and the afternoon happy hour are complimentary. With a three-day, two-night package, you get a day's bike rental and a pass to both Summer Waves and miniature golf. Four kinds of suites are available; the Lanai suites feature private hot tubs. Children 18 and under stay free (711 N. Beachview Dr., 912-635-2211 or 800-228-5150).

Best deal: Quality Inn Buccaneer, which has a free kids' recreation program which runs from Memorial Day to Labor Day and deluxe-sized efficiencies for those who want to eat in. There's also a tennis court, and children 16 and under stay free (85 S. Beachview Dr., 912-635-2261 or 800-228-5151).

Another option is the **Jekyll Island Campground,** an 18-acre, wooded location with 200 campsites and full amenities (on N. Beachview Dr., 912-635-3021).

WHERE TO EAT

With the exception of the Grand Dining Room at the Jekyll Island Club Hotel, which should be reserved for an adults-only dinner, all of the motel restaurants are suitable for family dining. Our pick of that bunch is Saint Andrews Landing, which is known for its pecan shrimp and its Friday night seafood buffet (at the Jekyll Inn, 912-635-2531). There's a Pizza Inn at the Comfort Inn Island Suites (711 N. Beachview Dr., 912-635-3733) which serves breakfast buffets, steak and seafood, besides pizza. Free-standing restaurants include Blackbeard's (200 N. Beachview Dr., 912-635-3522) and Zachry's (44 Beachview Dr., 912-635-3128), both of which specialize in coastal seafood.

If you're in the mood for a drive, zip on over to nearby St. Simons Island and have dinner at either the Crab Trap (1209 Ocean Blvd., 912-638-3552) or its newer, more polished sibling, Crabdaddy's (1219 Ocean Blvd., 912-634-1120). The atmosphere at the Crab Trap is very informal and there's a hole in the middle of every table for disposing of corn cobs and shrimp/crab shells. Crabdaddy's specializes in grilled fresh fish, and you toss your own salad.

SHOPPING/NEARBY FUN

Jekyll is not a shopper's paradise in the way that, say, Hilton Head is. The **Jekyll Shopping Center** (on Beachview Dr.) is the principal shopping area, and its offerings are pretty basic: beachwear, suntan lotion, snacks and drinks.

Cumberland Island is separated from Jekyll by St. Andrews Sound. This 16-by-3-mile wildlife sanctuary is run by the National Park Service. It also has beautiful beaches, but the island can be reached only by ferry—which leaves from nearby St. Mary's, Ga., twice a day. There is a fee for the ferry, but not for entrance to the island. No private vehicles are allowed on the island, and camping is limited to 120 persons per night. **Sea Camp,** which accommodates 60, is the only developed camp; four other areas have drinking water only. Reservations are required, and campers must carry all equipment and supplies to the campsites on foot. Nothing can be purchased on the island. To make ferry reservations (it's heavily booked during summer months) or for further information, contact: National Park Service, Cumberland Island National Seashore, Box 806, St. Mary's, GA 31558 (912-882-4335).

If your kids are starved for more commercial entertainment, take them to **Neptune Park** on St. Simons. Here you'll find miniature golf, picnic tables and access to the public beach. The **Neptune Park Casino** has a swimming pool, rollerskating rink, bowling lanes and a snack bar (912-638-2392). Neptune Park is also where you find the St. Simons Chamber of Commerce (912-638-9014) and the staff there can give you other suggestions for family fun, such as a visit to the **Fort Frederica National Monument.** This 18th-century English fort is surrounded by homes and shops built by soldiers and civilians (912-638-3639).

WHEN TO GO

Jekyll Island is 75 miles south of Hilton Head and its weather is virtually the same: average high temperatures in the 80s (May-September), 70s (April, October-November) and 60s (January-March, December). Pay close attention to these temps because even though Jekyll has lovely year-round weather, it isn't Florida. We can attest to that because we honeymooned there in early February and we still have a photo of one of us shivering in a bikini on the balcony of the Buccaneer Motel.

Jekyll's high season extends from late May to early September. Rates are lower until early February, but then golf season kicks in and they jump back up again.

FOR MORE INFORMATION

Contact:

Convention & Visitors Bureau
PO Box 3186, Jekyll Island, GA 31520
(912-635-3400 or 800-841-6586)

The Jekyll Island Welcome Center is located on the Jekyll Island Causeway next to the State Patrol headquarters.

MYRTLE BEACH

Myrtle Beach, S.C., is located on the Atlantic Ocean, 30 miles south of the North Carolina border at the intersection of U.S. 501 and U.S. 17. It is considered the hub of the Grand Strand, a 60-mile expanse of beach which runs from the North Carolina line south to Georgetown, S.C.

ABOUT THE AREA

The Grand Strand was colonized by Spanish settlers in 1526, and in 1730 the English laid out plans for Georgetown, South Carolina's third oldest city. But Myrtle Beach didn't exist until 1901, when a railroad was built from the Waccamaw River to the beach and a hotel was constructed. "New Town" was the original name of this impromptu beach community, but a local newspaper held a contest to rename it and Mrs. F.G. Burroughs, wife of the founder of the Burroughs and Collins timber- turpentine firm, submitted the winning entry. Mrs. Burroughs reasoned that with all the wax myrtle trees that grew along the beach, the name "Myrtle Beach" was appropriate. Even then, the area didn't really take off. It wasn't incorporated until 1938 and didn't become a city until 1957.

Fewer than 30,000 people live here year-round, but millions visit every year—which is Myrtle Beach's principal reason for being. And most Myrtle Beach visitors know what to expect: a wacky, tacky, carnival-type atmosphere that harkens back to the days when Elvis was king and resort areas weren't quite so upscale. Where else would you find an amusement park right in the middle of town? Or a strip of highway (Ocean Blvd.) known affectionately as "teenage Bourbon Street" where beach music and South Carolina's official state dance, The Shag, are still the rage? Yes, Myrtle Beach is gaudy and crowded. And parts of it do seem bent on setting new world records for neon, miniature golf, t-shirt shops and sideshow-type attractions like the Ripley's and Guinness "museums." But who says that's not fun—and doesn't everyone need a dose of kitsch now and then? We do, and we think Myrtle Beach offers more than that— particularly if you pick a nice place to stay. One way to escape the gaudiness is to choose a hotel in neighboring North Myrtle Beach, where the atmosphere is more soothing and the beach stretches more than an eighth of a mile from the dunes to the water at low tide.

THINGS TO DO

Since Myrtle Beach is, first and foremost, a family resort area— meaning it features lots of things that kids like to do, as well as adults— we'll start with the **Myrtle Beach Pavilion and Amusement Park,** which is located a half-block from the beach and has an assortment of stomach-churning rides, plus some tamer ones for kids. The landmark attractions at the Pavilion are "Big Eli," a 60-foot-high ferris wheel, and a single-loop roller coaster, The Corkscrew. Open daily, 1 p.m.-midnight, June-August, plus restricted schedule March-May and September (9th Ave. N. and Ocean Blvd., 803-448-6456).

We're big waterpark fans and we recommend nearby **Myrtle Waves** (see "Best of the Rest" in WATERPARKS). **Wild Water & Wheels,** a mini waterpark with go-karts, is also fun (Hwy. 17 and 10th Ave. S. in Surfside Beach, 803-238-9453).

If you and your kids like weird stuff, check out the **Guinness Hall of World Records** and **Ripley's Believe It or Not Museum.** Guinness is open daily 10 a.m.-midnight from mid-March to early October, but closed the rest of the year. Kids 6 and under are free (911 N. Ocean Blvd., 803-448-4611). Ripley's is open daily 9 a.m.-10 p.m., March-November, but closed the rest of the year. Kids 5 and under are free (901 N. Ocean Blvd., 803-448-2331).

The Grand Strand bills itself as the **"Seaside Golf Capital of the World"** and that nickname within a nickname reflects the fact that there are roughly 70 public courses from which to choose—meaning you can always get a tee time somewhere. It also means that Myrtle Beach has come a long way since 1948, when Pine Lakes International Country Club was the only place to play. Most courses are located on U.S. 17 (also known as Kings Hwy.) and some are on South Carolina 501. The most highly regarded, according to *Golf Digest*, are Arcadian Shores Golf Club, which winds through a grove of live oaks (803-449-5217), and Dunes Golf and Beach Club, an oceanfront course designed by Robert Trent Jones (803-449-5914). North Myrtle Beach courses of note include: Gator Hole (803-249-3543), Oyster Bay Golf Links (803-272-6399), Robbers Roost Golf Club (803-249-1471) and Marsh Harbor Golf Links (803-249-3449). You'll find three 18-hole layouts at the Bay Tree Golf Plantation (803-249-1487 or, outside South Carolina, 800-845-6191) and at the Myrtle Beach National Golf Club (803-448-2308 or 800-344-5590). Clubs with 36-hole layouts: Burning Ridge Golf Club (803-448-3141 or 800-833-0337), Myrtle West Golf Club (803-756-0550) and Myrtlewood Golf Club (803-449-5134). For a real treat, drive north to Calabash, N.C., just across the state line, and play the two seaside courses at the Pearl Golf Links (919-579-8132 or 803-272-2850).

If you're interested in what golf packages are available—and you should be—contact: Golf Holiday, Box 1323, Myrtle Beach, SC 29578 (803-448-5942 or 800-845-GOLF).

Most hotels and resorts have **tennis courts** on site, and you can also get court time at the Myrtle Beach Racquet Club (803-449-4031) and

Myrtle Beach Tennis and Swim Club (803-449-4486).

The waters around Myrtle Beach are warmed by the Gulf Stream, which means that **fishing** is usually good from early spring through December. As far as access goes, you can walk right out over the Atlantic on piers and jetties and angle for bluefish, channel bass, flounder, pompano and whiting. If you're good—or good and lucky—you could collect some prize money for the largest catch in the Grand Strand Fishing Rodeo's "fish of the month" contest, held April-October. Conveniently located marinas include Capt. Dick's (U.S. 17 Business, in Murrells Inlet, 803-651-3676) and Vereen's (U.S. 17 at 11th Ave. N. in North Myrtle Beach, 803-249-4333).

Body surfing and boogie-boarding are big at Myrtle Beach because the waves are usually strong. We love to crash and jump the surf with our kids, and one of the best places to rent surfboards and other watersport craft and equipment, including Hobie cats, jet-skis, sailboats and Windsurfers, is at Downwind Sails (Ocean Blvd. at 29th Ave. S., 803-448-7245).

Skindivers flock to the area off the coast of the Little River, just north of Myrtle Beach, where a variety of tropical fish—amberjack, barracuda, grouper and spadefish—congregate around outlying shipwrecks. Scuba gear and instruction are available at the Myrtle Beach Scuba Center (809 U.S. 501 W., 803-448-2832).

WHERE TO STAY

For deluxe North Myrtle Beach lodging choices, the Radisson Resort Hotel might solve all of your vacation needs in one fell swoop. This 20-story, all-suites hotel is part of the Kingston Plantation complex, which includes restaurants, shops, a 20-acre freshwater lake and 145 acres of oceanside woodlands. Hotel facilities include indoor/outdoor swimming pools, a wading pool and play area for kids, a volleyball court—and, of course, there's a nice beach out front. Children 16 and under stay free (9800 Lake Dr., 803-449-0006). Another choice in the deluxe category is the Myrtle Beach Hilton and Golf Club, a luxurious oceanfront high-rise with a 14-story atrium. The Hilton is part of the Arcadian Shores Golf Club, and it features a 600-foot private beach and 24-hour room service during the summer. Children of any age stay free (701 Hilton Rd., 803-449-5000). Both of these resorts have supervised children's activity programs at no charge. The Radisson's kids' program runs March-October, the Hilton's Memorial Day-Labor Day.

Deluxe accommodations in the midst of the Ocean Boulevard action include The Breakers Resort Hotel (2006 N. Ocean Blvd., 803-626-5000 or 800-845-0688) and the Best Western Landmark Resort (1501 S. Ocean Blvd., 803-448-9441 or 800-845-0658). The Breakers offers 250 rooms—181 of them with kitchenettes—in two towers. Children 15 and under stay free and the kids' activities program is free. The Best Western is a 14-story high-rise and some of the rooms have balconies and refrigerators. There is a kids' activities program and a game room. Children 17 and under stay free.

Less expensive choices include: Sheraton Atlantic Shores Hotel & Towers, which is one of Myrtle Beach's newest hotels and where children 16 and under stay free (2701 S. Ocean Blvd., 803-448-2518 or 800-992-1055); Beach Cove Clarion Resort, where children 15 and under stay free (4800 S. Ocean Blvd., 803-272-4044 or 800-331-6533); and of special interest to families, the Coral Beach Resort. The Coral Beach has—get this—six outdoor swimming pools, four indoor pools, a lazy river tube ride, an eight-lane bowling alley, an indoor putting green and driving range, pool tables and a game room. Children 15 and under stay free (1105 S. Ocean Blvd., 803-448-8421 or 800-843-2684).

A good-value choice is the Sea Mist Resort, which has most everything the Coral Beach has—except the bowling alley and driving range—for less money. It also has a kids' activities program (1200 S. Ocean Blvd., 803-448-1551 or 800-732-6478).

Before golf became king here, Myrtle Beach billed itself as the "Camping Capital of the World" and it still shines in that department. You can choose from seven private campgrounds and, with the exception of the KOA Kampground, all are located on the beach. But KOA is closest to Ocean Boulevard and all the Myrtle Beach Pavilion and Amusement Park action, which some people like better. The total number of campsites exceeds 7,000, and all seven campgrounds are conveniently located on U.S. 17 between U.S. 9 and U.S. 544. Most include hot showers, heated swimming pools, launderettes, general stores and snack bars. Three are located just north of Ocean Boulevard: Apache Family Campground (803-449-7323 or 800-553-1749), Barefoot RV Resort (800-272-1790) and Myrtle Beach Travel Park (803-449-3714 or 800-782-3816). And three are located south of both Ocean Boulevard and Myrtle Beach State Park: Lakewood Family Campground (800-258-8309), Ocean Lakes Family Campground (803-238-1451 or 800-722-1451) and Pirateland Family Campground (800-443-CAMP). KOA is all by itself in the middle (803-448-3421 or 800-255-7614), and there's also another KOA in North Myrtle Beach (Hwy. 17N, 803-272-6420). To get an idea of which one suits your family best, contact the Myrtle Beach Area Chamber of Commerce (see "For More Information") and ask for a brochure.

WHERE TO EAT

Two of the most popular seafood restaurants in Myrtle Beach are Rice Planter's (6707 Kings Hwy. N., 803-449-3456) and Sea Captain's House (3002 N. Ocean Blvd., 803-448-8082). Rice Planter's is housed in a large brick building with high ceilings, and multi-course meals here include shrimp/oyster cocktail, followed by clam chowder, filet of fish, fried shrimp, baked crabmeat and deep-sea scallops. Sea Captain's House starts you off with she-crab soup and the seafood platters are a good choice. Be sure to request a table on the porch, which overlooks the ocean.

Tony's is the oldest Italian restaurant on the Grand Strand. Cozy and casual, it features fresh veal, homemade pasta and fresh clams. Children have their own menu, and if they're not in the mood for Italian fare they can order a burger (1407 U.S. 17 across from Robbers Roost golf course, 803-249-1314).

On nearby Pawleys Island, 82 Queen is another must for families who like seafood. Specialties include baked snapper, broiled lump-crab cakes and shrimp provencale with fresh spinach pasta. There's also a children's menu, and be sure to request a table on the glass-enclosed porch of this antebellum-style inn (U.S. 17 in the Hammock Shops, 803-237-9033).

SHOPPING/NEARBY FUN

If you have little ones who despise shopping, **Myrtle Square Mall's full-size carousel** may change their minds (2501 N. Kings Hwy., 803-448-2513). We also recommend a visit to **Barefoot Landing,** a shopping and restaurant complex built over the water in North Myrtle Beach (4898 Hwy. 17 S., 803-272-8349).

Briarcliffe Mall has 100 shops (10177 Kings Hwy., 803-272-4040) and **Inlet Square Mall** (100125 U.S. 17 Bypass, Murrells Inlet, 803-651-6990) is brand-new.

Myrtle Beach is the home of **Waccamaw Pottery,** which has given birth to an entire complex of shops and outlet stores near the Intracoastal Waterway at U.S. 501. There's even a movie theater (3200 Pottery Dr., 803-236-4606).

Have you ever heard of a Pawleys Island hammock? Well, they're hand-made of rope and cord on **Pawleys Island, S.C.,** which is south of Brookgreen Gardens and Huntington Beach State Park. You'll find 17 boutiques and gift shops here, and they're all built from old brick that was brought from England as ballast.

Eighteen miles south of Myrtle Beach, on the grounds of a colonial rice plantation, is the world's largest outdoor sculpture garden. **Brookgreen Gardens** was created in 1931 by railroad magnate and philanthropist Archer Huntington and his wife. Adults will enjoy seeing works of art by the likes of Frederic Remington; the kids will get a boot out of the wildlife park and aviary, where deer, otters, alligators, raccoons, egrets, herons and ducks can be seen. For a history lesson, the entire family should stroll the avenue of massive 225-year-old oaks, dripping with Spanish moss, which leads to the former site of an antebellum home. The home burned in 1901, but the original kitchen has been restored as a museum for plantation tools and utensils. Open daily 9:30-4:45 except Christmas (off U.S. 17, 803-237-4218).

Across the highway from Brookgreen Gardens is **Huntington Beach State Park,** which is located on the former estate of the Huntingtons. The focal point of the 2,500-acre park is the beachside Moorish-style castle, Atalaya, which was once the Huntingtons' home and which is now open to visitors. But this isn't an adults-only kind of place because there's also a terrific beach, surf fishing, a salt-marsh boardwalk, picnic areas, bike trails and a campground (off U.S. 17, 803-237-4440).

WHEN TO GO

Myrtle Beach is roughly 250 miles north of Hilton Head and the weather is a bit cooler: High temperatures range from the 80s (May-September) to the 70s (April, October) to the 60s (March, November) to the 50s (December-February).

Tourist season begins in late February, when golfers from the North descend on the city. The Sun Fun Festival, held the first week of June, is the biggest event of the year. Past grand marshalls of the Sun Fun Festival parade include Vanna White and Willard Scott.

FOR MORE INFORMATION

Contact:

Myrtle Beach Area Chamber of Commerce
PO Box 2115, Myrtle Beach, SC 29578
(803-626-7444 or 800-356-3016)

CITIES

❖ **A**TLANTA

❖ **M**IAMI

❖ **N**ASHVILLE

❖ **O**RLANDO

CITIES

We consider ourselves to be city folk, having spent nearly the first decade of our married life living smack in the middle of Manhattan. But when our second child was born, we left for greener pastures—a place where we could live in a house with a swing set in the backyard. We still insist, however, that cities are great places to visit.

The four Southeastern cities we've chosen to highlight in this chapter—Atlanta, Miami, Nashville and Orlando—are all exciting places with much to offer family vacationers. For starters, there's the obvious: three of these four cities are home to at least one major theme/amusement park (Six Flags and White Water in Atlanta; Opryland U.S.A. in Nashville; Walt Disney World, Universal Studios and so on in Orlando). Miami's draw is its fabulous beach, plus a host of special attractions like Seaquarium.

But don't let these biggies keep you from sampling some of the less-advertised offerings. For instance, each of these cities boasts a number of excellent museums geared to children's interests (and fun for adults as well). Most of the ones we recommend are hands-on places where you get involved with the exhibits, rather than just looking at items in glass cases. Several of these museums have activity rooms for preschoolers, which may be the most fun of all. Check to see if a free pass is required for these special areas, since the number of children allowed in at one time may be limited. And be sure to allow plenty of time for your museum visit, because you don't want to rush your kids away from something they've gotten intrigued with.

Each of these cities has a planetarium connected to one of its museums, with intriguing shows that kids will enjoy. But be aware that preschoolers are generally not admitted—for fear they would fuss when the lights are turned out. The exception is the Space Transit Planetarium in Miami, which offers a special program for wee ones.

Both Miami and Atlanta have zoos, where it's easy to while away all or part of a day. And all four cities offer interesting sightseeing and recreational possibilities, as well as unique places to shop and eat. We haven't covered absolutely everything there is to see and do at each destination, but have focused on what we consider the best bets for families. If you discover a place or activity we've left out, we'd like to know about it for future editions.

We've also noted some of the annual festivals and special events held in these cities—like Nashville's Summer Lights and Carnaval Miami. For a more detailed calendar of events, write to the convention and visitors bureaus listed at the end of each section. They'll send you lots of literature to help you plan your trip. They can also answer any specific questions you may have.

If you'll be driving in these cities (a likelihood, since these are large metropolitan areas and attractions are spread out), be sure to get a detailed, up-to-date street map and know the route from where you are to where you're going; city streets can be confusing and getting lost is no fun. In some instances, you might want to take advantage of the local transit system, so you don't have to worry about driving and parking. We've provided phone numbers to call for information. If your kids haven't ridden on an elevated train—one of the transportation choices—they may think that getting there is half the fun.

Before you head for a museum, a zoo, a restaurant or whatever, call ahead to make sure it's open. While you're at it, ask for directions on how to get there and check the hours it's open and whether parking is available. You'll be glad you did.

P. S.

Though we don't go into them in as much detail, you'll find a number of other cities covered in various chapters in this book. For instance, one of our favorites —Asheville, NC—is under "Shopping/Nearby Fun" in the Grove Park Inn section of the RESORTS chapter.

A couple of last words of advice:

❑ Don't get caught in rush-hour traffic. People who live and work in big cities may have to deal with gridlock, but you don't. Arrange your schedule so that you're not trying to travel when people are going to work or heading home. And remember that Friday rush hour can start as early as 3:30 p.m.

❑ Exercise some ordinary safety precautions.
- ■ Lock your car doors (and stash any items you're leaving behind in the trunk).
- ■ Use the chain or dead bolt on your hotel/motel door when you're in the room.
- ■ When you're not, keep items like wallets, watches, cameras, etc. hidden from sight or even locked in a safe.
- ■ Don't let children ride elevators by themselves.

ATLANTA

We may be prejudiced since Atlanta is practically in our backyard, but frankly, my dears, we can't think of a more fun city to visit with kids, particularly in the summer. Six Flags keeps adding new rides and Zoo Atlanta new exhibits. American Adventures, a year-round amusement park, has opened next to White Water, one of the most popular waterparks in the U.S. Want to see a laser show with a mountain backdrop? Check the nightly summer spectacle at Stone Mountain Park. And if you choose to spend some time indoors, the city offers a collection of nifty museums, plus Underground Atlanta and, right next door, the World of Coca-Cola pavilion. What more could you want?

ABOUT THE CITY

As *Gone With the Wind* fans will vividly recall, the young city of Atlanta was razed by General Sherman on his infamous march to the sea in 1864. But it rose phoenix-like from the ashes and has been in a boom stage ever since. Today's skyline features a growing parade of tall buildings—luxury hotels and corporate offices—which attest to the city's appeal for business and tourism. Another measure of Atlanta's growing national and international reputation is the fact that within the span of a few years it was selected as the host city for the 1988 Democratic National Convention, the 1994 Super Bowl and the 1996 Summer Olympics.

Atlanta is not only the capital of Georgia but also the transportation hub of the Southeast. Just a few minutes south of the downtown area is Hartsfield International, one of the two or three busiest airports in the world. Three major interstates lead into the city: I-75 and I-85, which run basically north-south, and I-20, which runs east-west. A perimeter loop, I-285, encircles the metro area. These major arteries allow you to get where you're going quickly—provided you don't drive them during morning or evening rush hours.

Because Atlanta's attractions are spread out, you pretty much need a car to get around. The alternative is MARTA, the city's rapid-rail and bus transportation system, which is economical and fairly easy to negotiate. For schedules and information, call 404-848-4711.

The Convention and Visitors Bureau will send you an Atlanta map and a guide to attractions that is worth studying before your visit. The CVB also publishes *Atlanta Now*, a $3 guide which provides more extensive information. Write to the address at the end of this section.

If you're in town on a Saturday, pick up a copy of the *Atlanta Journal and Constitution* and consult the Weekend section. It lists "Kids Picks"—special events, performances and attractions—with all pertinent info.

Below we've highlighted some of our favorite things to do in Atlanta with kids. As time permits, you could add other activities like a visit to the Capitol (Capitol Hill at Washington St., 404-656-2844) or a trip to a Braves, Hawks or Falcons game. The Braves play at Atlanta-Fulton County Stadium (521 Capitol Ave. SW, 404-522-1967), which is also home to the Falcons until they move to the new Georgia Dome (slated to happen in 1992). The Hawks play at the Omni (100 Techwood Dr. NW, 404-681-2100).

Atlanta has lots of historic sites, but two that should interest children as well as adults are the Martin Luther King Jr. Historic District and the Wren's Nest, home of Joel Chandler Harris, who authored the Uncle Remus tales. The historic district on Auburn Avenue includes the Center for Nonviolent Social Change (449 Auburn Ave., 404-524-1956), where you can view King's grave and a film and exhibit on his life. There's also a small bookstore focused on black history materials for young people. At the Wren's Nest (1050 Gordon St. SW, 404-753-8535) storytelling sessions are a regular feature.

For a kid-oriented sampling of Atlanta's cultural offerings, you might want to schedule a visit to the Woodruff Arts Center (1280 Peachtree St. NE, 404-892-3600). The High Museum of Art is located in this complex, which also includes Symphony Hall and the Alliance and Studio Theaters. The High (as it's known) was devoting serious attention to interactive exhibitions for children long before most other art museums. Long-term exhibits are installed at the Junior Gallery, which is located on the ground floor. The current one, "Spectacles," will be on view through 1993. Excellent children's theater productions are also staged periodically at the center.

If your family likes to go "malling" together, head to Lenox Square, Atlanta's mega-shopping center, or to Perimeter or Cumberland malls, two other favorites of the shop-till-you-drop crowd. You'll find restaurants, food courts, movie theaters and miles of stores.

NOTE

$ $ $ A word about prices: They change, so we haven't included them. But be aware that admission is charged for most of the activities we've listed. With the exception of major attractions like Six Flags and White Water, you can generally plan to pay between $3-6 for adults, about half that for children. At Stone Mountain Park there's a per-car admission; some attractions are extra.

THINGS TO DO

Downtown/Midtown

Zoo Atlanta—What once was one of the city's biggest embarrassments is now one of its biggest attractions. The turn-around started in the mid-Eighties when the zoo became a private, nonprofit organization. A multimillion dollar redevelopment program has since taken many of the animals out of cages and placed them in natural habitats, which simulate such environments as an African rain forest.

The star and symbol of the zoo is longtime resident Willie B., a huge silverback gorilla. A pair of rare Sumatran tigers and a black rhinoceros, one of the world's most endangered species, were added to the collection in 1990.

The zoo covers 37 acres in Grant Park and includes a cafe at each entrance, a gift shop and a petting zoo (look out for the peacock!). Stroller rentals are available. Zoo Atlanta is open daily—except for a few major holidays—till 5 p.m., with extended weekend hours in the summer (800 Cherokee Ave. SE, 404-624-5678).

Just outside the entrance to the zoo is the **Atlanta Cyclorama** (404-658-7625), which houses a huge panoramic mural and diorama depicting the bloody 1864 Battle of Atlanta. Visitors sit in an amphitheater as the 358-foot-long mural rotates past and the story of this pivotal Civil War battle is recounted. An impressive 13-minute film, *The Atlanta Campaign*, is shown in a side auditorium before the audience is led to the amphitheater. First screened in 1990, this film is a mini-epic with narration by James Earl Jones and a 21-speaker sound system that makes it seem like cannons are actually firing in the room. Civil War buffs will love it, but the overall experience is saddening and may be too intense for young children.

Underground Atlanta—The new and improved Underground Atlanta opened in the summer of 1989. The six-block area under the streets of downtown Atlanta was revitalized by the Rouse Company, which also did Boston's Faneuil Hall Marketplace and Baltimore's Harborplace. While the nightclubs and many of the shops are aimed at adults, families can enjoy sightseeing and stopping in places like the Huggable Hut (stuffed animals), Dallas Alice (t-shirts), and the Candy Barrel (penny candy). Because waits can be long for the restaurants, consider the food court if hunger strikes. Good bets include Aleck's Barbecue Heaven (for ribs) and Southern Vittles (for fried chicken). For dessert, try some Gorin's homemade ice cream or a fresh-fruit drink at Udderly Cool. Most stores are open 10 a.m.-9:30 p.m. Monday-Saturday, noon-6 p.m. Sunday. The main entrance is at Peachtree and Alabama streets (404-523-2311) and parking lots are nearby.

When you visit Underground Atlanta, be sure to stop by **Heritage Row,** the 7,000-square-foot exhibit hall that stretches for nearly a block on Upper Alabama Street between Pryor Street and Central Avenue. You'll get an overview of Atlanta's history through a series of unique displays, including a Civil War bomb shelter, a trolley car and a jet cockpit. And take time to see the 15-minute film, *People: The Spirit of Atlanta,* shown in the Heritage Row theater—it's a stunner. Purchase tickets at the Delta clock tower near Pryor Street. Closed Mondays (404-584-7879).

World of Coca-Cola Pavilion—Located adjacent to Underground Atlanta, this three-story monument to the hometown soft drink is a company museum extraordinaire. You can visit a recreated 1930s soda fountain, view classic TV commercials, and marvel at an amazing kinetic sculpture called "The Bottling Fantasy." At the futuristic Club Coca-Cola, you can sample one of the 18 beverages the company distributes worldwide. Hours are the same as Underground stores (404-676-5151).

Science and Technology Museum (Scitrek)—One of Atlanta's newest museums (it opened in 1988) is housed in what used to be the Civic Center exhibition hall. A video presentation near the entrance orients visitors to the four areas of this scientific playground: Hall of Mechanics, Light and Perception, Magnetism and Electricity, and Kidspace (for those under four feet tall). In each, you'll find hands-on exhibits that entertain and inform—like the Van de Graaf generator which literally makes your hair stand on end. Open daily (395 Piedmont Ave. NE, 404-522-5500).

Center for Puppetry Arts—Located in an old school, this museum houses the largest private collection of puppets in the U.S. Kermit the Frog cut the ribbon when the center opened in 1978. Performances, classes and special programs are offered year-round. Closed Sundays (1404 Spring St., box office: 404-873-3391).

Metro Area

Six Flags Over Georgia—For details, see THEME PARKS chapter.
White Water/American Adventures—See WATERPARKS.
Stone Mountain Park—The focal point of the park is the 90-by-190-foot carving of Confederate heroes Robert E. Lee, Stonewall Jackson and Jefferson Davis begun by Mount Rushmore sculptor Gutzon Borglum in 1923. Located high on the mountain, it can be seen close up from a cable car. The massive carving also provides a dramatic backdrop for the popular laser shows shown nightly from May through Labor Day and weekends through October. Lots of families bring picnic suppers so they can stake out a nice grassy viewing area.

The 3,200-acre park has a lake and beach area, with a couple of water slides, a snack bar and picnic tables, and Toddler's Cove, a sandy playground for small fry. Other park activities include fishing, tennis and a Robert Trent Jones golf course. There's even an ice skating rink. A steam-driven locomotive and a paddlewheel boat offer ways to see the scenery at the base of the mountain. For the view from the top, take the Skylift or—if everyone's feeling energetic—walk up. Stone Mountain Park is open daily, with attraction hours extended in the summer. It's located 16 miles east of Atlanta off U.S. 78 (404-498-5600).

Fernbank Science Center—An eclectic exhibit area features some fairly lifelike dinosaurs plus an Apollo 6 space capsule. But the main draw here is the planetarium, one of the largest in the U.S. at 70 feet in diameter. Call for the schedule of shows and be on time—or you won't get in. Children under 5 are not admitted to the planetarium. Fernbank is located off Ponce de Leon Ave. on the way out of town to Stone Mountain (156 Heaton Park Dr. NE, 404-378-4311).

WHERE TO STAY

Many of Atlanta's most notable hotels—the 73-story Westin Peachtree Plaza, the Ritz-Carlton, the Marriott Marquis, etc.—are concentrated in the downtown area. That's fine for business travelers and conventioneers, who shuttle in from the airport, then get around on foot or by cab. But it's not so good for family vacationers with cars, because you have to negotiate lots of one-way streets and it's easy to get confused or lost.

We recommend staying north of the city and selecting a hotel or motel with easy access to I-285 so you can zip around the perimeter to various sites. There are lots of accommodations to choose from and because competition is stiff, you can frequently take advantage of special packages and other enticements.

Some deluxe properties in this vicinity include:

Hyatt Regency Ravinia (4355 Ashford-Dunwoody Rd., 404-577-1234). One block from I-285 and adjacent to Perimeter Mall. Kids under 18 stay free.

Stouffer Waverly (2450 Galleria Pkwy., 404-953-4500). Near the interchange of I-285 and I-75, across from Cumberland Mall. Kids under 18 stay free.

Ritz-Carlton Buckhead (3434 Peachtree Rd. NE, 404-237-2700). Across the street from Lenox Square shopping center. Young guests are pampered with kid-sized terrycloth robes and those under 18 stay free.

In a somewhat more moderate price range, we like all-suite hotels and motels, especially for extended stays. Among our recommendations in the area:

Guest Quarters (111 Perimeter Center West, 404-396-6800). Free breakfast buffet and kids under 18 stay free.

Embassy Suites Perimeter Center (1030 Crowne Point Pkwy., 404-394-5454). Free cooked-to-order breakfast is served in the lobby atrium. Kids under 12 stay free.

Residence Inn Atlanta-Dunwoody (1901 Savoy Dr., 404-455-4446). Free continental breakfast.

Sheraton Suites Cumberland (2844 Cobb Pkwy. SE, 404-955-3900). Opened in Sept. 1990. Treat for kids: VCRs and free videos. Free cooked-to-order breakfast.

If your main goal is to sleep cheap, budget chains abound in the area. You can use the 800-numbers listed in the appendix for information and reservations.

Another possibility is to stay at Stone Mountain Park. Options here include a campground with sites for tents and RVs (404-498-5710), the Stone Mountain Inn (404-469-3311) and the newer Evergreen Conference Center and Resort (404-879-9900 or 800-722-1000). The latter, which opened in 1989, offers packages which include breakfast and/or family passes to attractions.

WHERE TO EAT

If there's one thing Atlanta's got, it's restaurants. Hundreds of them. The noted ones—the ones recognized by both local and national critics as the city's best—are, for the most part, not places where people take children. They're elegant and expensive and are best saved for a special parents' night out when you can really savor your meal. Want to try one? Our favorite for very special occasions is Pano's and Paul's, which is located in a small shopping center on West Paces Ferry Rd. at I-75 (404-261-3662). Ask for one of the banquettes and order the fried lobster tail for an appetizer or entrée. You'll forget you even have kids.

On the other end of the eating scale, if you're interested in experiencing one of the world's largest drive-ins, head for the locally famous Varsity on North Avenue at I-75/85. Besides the usual burgers and hot dogs, regulars swear by the fried peach pies (404-881-1706).

Another Atlanta landmark is Mary Mac's Tearoom (224 Ponce de Leon Ave. NE, 404-875-4337). House specialties are baked or fried chicken and fresh vegetables. The child's plate is a real bargain.

Some of our favorite chain eateries in the area include Steak 'n Shake, Chili's and Red Lobster. Another popular family-style place is Black-eyed Pea. Each of these chains has multiple locations in the metro vicinity. Consult a phone book.

For a lavish—and expensive—Sunday brunch, head for the Stouffer Waverly Hotel (listed in "Where to Stay"). The array of food served up in the lobby atrium is truly astonishing; the dessert buffet alone is at least 20 feet long. And people do bring children.

WHEN TO GO

You can find things to do in Atlanta any time of the year. But if your kids will be disappointed if they don't get to Six Flags and/or White Water, you'd best plan to visit between Memorial Day and Labor Day or check the additional weekends they're open.

FOR MORE INFORMATION

Contact:

Atlanta Convention and Visitors Bureau
233 Peachtree St. NE, Suite 2000, Atlanta, GA 30303
(404-521-6600)
Visitor information centers are located in the Peachtree Center mall downtown, in Lenox Square shopping center and at Underground Atlanta.

MIAMI

Located on the southeastern tip of Florida, the city of Miami is separated from the Atlantic Ocean by Biscayne Bay and the islands of its sister-city, Miami Beach. The subtropical climate, sparkling sand and water, and elegant hotels have long made the area a major resort destination. More than one-third of the world's cruise ships dock at the Port of Miami.

ABOUT THE CITY

Miami has come a long way since Henry Flagler extended his East Coast Railway line here in 1896. In the early 1900s, Miami Beach was nothing more than a swampy strip of land where John Collins had tried unsuccessfully to grow coconuts and avocados. Collins sold 1,600 acres—much of it under water—to an Indianapolis industrialist, Carl G. Fisher, who promptly dredged up the bay, built a series of small islands, and offered a block of oceanfront property to anyone who would put a luxury hotel on it.

By the 1920s, the tourists were flocking to the beach, while across the bay, Miami was becoming a bustling business center. The stock market crash of 1929 hit hard, but as the national economy eventually recovered, so too did Miami's.

In the years immediately following World War II, more new hotels were built here than any other place in the world and Miami's draw as a tourist mecca seemed secure. Then came the Seventies and the opening of Walt Disney World, which began to siphon visitors to Central Florida. A spate of bad press about crime and the Cuban refugee flood also steered people away.

But like an aging star making a comeback, Miami is once again strutting its stuff. Worn-out beaches have been reclaimed, legendary hotels renovated, rundown neighborhoods revitalized. And the city is not content simply to restore its former self—it's moving in new directions with such projects as the Bayside Marketplace, Miami's version of Underground Atlanta and Baltimore's Harborplace. Located on 16 waterfront acres at Biscayne Boulevard and 4th Street, the complex of shops and restaurants is a fun place to browse and you'll often find street performers or other entertainment in the open plazas.

Greater Miami is made up of several neighborhoods, each with its own distinctive character. Be sure to visit Coral Gables, the nation's first planned community, which William Jennings Bryan extolled as "The City Beautiful" in 1921. Picturesque shops and restaurants line the central boulevard strip known as the Miracle Mile. And bring your bathing suits for a trip to the stunning Venetian Municipal Pool, often called the world's most beautiful swimming lagoon. Hewn from coral rock, the pool is adorned with caves, waterfalls and arched bridges and is open to the public for a nominal fee every day but Monday (2701 DeSoto Blvd., 305-442-6483).

Little Havana—the famous Latin Quarter of Miami—is another must-see. Located between downtown Miami and Coral Gables, the main thoroughfare is Calle Ocho (SW 8th St.), crowded with sidewalk cafes, colorful boutiques, exotic fruit stands and factories where workers make pinatas and roll cigars by hand. (Note: Many shopkeepers speak little English, so you may want to come prepared with a few rudimentary Spanish phrases.) The annual Carnaval Miami, held for a week in March, is the largest Hispanic celebration in the U.S. and culminates on Calle Oche with an all-day party spanning 20 blocks.

TRAVEL TIP

Driving in downtown Miami can be a headache; traffic is bad and parking is expensive. But there are alternatives: Metrorail, a sleek elevated train system, and Metrobus, which operates county-wide. Even more interesting is Metromover, individual motorized cars that run on a 1.9-mile elevated track looping around the downtown area and connecting to Metrorail at the Government Center station. For information on the transit system, call 305-638-6700.

On the professional sports scene, the 1988 opening of the Miami Arena (721 NW 1st Ave., Overtown, 305-577-HEAT) adds another season to the calendar, which already included football in the fall and baseball in the spring. The arena is the home court for the NBA expansion team the Miami Heat. The Miami Dolphins play at Joe Robbie Stadium (2269 NW 199th St., Greater Miami North, 305-623-6262), while the Baltimore Orioles hold spring training here from mid-February to early April, with exhibition games in Miami Stadium (2301 NW 10th Ave., 305-633-9857). Miami is also the site of college football's Orange Bowl, played New Year's Day at Orange Bowl Stadium (1400 NW 4th St., 305-642-5211). It's preceded by the lavish King Orange Jamboree Parade.

THINGS TO DO

Metrozoo—This 290-acre habitat is one of the largest cageless zoos in the nation. Residents include koalas and rare white Bengal tigers, who roam around a replica of an ancient Cambodian temple. A 1.5-acre free-flight aviary, Wings of Asia, contains more than 300 exotic birds in a tropical rain forest setting. Pick up a map and daily schedule when you arrive so you can plan your visit around the various animal shows, which are both entertaining and educational. The petting zoo, PAWS, opened in 1989 and is the place to go if you want to ride an elephant. Metrozoo has four restaurants and a monorail to help you get around (12400 SW 152nd St., Greater Miami South, 305-251-0400).

Parrot Jungle & Gardens—If you've never seen a bird jump rope, rollerskate or ride a bicycle on a high wire, then you've obviously never been to Parrot Jungle. Macaws, flamingos, peacocks, cockatoos and, of course, parrots are among the plumed creatures you'll find in this authentic subtropical jungle setting. In addition to trained bird shows, you'll see wildlife exhibits featuring alligators, giant tortoises and iguanas. There's a children's petting zoo, playground, gift shop and Parrot Cafe (11000 SW 57th Ave., Greater Miami South, 305-666-7834).

Monkey Jungle—Monkeys are fascinating, and at Monkey Jungle you can watch them roam freely in habitats simulating the jungles of Asia, South America and Africa. Here, it's the people who are "caged"—in enclosed walkways that run through the park. Special shows feature talented chimps and other species. This attraction, like Parrot Jungle, has been in operation for more than 50 years (14805 SW 216th St., Greater Miami South, 305-235-1611).

Miami Youth Museum—Since the exhibitions change, we can't tell you exactly what you'll find at this cultural arts museum. But the hands-on activities which are its hallmark will doubtless be enjoyed by the whole family. Closed on Thanksgiving and Christmas Day (5701 Sunset Dr., Greater Miami South, 305-661-3046).

Miami Seaquarium—A 10,000-pound killer whale and TV's Flipper are the stars at this marine attraction. Sea lions and dolphins share the spotlight during daily shows, while dozens of aquariums showcase the various inhabitants of the Atlantic Ocean and the Caribbean Sea—including sharks, manatees and sea turtles (4400 Rickenbacker Causeway, Key Biscayne area, 305-361-5705).

Planet Ocean—Want to touch an iceberg? Climb inside a submarine? Churn up your own ocean storm? You can do it all at this 100,000-square-foot indoor exhibit area—a great place to introduce kids to oceanography. Dozens of exhibits, plus fiber-optics shows and special films help explain why the sea is important in our lives (3979 Rickenbacker Causeway, Key Biscayne area, 305-361-9455).

Museum of Science & Space Transit Planetarium—Intriguing mysteries of science and space are revealed through more than 150 hands-on exhibits and live demonstrations of scientific phenomena. Kids will be drawn to such items as the anti-gravity mirror that makes you appear to fly and the killer whale skull, complete with ivory teeth. The planetarium features multimedia astronomy and laser shows, including "A Child's Garden of Stars," especially for preschoolers (they don't turn off all the lights). For show times, call 305-854-2222. The observatory is open weekend evenings free of charge. A wildlife center behind the museum houses native snakes, turtles and birds. Closed Thanksgiving and Christmas Day (3280 S. Miami Ave., Coconut Grove, 305-854-4247).

THINGS TO DO NEARBY

Miami is the only city in the U.S. with two national parks in its backyard. See the Everglades and Biscayne sections in the NATIONAL PARKS chapter for details.

To the north, in Hollywood, you'll find **Atlantis, The Water Kingdom** (formerly Six Flags Atlantis), a 65-acre waterpark (see "Best of the Rest" section in the WATERPARKS chapter).

WHERE TO STAY

If you're going to take a family vacation to Miami, you really should stay on the ocean. That means choosing from accommodations on Key Biscayne or on Miami Beach. Not that there aren't many fine hotels elsewhere in the Greater Miami area, but there's nothing like being right on the beach.

Key Biscayne is less than a half-hour drive from downtown Miami and is convenient to the various attractions we've listed, especially Planet Ocean and the Seaquarium. You'll find two plush resorts here: the Sonesta Beach Hotel and the Sheraton Royal Biscayne (for details, see "Where to Stay" for Biscayne National Park in NATIONAL PARKS chapter).

Miami Beach offers a wide, 12-mile stretch of powdery sand handsomely restored by the U.S. Army Corps of Engineers. With an aquamarine ocean stretching to the horizon, the setting is as beautiful as its picture-postcard image. Here's a rundown of our choices for the best places for families to stay.

The Fontainebleau Hilton—after undergoing a $43 million renovation—continues to be the "queen of the beach." With more than 1,200 rooms and a rebuilt 300-foot-wide white sand beach, it's the biggest and most impressive of the grand hotels that line Collins Avenue. The 18 acres of grounds include a half-acre pool with an island and a five-story-high "magic mountain" with four waterfalls, plus lighted tennis courts and a state-of-the-art health spa. As you would expect, prices aren't cheap. On the other hand, package deals are available and the hotel follows the Hilton policy of not charging for children who share their parents' rooms. To entice families to visit during the summer months, a free children's activities program is offered from June through Labor Day (4441 Collins Ave., 305-538-2000).

Not as big as the Fontainebleau (what is?), but otherwise on a par with it is the Doral-on-the-Ocean Beach Resort, whose guests can enjoy use of five 18-hole golf courses and 15 tennis courts at the Doral Country Club over in Miami (with free transportation, of course). Recently renovated rooms are luxurious and include refrigerators. The Doral offers a kids' activities program and a game room, and guests under 17 stay free (4833 Collins Ave., 305-532-3600 or 800-327-6334).

If you prefer two- or three-story motels to high-rises, we recommend the Radisson Pan American Ocean Hotel and the Suez. They're not small (with nearly 150 and 200 rooms, respectively), but they're not as overwhelming as the Fontainebleau and the Doral (650 rooms). You'll find refrigerators in all of the Radisson's rooms and most of the Suez's. The Radisson, which was completely renovated in 1988-89, has an Olympic-size pool, shuffleboard, a game room and a nine-hole putting green. Kids under 17 stay free (17875 Collins Ave., 305-932-1100). The less-expensive Suez is well-geared to families, with a wading pool, a playground and a free kids' activities program (18215 Collins Ave., 305-932-0661 or 800-327-5278).

WHERE TO EAT

No matter where you stay in Miami Beach, it's fun to look in on other hotels. Most have a casual restaurant or coffee shop on-property, so you can sightsee and feed the family at the same time. Some good bets include Chez Bon Bon at the Fontainebleau, Seabreeze at the Doral, Ponderosa Grill at the Deauville and the Terrace Cafe at the Radisson Pan American.

In the Art Deco district, the Roney Pub offers lots of food at very reasonable prices. You may run into a line (no reservations), but it will probably move quickly. The pub is located in the Roney Plaza Apartment Hotel (2301 Collins Ave.), where you'll also find the Villa Deli, which we recommend for soups and sandwiches.

In Miami, you'll find several fun places to eat at Bayside Marketplace. Dick Clark's American Bandstand Grill features Philly cheese steaks, burgers and milkshakes, with American Bandstand reruns playing continuously on TV monitors. Pete's Fountain & Bar is a Fifties-style hangout with a freestanding bar where you can create a shake or something more potent. The Dockside Terrace is an indoor/outdoor restaurant on the bay with a good selection of munchies, exotic tropical drinks and delectable desserts.

You can't be in Miami for long without hearing about stone crabs, a South Florida specialty, and where to eat them. Joe's Stone Crab Restaurant (227 Biscayne St., 305-673-0365) is a Miami institution dating back to 1913. It's a big place—350 seats—but so popular that lines can be exceedingly long (no reservations). If you decide to give it a shot, do so without the kids. If you want stone crabs with kids in tow, try Cye's Rivergate Restaurant (444 Brickell Ave., 305-358-9100), which does take reservations. Located in the financial district, it offers a nice view of the Miami River.

For an elegant, adults-only dinner, two excellent choices are The Dining Galleries at the Fontainebleau, specializing in veal Romanoff and pompano with crab, and Dominique's at the Alexander Hotel (5225 Collins Ave., 305-865-6500). The latter is a sister-restaurant to the world-famous Dominique's in Washington, D.C. Both require jackets and offer sumptuous Sunday brunches.

WHEN TO GO

Miami is becoming a year-round resort, though the official high season continues to be from mid-December to mid-April. That's an excellent time to visit, especially if you'll be escaping cold weather back home. Hotel rates will be somewhat higher than other times of the year, but these are the best months for catching various festivals and special activities (like the annual Dade County Youth Fair held at the end of March). And if you're planning a side trip to the Everglades, it's the only time of year when the mosquitos aren't out in killer force.

FOR MORE INFORMATION

Contact:

Greater Miami Convention & Visitors Bureau
701 Brickell Ave., Miami, FL 33131
(800-283-2707 or 305-539-3000)

They'll send you maps and brochures, plus a copy of *Destination Miami*, a slick guide to entertainment, shopping, sightseeing and dining published bimonthly.

NASHVILLE

Nashville is famous as the home of the Grand Ole Opry, but this fast-growing capital of Tennessee has lots of other things going for it. So besides heading for the Opryland USA music and entertainment complex, families can have fun in Nashville exploring an old fort, riding a trolley through downtown, boarding a paddlewheel boat for a cruise on the Cumberland River, or visiting a museum dedicated to toys. And that's just a sample of the things to do in this vibrant Southern city, located at the confluence of three interstates (I-65, I-40 and I-24).

ABOUT THE CITY

Nashville is sometimes called the "Athens of the South" because of the abundance of academic institutions located here. To enhance the point, the city boasts a full-size replica of the Parthenon, the many-columned architectural wonder of ancient Greece. Inside is a 42-foot-tall statue of Athena, the goddess of wisdom.

In recent years, a massive redevelopment program has given birth to new highways, parks and buildings. Yet Nashville retains a reverence for its history, which dates back to 1779, when a band of pioneers built a log stockade on the west bank of the Cumberland River and named it Fort Nashborough.

Today, the fort has been painstakingly recreated and is a must-see stop (see "Things to Do") on a visit to Riverfront Park, a popular setting for summertime picnics and concerts. The park offers an expansive view of the boat traffic on the river, and down at the dock you can board one of the paddlewheelers operated by the Belle Carol Riverboat Company for a sightseeing cruise (615-244-3430 or 800-342-2355).

From Fort Nashborough, you can walk to Church Street to visit the new Church Street Centre, a 180,000-square-foot, glass-domed complex of shops and restaurants. Or, if you like, board one of the shiny red trolleys that run through the central business district and ride to any number of destinations: the Tennessee State Museum (see "Things to Do"), the Capitol or Union Station, for example. Or just take a whirl around downtown for the fun of it. It will only cost you 25 cents per person and trolleys come along about every 10 minutes. Stops are marked with red-and-gold signs with the route map on one side.

When you do head back to Riverfront Park, go by way of Market Street and try to imagine what these renovated Victorian warehouses looked like in the horse-and-buggy era of the 1870s. If you happen to be visiting on the first Saturday in October, you can catch the annual Market

Street Festival, featuring clowns, street vendors, face painting and pony rides.

To see the other Nashville-with-kids attractions which we've listed below, you need a car. However, with three interstates (I-65 and I-40 heading generally north-south, and I-24 stretching east-west), plus the Briley Parkway, you can get around fairly quickly.

To help plan your trip, you may want to write for a copy of the annual Nashville Visitor's Guide (1719 West End Ave., Nashville, TN 37203, 615-329-3899). It includes a page of discount coupons.

THINGS TO DO

Opryland USA—See THEME PARKS chapter.

Fort Nashborough—At this replica of the original fort, costumed interpreters demonstrate what work and play were like for settlers in the 1780s. You may find them spinning and weaving wool, tending herb gardens or cooking over a fire. Open Tuesdays-Saturdays, 9 a.m.-4 p.m. (170 1st Ave. N., 615-255-8192).

Tennessee State Museum—A working gristmill stands at the center of the museum, surrounded by a reconstructed log cabin and exhibits depicting Tennessee life in various times. Children will like the Museum Experience Room, where they can touch a foxskin cap and participate in other sensory experiences. The museum gift store is a good place to shop for souvenirs. Open daily; free (505 Deaderick St., 615-741-2692).

Cumberland Science Museum—The welcome mat is out for children and families at this interesting museum with hands-on exhibits, live animals and a planetarium. At the Curiosity Corner, younger children can hide in a fox's den or try on a Japanese kimono. Open daily mid-June to mid-August; Tuesday-Sunday the rest of the year (800 Ridley Blvd., 615-259-6099).

The Nashville Toy Museum—Located near Opryland, this museum is a wonderland of toy soldiers, antique dolls, teddy bears, and toy trains and cars. Open daily (2613-B McGavock Pike, 615-883-8870).

Centennial Park—The focal point of this park, which is located on West End Avenue, is the Parthenon, described in the introduction. Approaching the structure from the front side, you'll find a nice play area if your kids need some blow-off-steam time. There are swings, a tree house,

NOTE

The Metropolitan Board of Parks and Recreation provides free entertainment during the summer through its Family Outings Series, which includes children's theater and concerts at Centennial, Riverfront and Hadley parks. For a schedule, contact the board's Centennial Park office (615-259-6314).

a climbing apparatus and a large sandbox. Behind the Parthenon is Lake Watauga, where you can rent paddle boats in the summer. Another feature of the park is Ice Centennial, an indoor ice-skating rink open mid-September to mid-May (333 23rd Ave. N., 615-320-1369).

The Hermitage—This was the home of Andrew Jackson, the country's seventh president, and his wife, Rachel. Stop at the visitor center to see a biographical film and pick up cassettes of the fine audio tour for children. Besides the mansion, the tour includes some of the original log cabins where the family lived before the house was built. The Hermitage is 11 miles east of Nashville on I-40. Take the Old Hickory Boulevard exit and follow the signs. Open daily except Thanksgiving and Christmas (615-889-2941).

Belle Meade Mansion—A guided children's tour with lots of fun facts keeps a visit to this antebellum mansion from being a dull house tour. Belle Meade was renowned in the 1800s for the breeding of thoroughbred race horses, and you can visit the carriage house and stable along with other buildings on the grounds. Open daily except Thanksgiving, Christmas and New Year's Day (110 Leake Ave., 615-356-0501).

THINGS TO DO NEARBY

If you have time, stop by **Murfreesboro,** some 30 miles southeast of Nashville, to visit the **Cannonsburgh Pioneer Village** and the **Children's Discovery House.** The pioneer village on South Front St. recreates 19th-century rural life with a log house, blacksmith shop, general store, one-room schoolhouse, etc. (off I-24 at Hwy. 96). Open daily except Mondays from May through September. Free. For information, contact the Rutherford County Chamber of Commerce, PO Box 864, Murfreesboro, TN 37133 (615-893-6565).

Children's Discovery House is an amazing place for kids aged 2-12—with bubble blowers on the front lawn, colored chalk by the sidewalks and a fire engine parked in the carport. Inside, kids will find dress-up clothes, a play store, art materials and more. The tough part is getting them to leave. Open daily except Mondays (503 N. Maple St., 615-890-2300).

WHERE TO STAY

Our thinking is that you might as well stay near Opryland, since you can find accommodations in all price ranges. Of course, you can't get any closer than the Opryland Hotel, on the Briley Parkway in Opryland. Rooms don't come cheap in this mammoth complex, but kids under 12 stay free and off-season rates are offered. Even if you don't stay here, at least stop for a look: The attached conservatory has two acres of glass-covered nature (2800 Opryland Dr., 615-889-1000).

Just a couple of miles away is the Holiday Inn-Briley Parkway, which has a Holidome indoor recreation center. Kids 17 and under stay free (2200 Elm Hill Pike, 615-391-4521). On the same stretch of road, there's a Residence Inn by Marriott, an all-suite property which offers a complimentary continental breakfast buffet (2300 Elm Hill Pike, 615-832-0093). Further on is the economy-priced Hampton Inn-Briley Parkway. Kids under 18 stay free and there's a free continental breakfast (2350 Elm Hill Pike, 615-871-0222).

Other good deals in the area include:

Comfort Inn Opryland (2516 Music Valley Dr., 615-889-0086). Kids 18 and under stay free.

Econo Lodge Opryland (2460 Music Valley Dr., 615-889-0090). Kids under 12 free.

Ramada Inn across from Opryland (2401 Music Valley Dr., 615-889-0800). This is the closest location to Opryland other than the Opryland Hotel, but rates are higher than the above two listings.

If you want to stay downtown, there are a number of deluxe hotels to choose from. We're partial to Stouffer's, which has glass-enclosed elevators and spacious rooms. It's attached by covered walkway to the Church Street Centre complex of shops and restaurants. Kids 18 and under stay free and weekend packages are offered (611 Commerce St., 615-255-8400).

WHERE TO EAT

Nashville offers a number of dining spots which are good choices for families. Here are some of the more unique:

Crawdaddys (14 Oldham St., 615-255-5434) specializes in Cajun seafood and steak in an old-time wharf atmosphere overlooking the Cumberland River with a view of downtown Nashville.

Darryl's 1827 Restaurant and Tavern (4319 Sidco Dr., 615-832-1827) features seating in or near such unusual settings as a jail house, an elevator or a double-decker bus. The food is of the pasta-chicken-ribs variety.

Major Wallaby's (741 Myatt Dr., 615-868-6766) is another place with fascinating decor—in this case a huge overhead aquarium. Request a table with a good view.

The Old Spaghetti Factory (160 Second Ave. N., 615-254-9010) is a renovated Market Street warehouse with stained glass windows, high ceilings and an old-fashioned trolley car (with seating inside).

101st Airborne Restaurant (1362-A Murfreesboro Rd., 615-361-4212) offers you a chance to watch planes take off and land and listen to the control tower's instructions on the headphones at the table while you eat in the recreated atmosphere of a French farmhouse during World War II. A tank is stationed along the road leading to the restaurant and a plane, jeep and truck are parked outside.

In terms of ethnic eateries, if you're hungry for Chinese food, you can't go wrong at Peking Garden Restaurant (1923 Division St., 615-327-2020). Los Cunados (1910 Belcourt Ave., 615-383-8920) is the place for Tex-Mex.

We'd also recommend at least one adults-only dinner if you can swing the arrangements. The problem is which restaurant to choose. In the elegant and expensive group, the top picks are Arthur's (now located in Union Station, 1001 Broadway, 615-255-1494), Mario's (2005 Broadway, 615-327-3232) and Julian's (2412 West End Ave., 615-327-2412). Arthur's is the most romantic of the three, Mario's is the place to see visiting celebrities, while Julian's serves some of the best French cuisine this side of the Atlantic. Jackets and reservations are needed for all three. If you'd prefer a more informal atmosphere, try Maude's Courtyard (106 Harding Pl., 615-356-1300), which is also a great place for Sunday brunch with live jazz.

WHEN TO GO

A fun time to visit Nashville (though a busy time) is during the annual Summer Lights Festival, which takes place the first weekend in June. Top names and newcomers in pop, rock, jazz and—of course—country music are showcased on outdoor stages downtown. Art exhibits in storefronts, street entertainers and food booths on the plaza are part of the festivities as well. The city also makes a big to-do about Christmas, with an extravagant parade and lots of other "country holiday" events scheduled from late November through December.

FOR MORE INFORMATION

Contact:

Nashville Area Chamber of Commerce
161 4th Ave. N., Nashville, TN 37219
(615-259-4700)

A visitor information center is located on I-65 at the James Robertson Parkway (exit 85). It's open 8 a.m.-5 p.m. daily, and till 8 p.m. from Memorial Day to Labor Day (615-259-4747).

ORLANDO

Orlando, home of Walt Disney World, Sea World, Universal Studios and assorted other attractions, is the tourist mecca of central Forida—and, for that matter, the world. Located at the intersection of I-4 and the Florida Turnpike, it's within easy driving range of the Kennedy Space Center on the Atlantic coast to the east, and Tampa and nearby Gulf beaches to the west.

ABOUT THE CITY

Orlando has been called the "most-visited and least-seen town in America." And for obvious reasons. The world's No. 1 tourist attraction, Walt Disney World, is located here. But most Disney visitors don't see much else. And with the opening of MGM Studios and Typhoon Lagoon, it now takes even more time (and money and energy) to do the Disney empire.

Nevertheless, there's more to Orlando than Walt Disney World—much more. While it's hard to imagine visiting the area with kids and not taking in at least the Magic Kingdom, those who choose to do so can easily spend a busy week doing other things that are very enjoyable.

Orlando is one of the fastest-growing cities in the country—and the boom is likely to stretch on and on into the future. A main reason, of course, is the seemingly endless expansion of Walt Disney World. But that's not the whole story. Universal Studios has joined MGM as the city's second major film studio—providing both another industry and another lure for visitors eager to tour backlots and try out movie-themed rides. And a number of major corporations are choosing Orlando for their headquarters.

As a measure of the city's current and projected growth, consider that Orlando International Airport added a third runway and airside terminal as part of a $430 million expansion project completed in 1990. Or the fact that Orlando boasts more hotel/motel rooms than any other city in the U.S.—with more groundbreaking under way.

Orlando's sports scene is growing, too. The $100 million Orlando Arena (407-849-2020) in the downtown Centroplex opened in January 1989. It's home to the city's National Basketball Association franchise, the "Orlando Magic," and is also the site of concerts, ice shows and other entertainment. Meanwhile, Orlando Stadium, where the Florida Citrus Bowl is played on New Year's Day, has undergone a facelift and can now accommodate 90,000 spectators.

Everywhere you look, you'll see new development, expansions and renovations. Still, with the possible exception of busy International

Drive, Orlando doesn't look overgrown. Thanks to the more than 50 lakes within the city limits, it retains a parklike atmosphere with lots of greenery and open spaces.

THINGS TO DO

Theme parks—The No. 1 tourist draw, obviously, is Walt Disney World—which includes the Magic Kingdom, EPCOT and MGM Studios. The No. 2 attraction traditionally has been Sea World, but it is being challenged by Universal Studios, which opened in 1990. All are covered in detail in the THEME PARKS chapter.

Waterparks—Orlando is the site of two of the best waterparks in the U.S.—Wet 'n Wild and Disney's Typhoon Lagoon. A third, smaller park, Watermania, is located in nearby Kissimmee. See WATERPARKS for more information.

Orlando Science Center—Both a museum and a planetarium, the center features a variety of see-and-do exhibits on such topics as black holes, the human body and Florida's natural history. The planetarium offers daily multimedia space shows projected on a 40-foot domed screen and on weekends you can catch a "Cosmic Concert"—a laser show choreographed to music (810 E. Rollins St., in Loch Haven Park, 407-896-7151).

Gatorland Zoo—This is the place to learn all about alligators, and see them in all sizes from babies to 1,000-pound adults. The main event, repeated several times a day, is the "Gator Jumparoo," where giant alligators leap out of a pool to retrieve food suspended above them. Creepy, but fascinating. At the Reptile Photo Area, you can get your picture taken with a boa constrictor or a small gator (14501 S. Orange Blossom Trail, 407-857-3845).

Church Street Station—This shopping and entertainment complex, open 11 a.m.-2 a.m., is mainly for adults, who will enjoy the interesting night spots. If you visit with kids, head for Commander Ragtime's Midway of Fun, Food and Games on the third floor of the Church Street Station Exchange, the newest addition to Church Street Station. Here you'll find state-of-the-art video games surrounded by turn-of-the-century circus memorabilia, antique autos and replicas of World War I planes. There's food, too—hot roasted peanuts, chicken wings, ice cream and more—and the waitresses traverse the Midway on roller skates (129 W. Church St., 407-422-2434).

Fun 'N Wheels—This "family activity park" features go-karts, bumper cars and bumper boats, a 65-foot ferris wheel, mini golf and more. There is no overall admission charge; you buy tickets only for the rides you select. Open daily till midnight in the summer, shorter hours the rest of the year. The Orlando park is at International Drive and Sand Lake Road (407-

351-5651). There's a second one in Kissimmee on Rte. 192 at Osceola Square Mall (407-870-2222).

Turkey Lake Park—This 300-acre park in southwest Orlando is a recreational haven for visitors and residents alike. For a nominal fee you can use all the facilities, including two beaches, a swimming pool, hiking trails, a 200-foot fishing pier, a petting zoo and playground. A good place for some low-key fun and it's open every day except Christmas (3401 Hiawassee Rd., 407-299-5594).

THINGS TO DO NEARBY

The *John F. Kennedy Space Center* is located 47 miles east of Orlando on the Atlantic Coast. From launch pads here, Apollo astronauts left earth for man's first voyage to the moon. Today it is the launch and landing site of the Space Shuttle. Bus tours of the Kennedy Space Center and of the Cape Canaveral Air Force Station, launch site of the earlier Mercury and Gemini missions, are offered at Spaceport USA. Each takes about two hours, which may be a bit long for young children since much of that time is spent on the bus.

Even if you don't take one of the bus tours, there are other things to do—most of them free—that make this a worthwhile side trip. One highlight is the $3.5 million "Satellites and You" exhibit, which opened in 1989 and uses animatronics and audiovisual effects to simulate working conditions on a space station. Though there's an admission charge, you'll also want to see *The Dream Is Alive*, a 40-minute IMAX film projected onto a 5 1/2 story screen (it's also shown at the Air and Space Museum in Washington, D.C.). The film takes you aboard the space shuttle from lift-off to touchdown, with some sequences shot by the astronauts themselves. A shorter film, *The Boy from Mars*, tells the story of a 10-year-old raised on Mars who visits Earth for the first time; it is shown free in the Galaxy Theater. Spaceport USA is normally open from 9 a.m. to dusk every day except Christmas, but Space Shuttle launch/landing operations occasionally disrupt the schedule. Call ahead to make sure the facility is open before you make the drive (407-452-2121).

WHERE TO STAY

With so many possibilities to choose from, deciding where to stay in Orlando can be a daunting prospect. We don't have enough space for all-inclusive coverage, but we'll list what we consider to be some of the best choices in various locations.

The first decision for many families is whether to stay in or near Walt Disney World. If you plan to spend several days at any of the WDW theme parks, we recommend staying as close by as your budget will allow; you'll find the convenience worth the price. For information on the Disney-owned hotels, see the Magic Kingdom section of the THEME PARKS chapter.

Several Lake Buena Vista properties are also handy to Disney World action. Some deluxe hotels, though not owned by Disney, are actually located on Disney property and are designated as "official" Walt Disney World hotels. The largest of these—and one of our favorites—is the 27-story Buena Vista Palace just across the street from the Disney Village Marketplace. If you get a room on an upper floor facing that direction, you can watch the nighttime fireworks display at Pleasure Island from your balcony. Facilities include a recreation island with swimming pools, lighted tennis courts and playground. A summer activities program, Kids Stuff, is offered for ages 3-12 and includes special evening functions like an "un-birthday" party. A variety of family packages are offered (1900 Buena Vista Dr., 407-827-3333, 800-327-2990 or, in Florida, 800-327-2906).

The nearby Hilton, another official WDW hotel, offers many of the same amenities as the Buena Vista Palace and features a Youth Hotel—open daily till midnight—where kids ages 3-12 can participate in super-vised activities, watch a large-screen TV in the video room or even take a nap in a pint-sized dormitory while parents enjoy some time on their own (1751 Hotel Plaza Blvd., 407-827-4000).

A new Holiday Inn opened in Lake Buena Vista in the summer of 1990. It bills itself as "an official hotel for kids" and features a complimen-tary evening activity program for ages 4 and up, plus a child care center which operates days and evenings. At Maxine's, the hotel's family-style restaurant, kids can choose from their own buffet and eat in a special area where they can watch cartoons on a wide-screen TV. Guest rooms each have a refrigerator, microwave oven and coffee maker (State Rd. 535, 407-396-8915).

An alternative to high-rise hotels is the Vistana Resort, where the ac-commodations consist of two-bedroom, two-bath villas which sleep six to eight people. If you're traveling with relatives or friends, this is well worth considering. Besides swimming pools and playgrounds, the complex has 14 tennis courts. A full-time rec staff plans a wide range of activities for kids ages 4-15 (State Rd. 535, 407-239-3100, 800-327-9152 or, in Florida, 800-432-9197).

Less expensive accommodations in Lake Buena Vista include a Comfort Inn (8442 Palm Pkwy., 407-239-7300) and Days Inn Resort (State Rd. 535, 407-239-0444).

Moving on from Lake Buena Vista, the area in and around Interna-tional Drive is loaded with hotels, motels and restaurants. International parallels I-4, so a few minutes' drive south puts you at Disney World, while a few minutes drive north takes you to downtown Orlando (provided you don't run into traffic in either direction). Various attractions—from Wet 'n Wild to dinner theaters—are located along this strip.

The classiest hotel on International Drive is the Peabody Orlando. Like its famous sister hotel in Memphis, it features a resident family of ducks which parade to the indoor fountain each morning at 11 a.m. The Peabody offers all the facilities of a deluxe resort, including some first-rate restaurants. It also operates a Children's Hotel from 6-10 p.m. daily for kids ages 3-12. The Peabody is at the north end of International—closer to Universal Studios than WDW (9801 International Dr., 407-352-4000, 800-PEABODY).

A short distance from International Drive and near the main entrance to Universal Studios is the Delta Orlando Resort (formerly Delta Court of Flags). It bills itself as "Orlando's affordable resort" and it is just that—offering many of the amenities you pay more for elsewhere. The property was purchased a few years ago by a Canadian resort company and they've been refurbishing and upgrading ever since. OK, so the pool's not as big as some and the tennis courts needed some work when we were there; this is still an excellent value. And the kids' program is free, except for a meal charge (5715 Major Blvd., 407-351-3340 or 800-877-1133).

The largest hotel on International Drive is the Orlando Marriott, with more than 1,000 guest rooms in 16 two-story stucco buildings. It's been newly renovated and features three free-form swimming pools, two game rooms and the Munchkin Maze jungle gym and playground. A tram service whisks guests around the beautifully landscaped 48-acre grounds. A 1990 "Room to Breathe" promotion—which may be continued— offered families a good deal: a second room for half price during certain seasons (8001 International Dr., 407-351-2420). Marriott's Orlando World Center is even bigger, with more than 1,500 rooms surrounded by an 18-hole golf course. It opened in 1986, but gets so much traffic because of its prime location near WDW that renovations were already underway in 1990. We found the rooms not particularly memorable, but the outdoor pool area (complete with waterfalls and a water slide) is spectacular. The Lollipop Lounge, open 4-11 p.m., offers activities for kids ages 5-12 (8701 World Center Dr., 407-239-4200).

Near the south end of International Drive is another landmark Orlando hotel: Stouffer Orlando Resort. It's located directly across the street from Sea World and boasts the "world's largest hotel atrium lobby"—longer and wider than a football field. The lobby features a large aviary housing tropical birds and ponds stocked with exotic koi fish (which kids can feed). Guest rooms are also generous in size and Shamu's Playhouse is one of the best-equipped child care centers we've seen at any hotel. Just outside the center, there's a nice playground near the huge outdoor pool (6677 Sea Harbor Dr., 407-351-5555).

If you're not interested in on-site child care, tennis courts and so forth, you'll find less expensive accommodations offered by various chains up and down International Drive. The Comfort Inn, Econo Lodge and Days Inn are all good bets. Just be aware that each of these chains has several locations in the Orlando area (Days Inn, for instance, has more than two dozen), so be sure you know which property you're making your reservations at and how to get there.

You can also find good lodging deals in Kissimmee (pronounced Kis-SEM-mee), just south of Orlando. Hotels and motels closest to WDW will usually have "main gate" in their name, like the Holiday Inn Main Gate East and the Radisson Inn Maingate. For a directory of accommodations (including maps of their locations), contact Kissimmee-St. Cloud Convention & Visitors Bureau, PO Box 422007, Kissimmee, FL 34742-2007 (407-847-5000, 800-327-9159 or, in Florida, 800-432-9199; central reservations: 800-333-KISS).

WHERE TO EAT

You'll find lots of places to eat at Walt Disney World, Sea World and Universal Studios, and we cover these in the THEME PARKS chapter.

Where else can you go for a family meal? Again, the choices are virtually endless. For starters, even if you're not staying at one of the grand hotels on or off Disney property, you can stop in for a meal (and a look around). You'll always find a casual, family-style restaurant in addition to the more elegant eateries. For example, we recommend the Watercress Cafe at the Buena Vista Palace or the Garden Terrace at Marriott's Orlando World Center.

We might also mention here that the Stouffer Orlando Resort offers a Champagne Sunday Brunch that's to die for, served in that spectacular atrium we discussed under "Where to Stay." While adults sip unlimited champagne and choose from 150 hot and cold items at 16 food stations, kids can enjoy their own buffet hosted by Peaches the Clown.

Back to dinner, you'll find lots of choices on International Drive, from fast food to dinner theaters. Some of our favorite chains are along here: Chili's (burgers and more), Red Lobster (seafood), Olive Garden (Italian), Morrison's (cafeteria-style Southern) and Sizzler (which offers an extensive, all-you-can-eat buffet). All offer ample portions of good food at reasonable prices. Consult the phone book for locations on International Drive and elsewhere in Orlando. If you like Mexican food, try the Casa Gallardo (8250 International Dr., 407-352-8121), or if you've got a taste for ribs, head for Damon's at the Mercado Village shopping center

(8445 International Dr., 407-352-5984). If you're not sure what you're hungry for, you can find most anything on the varied menu at Darryl's 1883 Restaurant (8282 International Dr., 407-351-1883).

Slightly further afield is Gary's Duck Inn (3974 S. Orange Blossom Trail, 407-843-0270), a family seafood house that's an Orlando institution.

If you have the opportunity for an adults-only meal, we have several recommendations. Haifeng (at Stouffer's Orlando Resort) provides the perfect atmosphere to unwind after a frantic day of theme-parking. The setting is tranquil and utterly soothing, and the food—traditional Hunan fare—is superbly prepared. Jackets requested (407-351-5555).

If you don't mind dressing up (as in jacket and tie) and dropping a few bucks, you'll find a spectacular view of Walt Disney World from Arthur's 27 on the 27th floor of the Buena Vista Palace. The setting is elegant and the international menu first-rate (407-827-3450).

Dux is the name of the excellent gourmet restaurant at the Peabody Hotel, where you'll also find Capriccio, a slick Italian eatery with both traditional and innovative pasta dishes.

The Royal Orleans in the Mercado shopping village serves some of the finest Louisiana cooking this side of New Orleans. Try the blackened shrimp or stuffed andouille, a Cajun sausage filled with crabmeat and served with a mustard and red pepper sauce (407-352-8200).

The Royal Orleans, incidentally, is among the growing list of restaurants and dinner attractions run by Robert Earl's Mecca Leisure USA. Earl, a pioneer of Orlando-area dinner theaters since 1979, has two young daughters and says he keeps them in mind when planning new family-entertainment concepts. Among his creations:

▲ Mardi Gras (next door to Royal Orleans at the Mercado shopping village), a carnival-themed revue;

▲ Fort Liberty (on U.S. Hwy. 192 in Kissimmee), with cowboy and Indian acts;

▲ King Henry's Feast (8984 International Dr.), with jugglers, jesters and magicians.

NOTE

Fairy Godmother's provides licensed and bonded baby-sitters to all hotels within a 50-mile radius of Orlando, and will also provide sitters to accompany kids to area attractions. Services are available 24 hours a day, seven days a week. Rates are on a per-hour basis with a four-hour minimum (407-277-3724 or 407-275-7326). Super-Sitters (407-740-5516) and Mothers Sitting Service (407-857-7447) provide similar services.

For reservations and information about any of these three, call 407-351-5151 or 800-347-8181.

Following in Earl's footsteps, two other dinner attractions (both on Hwy. 192 in Kissimmee) opened in the late Eighties. Medieval Times features jousting knights, while Arabian Nights showcases eight breeds of horses in various acts. For information, call Medieval Times (407-239-0214, 800-327-4024 or, in Florida, 800-432-0768) or Arabian Nights (407-239-9223 or 800-553-6116).

WHEN TO GO

If your primary purpose in visiting Orlando is to see Disney World or another such major attraction, you should plan according to the information provided in the THEME PARKS chapter. Even if you're doing other things, this will clue you in about the crowds to expect in the area at various times of year.

FOR MORE INFORMATION

Contact:

Orlando/Orange County Convention and Visitors Bureau
7208 Sand Lake Rd., Suite 300, Orlando, FL 32819
(407-363-5800)

Tourist Information Center
Mercado Mediterranean Shopping Village
8445 International Dr.
(407-363-5871)

It's open 8 a.m.-8 p.m. year-round. You can get a copy of the Official Visitors Guide to Central Florida by calling or stopping by the Tourist Information Center.

HISTORY PLACES

❀ COLONIAL WILLIAMSBURG

❀ MUSEUM OF AMERICAN FRONTIER CULTURE

❀ OLD SALEM

❀ ST. AUGUSTINE

HISTORY PLACES

No book or movie can recreate the sights and sounds of the past as vividly as a visit to a living history village. We've selected four notable examples which cover various eras in the development of our nation—dating from the 16th through the 18th centuries. At these sites, you can watch staff people dressed in authentic costumes perform day-to-day activities from these former times, thus enabling you to experience first-hand what life was like when there was no electricity or running water or any of the other conveniences we take so much for granted.

Virginia's Colonial Williamsburg is, in a sense, the Disney World of living history villages. It attracts tourists from all over the country and the world, and offers so many things to see and do that you need several days to take it all in.

St. Augustine is another popular destination tourists flock to—for the Florida sunshine and beaches, as well as to see the restored Spanish Quarter and ancient fort.

Less well-known, and therefore quieter, are Old Salem in central North Carolina and the Museum of American Frontier Culture in Virginia's Shenandoah Valley. The latter opened in the fall of 1988 and is an ongoing reconstruction.

Besides the fact that living history villages offer a unique learning experience, we like them because they offer a respite from our hectic modern lives—and a gentle reminder of the important things that transcend time, like a sense of family and community.

In Colonial Williamsburg, St. Augustine and Old Salem, you can stroll the streets of the historic district and go into shops and eating places for free. There is an admission charge for entrance to Colonial Williamsburg's exhibit buildings; St. Augustine's Spanish Quarter, Castillo de San Marcos and a few other exhibit buildings; Old Salem's exhibit buildings; and the grounds of the Museum of American Frontier Culture.

Reduced rates are offered for children—variously defined as under 16 or under 12.

These are not commercial ventures, however. All are administered by non-profit foundations, in some cases assisted by state or city government. St. Augustine's Castillo—the bargain admission of the lot—is administered by the National Park Service.

Exhibit buildings generally close around 5 p.m. (though there may be extended hours at some sites in the summer months). We find the end of the day a wonderful time to walk the streets of these old villages, as the crowds disappear and the sun begins to set. This is when you can really imagine that you're in another century.

When visiting these sites by day, try to take your time and explore the area thoroughly in an unhurried way. Ask questions of the interpreters and encourage your children to do the same. Check the visitor centers for schedules of special programs and activities and take advantage of them. Don't overlook the gift shops either, which carry olden toys and crafts made on site, plus informative books about the area's history.

To enhance your trip, stop by the public library before you go and do some research on the historical places you'll visit. If you write ahead, you can also get free materials from your destination. Be sure to share background information with your children to prepare them for what they'll see and get them excited about the prospect. They may complain beforehand that they'd rather go to an amusement park, but just tell them that this is a different kind of fun—like traveling in a time machine. All you need is a good imagination and a comfortable pair of walking shoes.

NOTE

To enhance your trip:
❑ Stop by the public library before you go and do some research on the historical places you'll visit.
❑ Write ahead to get free materials from your destination.
❑ Be sure to share background information with your children to prepare them for what they'll see and get them excited about the prospect.

COLONIAL WILLIAMSBURG

Colonial Williamsburg, located in Williamsburg, Va., about midway between Norfolk and Richmond, is the largest restored 18th-century town in America. It is considered part of Virginia's "Historic Triangle," along with Jamestown, the site of the first permanent English settlement in America, and Yorktown, where the Revolutionary War ended. The three are connected by the Colonial Parkway.

HISTORICAL BACKGROUND

From 1699 to 1780, Williamsburg was the capital of the colony of Virginia, which at one time stretched west all the way to the Mississippi River and north to the Great Lakes. It was a gathering place for the movers and shakers of colonial America, who came to politic and socialize.

But after the American Revolution, Williamsburg's fortunes declined and it became a sleepy little Southern town of dilapidated buildings and overgrown gardens. Until 1926 that is, when John D. Rockefeller Jr. began to restore the old city to its former glory. Today, the 173-acre historic area is administered by the non-profit Colonial Williamsburg Foundation and includes 88 original 18th- and early 19th-century buildings, plus many others that have been reconstructed on their original foundations. Some of these are occupied by Colonial Williamsburg staff members and their families or are used as public lodging.

Duke of Gloucester Street runs through the center of the historic area, from the College of William and Mary (where Thomas Jefferson studied) to the Capitol (where Patrick Henry denounced King George III's stamp tax). It's about a mile long and closed to vehicular traffic during the day. Among other exhibit buildings are the Governor's Palace, home to seven British governors and Patrick Henry and Thomas Jefferson when they served as governors of the new state, and the Public Hospital, the first American institution devoted to treating mental illness.

A short distance away is Jamestown, where in the spring of 1607—13 years before the Pilgrims landed at Plymouth Rock—104 English men and boys selected a site for a settlement on the banks of the James River. The expedition was sponsored by a group of businessmen called the London Company, whose investors hoped to find gold and silver and new trade routes to the Orient.

The early settlers were unprepared for the hardships of the new land and seven months later, less than 35 were still alive. New settlers, including a handful of women, did little to stabilize the colony. In 1608, Captain John Smith took command, established trade relations with the Indians and was able to create a degree of order and cooperation. But when he left for England the next year, chaos returned and only a handful of people survived the winter. The colony was rescued from destruction by the arrival of more settlers and supplies.

After that, immigration and stability increased and Jamestown became the center of an expanding colony until 1699, when the capital was moved to the Middle Plantation, later renamed Williamsburg. Today, little evidence remains of the once-bustling seaport, though Jamestown Settlement—a large outdoor museum operated by an agency of the state of Virginia—re-creates its earliest days.

Yorktown, the third leg of the "Historic Triangle," is at the opposite end of the Colonial Parkway from Jamestown. Here, the troops of General George Washington defeated the British in the last major battle of the Revolution. The site is administered by the National Park Service and you can walk the battlefield and scale the redoubts. The Yorktown Victory Center provides an instructive prelude.

ABOUT THE TOURS

Because there are so many things to see and do in Colonial Williamsburg, it's worthwhile to spend some time getting oriented and figuring out a schedule for your visit. A good place to start is the visitor center, where you can park your car for free, get questions answered and view an excellent 35-minute film, *Williamsburg—The Story of a Patriot*, shown continuously throughout the day.

While you can stroll through the historic district for free, an admission ticket is required for entrance into various buildings. Three combination passes are available:

❑   The most inclusive and expensive is the Patriot's Pass, which provides admission to everything but Bassett Hall (the Rockefellers' Williamsburg estate) and includes Carter's Grove (a nearby plantation) and the Patriot's Tour, a special one-hour guided tour. The ticket is valid for a year from the date of purchase.

❑   The Royal Governor's Pass is the same as the Patriot's Pass except that it does not include Carter's Grove and is good for four consecutive days.

❑   The Basic Ticket provides admission for your choice of up to 12 exhibits in the historic area but does not include the Governor's Palace, DeWitt Wallace Decorative Arts Gallery, Carter's Grove or Bassett Hall.

Tickets can be purchased at the visitor center, Merchants Square Information Station, Greenhow Lumber House (opposite the Palace Green on Duke of Gloucester Street), Williamsburg Inn, Williamsburg Lodge and participating area hotels. With your ticket, you get a tabloid newspaper, *Visitor's Companion*, which lists special programs and activities for the week and includes a detailed map. Your ticket also entitles you to use the transportation system which circles the perimeter of the historic area with various stops where you can get off and on.

From mid-June to late August, special programs are offered for children and families. An additional ticket is required for each of these and can be purchased at the Greenhow Lumber House, where the tours begin.

❑ "Once Upon a Town" (ages 4-6) is a walking tour of the Palace Green neighborhood led by an interpreter and a local 4-H youth in costume. It includes games, storytelling, puppets and animals. Offered daily, 10 a.m.-noon; 15 children per tour.

❑ "Young Apprentice Tour" (ages 7-12) allows participation in varied 18th-century work and play activities in the historic area. Offered daily, 10 a.m.-noon; 20 children per tour.

❑ "Stepping into the Past" gives 20th-century families an opportunity to see what family life was like in colonial times through participatory activities for parents and children (over age 7). Offered daily, 2-4 p.m.; 20 participants per tour.

Other tours of special interest—each of which requires an additional ticket purchase—include:

❑ "According to the Ladies," a two-hour walking tour offering a feminine perspective of the community (offered spring, summer and fall).

❑ "Other Half Tour," an innovative tour exploring African-American experiences in 18th-century Williamsburg, where blacks composed 50 percent of the population (spring, summer and fall).

❑ "Lanthorn Tour," an evening walking tour which includes four candlelit shops where craftspeople ply their trades (year-round).

THINGS TO DO NEARBY

The story of the people who founded Jamestown and of the Native Americans they encountered is told at **Jamestown Settlement** (formerly Jamestown Festival Park), six miles away on the Colonial Parkway. We've visited several times with our kids at various ages, and they've never failed to be fascinated by the re-created Indian village, colonial fort and full-size replicas of the three ships which carried settlers to Virginia in 1607. The largest of the ships, the *Susan Constant,* can be boarded.

At the **Powhatan Indian Village,** costumed interpreters grow and prepare food, tan hides and make tools and pottery. At the **James Fort**—a triangular wooden stockade with primitive early buildings, including homes, a church, a storehouse and a guardhouse—interpreters engage in a variety of activities typical of daily life in the early 17th century. Periodically, "soldiers" conduct militia musters in which visitors can participate.

In 1990, a new lobby and exhibit area opened. Here you can see a film, *Jamestown: The Beginning*, which provides an overview of the colony's first 25 years.

At the opposite end of the Colonial Parkway is **Yorktown Victory Center,** where you can experience the entire spectacle of the Revolutionary War and George Washington's final victory in a brief, entertaining visit. Start with a stroll down Liberty Street, an indoor re-creation of an 18th-century lane, where recorded voices recount major events from the Revolution. Then watch the dramatic film *The Road to Yorktown*, shown continuously in the museum theater. Before you leave, visit the military encampment outside the center where interpreters dressed as soldiers and camp followers will tell you stories of what their lives were like 200 years ago.

Jamestown Settlement and Yorktown Victory Center are open year-round except Christmas and New Year's Day. A combination ticket can be purchased for admission to both places. For more information, contact: Jamestown-Yorktown Foundation, PO Drawer JF, Williamsburg, VA 23187 (804-253-4138).

Just a few miles from Colonial Williamsburg is a 20th-century attraction the kids won't want to miss—**Busch Gardens/The Old Country** (see THEME PARKS).

If you're visiting in the summer and want to cool off and have a barrel of fun at the same time, head for **Water Country USA** (see "Best of the Rest" in WATERPARKS).

N O T E

Special programs for children—featuring hands-on activities, stories, games and take-home crafts—are offered periodically throughout the year (including six weeks in July and August) at both Jamestown Settlement and Yorktown Victory Center. The age groups are 4- to 6-year-olds, first and second graders, and third and fourth graders. For fee information and schedule, call 804-253-4939.

WHERE TO STAY

Colonial Williamsburg operates several "official hotels" (like the "official hotels" of Walt Disney World). If you choose to stay at one of these, not only are you very handy to the historic district, but you can also purchase a hotel guest admission ticket that gets you into everything you could possibly want to see at a bit of a discount over what the general public pays. Additionally, you get a complimentary guided walking tour from your hotel, preferred seating times when you make advance reservations at the colonial taverns and hotel restaurants, and use of the Tazewell Club Fitness Center (see Williamsburg Lodge).

While there are several choices of "official hotels," the best bet for families is either the Motor House or the Cascades, which are located next to each other near the visitor center (where you can get complimentary transportation to the historic district). Of the two, the Cascades is a bit more secluded and offers mini-suites furnished in contemporary design. Corner suites are available at the Motor House, along with standard rooms. The complex shared by the two has swimming pools, a playground, miniature golf, shuffleboard and ping-pong tables. The Cascades Restaurant (see "Where to Eat") and Motor House Grill serve breakfast, lunch and dinner, the latter cafeteria-style.

If you want to go more upscale, try the Williamsburg Lodge and Conference Center, within walking distance of the historic district and across the street from the Golden Horseshoe Golf Course. The most expensive rooms and suites are found in the Tazewell and West wings, which are built around a landscaped interior courtyard. The Tazewell Club Fitness Center includes an exercise room with Keiser and Nautilus equipment, indoor lap pool, sauna and so forth.

If, on the other hand, you'd like to economize, stay at the Governor's Inn, Colonial Williamsburg's newest property. Besides lower rates, you get a complimentary continental breakfast and shuttle bus service to the visitor center.

Make advance reservations for all of the above by calling 1-800-HIS-TORY.

Of course, you don't have to stay in a Colonial Williamsburg hotel property to be near the historic district; there are other possibilities. For instance, the newest of five Days Inns in Williamsburg is just three blocks away. It's a cut above the usual, with suites and rooms with jacuzzis available, and a heated outdoor pool, too. Kids under 18 stay free (331 Bypass Rd., 804-253-1166).

Nearby is the Econo Lodge Williamsburg Center, the most convenient to the historic district of four Econo Lodges in the area. It also offers suites, plus less expensive kitchen units, and has a pool, playground, game room and fitness center. Kids under 18 stay free (600 Bypass Rd., 804-220-2800).

Another chain with lots of properties in Williamsburg is Quality International—with three Comfort Inns, five Quality Inns and a Quality Suites all within a relatively short distance of each other. The Quality Suites is 1.5 miles from the historic district and features two-room suites with microwaves and VCRs, and an indoor pool. A complimentary breakfast and evening manager's reception are offered. Kids under 18 stay free (152 Kingsgate Pkwy., 804-229-6800).

If you're looking for something a bit different, go for a cottage at the Governor Spottswood, located about a mile from the historic area. These can sleep up to six people and are equipped with kitchens. Regular motel rooms, plus suites and kitchen units, are also available and rates are moderate. There's a pool and playground on the wooded premises, along with picnic tables and grills (1508 Richmond Rd., 804-229-6444, 800-368-1244 or, in Virginia, 800-572-4567).

WHERE TO EAT

Four restored taverns in the historic area are once again serving food to visitors as they did 200 years ago. You'll want to try at least one of them. Shields Tavern on Duke of Gloucester Street near the Capitol is both the oldest and the newest—it predates the others by about 25 years, but opened most recently (1989). Dining rooms are located on three levels and are decorated according to their use in colonial times: the room used as the kitchen features a working fireplace and large trestle tables; the brick-floored basement, originally used for storage, is lined with barrels and shelves. In summer months, patrons are entertained in the garden after dinner by 18th-century-style magicians, musicians, puppeteers and theatrical performers.

Josiah Chowning's Tavern, adjacent to Market Square, is a typical colonial alehouse, where lunch and dinner are served in the garden and nightly "gambols" commence at 9 p.m., featuring strolling musicians and magicians and 18th-century table games like backgammon. Even if you eat elsewhere, you can show up for the gambols, but be aware that seating is on a first-come, first-served basis.

Christiana Campbell's Tavern, on Waller Street across from the Capitol, was one of George Washington's favorite eating places. It's a good spot for brunch, which is offered daily and features pecan waffles, specialty omelets and even skillet-fried chicken. The dinner menu includes seafood specialties and spoon bread.

The fourth tavern, King's Arms on Duke of Gloucester Street, is somewhat more genteel than the others and perhaps best reserved for an adults-only meal.

Definitely for adults-only is dinner in the elegant Regency Room of the Williamsburg Inn. It's expensive, but worth every penny to sit under bronze and crystal chandeliers and taste such delicacies as croustade of lobster au whisky or French lamb chops with minted pears. Try to save room to sample one of the extraordinary desserts. Jacket and tie required.

If you've timed your visit right, you can take in the Chesapeake Bay Feast offered Friday and Saturday evenings in the Bay Room of the Williamsburg Lodge. The biggest problem is figuring out how to sample some of everything from the overflowing buffet. In addition to every kind of seafood imaginable, there's Virginia ham and prime rib.

Another bountiful buffet is the Hunt Breakfast at the Cascades

Restaurant, served Monday through Saturday starting at 7:30 a.m. You can refill your plate as many times as you want with eggs, bacon, sausage, ham, fried chicken, muffins, etc. A slightly more expensive brunch is served on Sundays, and there's also a dinner buffet.

Dinner reservations for all of the above places should be made before you leave home and reconfirmed when you arrive in Williamsburg. Write or call Colonial Williamsburg Dining Reservations, PO Box B, Williamsburg, VA 23187 (804-229-2141).

In Merchants Square (on Duke of Gloucester Street between the historic area and the College of William and Mary), you can get sandwiches, burgers and great ice cream at A Good Place to Eat or more varied fare at the Trellis. The latter offers seating in five rooms: the Cafe Bar, the elegant Garden Room, the Grill Room, the Vault Room and the airy Trellis Room. The food is as pleasing as the decor. Make reservations for dinner (804-229-8610).

If you visit Yorktown, you may want to stop at Nick's Seafood Pavilion, which serves both lunch and dinner and offers a children's menu. The seafood is the freshest, but the wait for a table can be long (no reservations). Open every day except Christmas (on Va. 238—Water Street—at the south end of the bridge, 804-887-5269).

WHEN TO GO

Colonial Williamsburg is open 365 days a year and the off- season is short: January and February. Although it's crowded in the summer, the best time to visit with kids is mid-June to late August because you can take advantage of special tours and activities that are offered only then. That's also the best time, weather-wise, to take in Busch Gardens and Water Country U.S.A. If you visit in the summer, be sure to book accommodations well in advance. Restaurants will be busy, too, so make reservations whenever possible.

FOR MORE INFORMATION

Contact:

The Colonial Williamsburg Foundation
Williamsburg, VA 23187 (1-800-HISTORY)

They'll send you a free vacation planner, with information about rates and packages for the "official hotels." A directory of accommodations, attractions, camping and dining facilities is published by the Williamsburg Area Convention and Visitors Bureau, PO Box GB, Williamsburg, VA 23187 (804-253-0192). The Williamsburg Hotel and Motel Association can also assist with reservations (800-446-9244 or, in Virginia, 800-582-8977).

MUSEUM OF AMERICAN FRONTIER CULTURE

The Museum of American Frontier Culture in Staunton, Va., explores the important contributions made by the early settlers of the Appalachian frontier. The outdoor museum consists of four authentic farmsteads, three of which come from the European nations the pioneers left behind and one of which represents the American synthesis of these cultures. All four farms are living history demonstrations, where costumed interpreters carry out day-to-day and seasonal activities. The museum is located at the intersection of I-84 and I-64 in the beautiful Shenandoah Valley of Virginia. Take exit 57 off I-81 to Route 250 west and follow the signs.

HISTORICAL BACKGROUND

Much of America's frontier heritage began here in the "Great Valley" of Virginia, where pioneer farmers and artisans adapted Old World experiences to a new environment.

The land was first claimed in 1716 by Governor Alexander Spottswood, who led an expedition of 63 men from the colonial capital of Williamsburg. Later, successive waves of settlers came down the valley from Maryland and Pennsylvania, as well as from the Tidewater area of Virginia to the east. By the mid-1700s, the road through the valley came to be known as "The Great Wagon Road," the gateway to the Western frontier.

The Museum of American Frontier Culture was conceived by an international committee during our nation's Bicentennial. Development began in 1982 and complex arrangements were made to dismantle, ship and reconstruct the historic buildings from farmsteads in Europe. The museum opened in the fall of 1988, with two farms—the American and Scotch-Irish—completed and two others—the English and German—still in the process of being reconstructed. The ongoing project is funded and supported by the Commonwealth of Virginia and by contributions from private individuals and businesses through the American Frontier Culture Foundation.

ABOUT THE TOUR

Tours begin at the orientation building in the visitor center, where you can watch a film and learn about the day's activities. From the orientation area, you travel on foot over a three-quarter mile loop that takes you past the four farms. Costumed interpreters at each site will gladly answer questions about the day-to-day activities you see them performing—tending livestock, growing crops, doing domestic chores and practicing the crafts of early artisans.

The English farm, dating from the 17th century, is scheduled to be completed by 1991. It is comprised of several separate buildings, including the farmhouse, barns and cattleshed. Livestock you'll see here include cattle, draft horses, sheep, pigs and oxen. Of particular interest is the beekeeping operation and the lime kiln.

The late 17th-century German farm is one main building: a large farmhouse with attached barns. Livestock includes cattle, pigs, chickens and horses, and tobacco is among the crops grown.

The Scotch-Irish farm, which dates from the early 19th century, has a house with attached barn, plus a separate barn and a pig sty. Crops include cabbages, potatoes and turnips.

The American farm also dates from the early 19th century and, like most of the Appalachian farms of the period, is a symbol of the cultural mesh of the frontier. The farmstead includes a separate home and two barns—one used for tobacco—plus outbuildings: a smokehouse, a buggy shed, chicken houses and more.

A number of workshops and special events are scheduled at the Museum of Frontier Culture throughout the year, both for children and adults. A Traditional Frontier Festival is held annually in September, with entertainment, food and craft demonstrations in a country fair atmosphere. From late June through early August a "Summer on the Farms" program for children ages 4 through 12 allows them to take part in chores, games and special craft projects—even a taffy pull. The program is offered daily from 10 a.m. to noon. Traditional Christmas celebrations are held in December, focusing on the customs of the different countries represented at the museum. Special celebrations are also scheduled for St. Patrick's Day, the Fourth of July and Halloween, as well as for spring planting and fall harvesting.

For information on upcoming events, write or phone the museum for a schedule. In some cases, preregistration and an additional fee are required.

THINGS TO DO NEARBY

Staunton is about a half-hour drive from Waynesboro, at the southern entrance to **Shenandoah National Park.** For more information about the park see NATIONAL PARKS.

Woodrow Wilson's Birthplace is a restored mansion with many mementos of the 28th president and his family, including his 1919 Pierce-Arrow limousine. A 20-minute video covers Wilson's life and times. Closed Sundays in January and February, plus Thanksgiving, Christmas and New Year's Day (24 N. Coalter St., 703-885-0897).

Gypsy Hill Park is the center of outdoor activities in Staunton. In addition to tennis courts and an 18-hole golf course, you'll find a lake stocked with fish, a miniature train ride and playgrounds. Open daily (off Churchville and Thornrose avenues, 703-886-8435).

If you happen to be visiting in the winter, you may want to make a trip to **Massanutten Ski Resort,** less than an hour away. Located just 13 miles from Harrisonburg and I-81, this is Virginia's second biggest ski area. It has a good ski school with programs for children ages 4-5 and 6-12. For information, contact: Massanutten Resort, PO Box 1227, Harrisonburg, VA 22801 (703-289-9441).

WHERE TO STAY

Staunton is a charming city, but not a big one, so the choices of where to stay are somewhat limited. These are our picks for families:

The best deal for the money is the Ingleside Red Carpet Inn, a modestly priced four-story resort motel on 200 landscaped acres. All rooms have refrigerators, plus patios or balconies overlooking the 18-hole golf course. There's also tennis, swimming pools and a playground. Kids under 12 stay free. It's located on U.S. 11, just a few miles from I-81 (703-248-1201).

The Sheraton Inn, off I-81 at Woodrow Wilson Parkway (703-248-6020), offers golf and tennis privileges at the Country Club of Staunton. It has an indoor/outdoor pool and kids under 17 stay free.

Adjacent to the Museum of Frontier Culture off I-81, you'll find a Comfort Inn and Shoney's Inn. At either one, you'll get comfortable accommodations at a good price. The Comfort Inn (703-886-5000) offers a continental breakfast and kids under 18 stay free. The Shoney's Inn (703-885-3117) has an exercise room in addition to an indoor pool, and some rooms have whirlpools. Kids under 18 stay free.

WHERE TO EAT

The Wharf Deli & Pub, as its name implies, is located in the wharf area (on Middlebrook Ave., 703-886-2329). Save room for the German chocolate pie—it's sinful.

Edelweiss offers a robust German menu in a log cabin setting. Closed Mondays (at the junction of U.S. 340 and 11, 703-337-1203).

Rowe's Family Restaurant has been operated by the same family since 1947. It's a homey place, where good food can be had inexpensively. Specialties include Virginia ham, steak and chicken (exit 57 off I-81, 703-886-1833).

Take a drive to the Buckhorn Inn restaurant in nearby Churchville for a nice dinner or Sunday brunch. Located in a colonial country inn in the Shenandoah Valley, it specializes in regional country dishes (Rte. 250, 703-337-6900).

WHEN TO GO

The Museum of American Frontier Culture is open daily from 9 a.m. to 5 p.m. except Christmas Day and New Year's Day. Hours are extended to 8 p.m. in the summer. Because a lot of walking around outdoors is required to see the various farms which make up the museum, you may prefer visiting between April and November, when the weather is most pleasant. Special programs and workshops are offered periodically year-round, but the "Summer on the Farms" children's program is available daily from late June to early August.

FOR MORE INFORMATION

Contact:

Museum of American Frontier Culture
PO Box 810, Staunton, VA 24401
(703-332-7850)

For more information on Staunton, contact the Chamber of Commerce Travel Info Service, 30 N. New St., Staunton, VA 24401 (703-885-8504).

OLD SALEM

Old Salem is a faithfully restored planned community which was the 18th-century trade and cultural center of North Carolina's Piedmont. The village consists of 60 original brick and wooden structures, some of which are open to the public and some of which are private residences. Old Salem is located a short distance from downtown Winston-Salem, just off I-40 (take the Old Salem/Salem College exit and follow the signs).

HISTORICAL BACKGROUND

Among early American towns, Salem was an unusual community. It was founded in 1766 by emigres from Moravia, a state in present-day Czechoslovakia, who came to the New World to escape religious persecution. Having earlier established a successful colony in Bethlehem, Pa., the Moravians were offered a tract of land in North Carolina by a British nobleman, Lord Granville, who had heard of their industrious, law-abiding ways. The settlement came to be known as Wachovia, and Salem was planned as its trade center, a town of craftsmen and merchants.

By 1772, most of the major buildings had been completed and for more than 50 years Salem flourished as a congregation town—the Moravian church owned all the land, leasing lots to individual church members.

Moravians did not separate church and state, and important questions—from business matters to selecting a mate—were decided through a practice known as the lot. Three hollow reeds were placed in a wooden bowl: one contained a paper marked "ja," another "nein." The third was blank, indicating that the question was premature or needed rephrasing. After deliberation and prayer, one reed was drawn; its message was considered the Lord's will.

Though strict by today's standards, life in early Salem nonetheless included laughter and music. Most Moravians played at least one instrument and nearly every occasion was celebrated with song. There was a strong emphasis on family and children, and education—for girls as well as boys—was highly regarded.

However, as the area surrounding Wachovia grew more populated, the regimented congregation system of Salem lost much of its appeal. Gradually, the old rules were either relaxed or abandoned, and by the mid-19th century, the church relinquished economic control of the town.

About the same time, a new town, Winston, was founded on Salem's northern borders. In 1875, R.J. Reynolds started his tobacco company there and Winston began to thrive as an industrial center. In 1913, the two towns merged, and as the years passed the old Moravian village gradually deteriorated.

But just when it seemed on the verge of extinction, the citizens of Winston-Salem formed a non-profit organization to bring together Moravians and non-Moravians in an effort to preserve the historic area. Since 1950, when the restoration project began, some 60 buildings have been restored or reconstructed on their original sites, street signs and lamp posts have been redesigned to their former look, and open spaces have been planted with fruit trees and flowers of the period. Today, just minutes from downtown Winston-Salem, you can step back in time and sample the culture and daily lives of the people who lived here two centuries ago.

ABOUT THE TOUR

At the visitor center on Old Salem Road, you can view a slide show on Moravian history and purchase tickets which will admit you to nine restored buildings. You can buy either individual admissions or a combination ticket; there's a family rate for the latter.

The most interesting building to tour is the Single Brothers House, where young men lived communally and learned various trades through a seven-year apprentice system. One wing houses workshops where shoemakers, tailors, coopers, tinsmiths and other craftsmen demonstrate their skills.

Other museum buildings include the Market-Fire House, which contains an exhibit of early fire-fighting equipment; the Boys School, which includes exhibits on the history of Wachovia and a restored classroom; the Miksch Tobacco Shop, with reproductions of early tobacco-making implements; the Vierling House, which contains the medical offices of a renowned physician; the John Vogler House, which includes a silversmith shop; and the Schultz Shoemaker Shop, with displays of tools and products. The Salem Tavern accommodated travelers of yesteryear—including George Washington, who indeed slept here. Today's visitors can stop for a meal in the dining rooms next door (see "Where to Eat").

No admission ticket is needed for the Winkler Bakery, where 18th-century processes are still used to make breads, sugar cookies and tantalizing Moravian Lovefeast buns. The aroma emanating from the bakery is irresistible.

> **NOTE**
>
> Visitors are always welcomed to services at the Home Moravian Church, located on the square. Hundreds show up for the Easter Sunrise Service, the Christmas Lovefeast (December 24) and the New Year's Eve Watch Night Service.

For interesting souvenirs, check T. Bagge-Merchant, the Old Salem Museum Store, or one of the two book and gift shops also found on the village square.

THINGS TO DO NEARBY

Historic **Bethabara Park** is the site of the Moravians' first settlement when they came to North Carolina in 1753. Archeological research has uncovered the foundations and cellars of many of the original buildings; it's interesting to imagine how people lived in what was essentially one smallish room. Three larger buildings have been restored and the palisade fort, built in 1756 during the French and Indian Wars, has been reconstructed. The visitor center contains exhibits on the early settlers, including many artifacts found on the site. This is an excellent spot for an afternoon picnic or a hike on the trails that lead to the Moravian graveyard called God's Acre. The visitor center is closed from mid-December to April, but you can take in the rest of the park anytime (2147 Bethabara Rd., 919-924-8191).

Located on 31 acres of scenic woodland, the **Nature Science Center** is a combination science museum, planetarium, barnyard and nature trail. For good measure, there's a 1,000-gallon tidal pool inhabited by small sea creatures. The center's Discovery Room features some nifty experiences like a photo shadow wall that momentarily freezes your silhouette and a kaleidoscope of mirrors that allows you to see yourself projected into infinity. If you've ever wanted to pet a skunk (de-scented) or stick your hand into a dinosaur's jaw, this is the place to do it. Open daily except Thanksgiving, Christmas and New Year's Day, 10 a.m.-5 p.m. Monday-Saturday, 1-5 p.m. Sunday (Museum Dr., 919-767-6730).

Woodsy, 1,152-acre **Tanglewood Park**—located 12 miles southwest of Winston-Salem off I-40—was once the country estate of tobacco tycoon William N. Reynolds. It's been open to the public since 1951 as a non-profit resort operated under county auspices. The recreational activities available are as varied as you'll find at commercial resorts—and, for the most part, less expensive. There's a bigger-than-Olympic-size pool with water slide, a nine-court tennis center, two fine 18-hole golf courses and two driving ranges, stables, playgrounds, a stocked fishing lake, plus canoes and paddleboats. On summer weekdays you can take advantage of an on-site YMCA camp for kids ages 6 to 12. See "Where to Stay" section for further details.

Reynolda Village is another restored area that's worth a visit. Built in 1917, the village was originally part of Reynolda, the 1,000-acre estate of R.J. Reynolds. Today, the quaint cottages and buildings belong to Wake Forest University and house a collection of interesting shops and restaurants, such as the Village Book Shop, which includes a children's room; the Great Kids Company, crammed with toys and stuffed animals; and Breads and Spreads, which features home-baked goodies. Most shops are closed Sundays.

WHERE TO STAY

The choices of accommodations in the Winston-Salem area range from deluxe to rustic. Starting with the former, you'll find two swanky hotels downtown within a block of each other: the Hyatt and the Stouffer Winston Plaza. The Hyatt (300 W. 5th St., 919-725-1234) is the older of the two, but underwent a $4 million renovation fairly recently. Its 293 rooms overlook a nine-story atrium. Stouffer's (425 N. Cherry St., 919-725-3500) is 17 stories high, with 315 rooms. Both hotels offer indoor pools, exercise facilities, and golf and tennis privileges. And if you want to be further pampered, you can stay on the "club level" at either place and enjoy such amenities as complimentary continental breakfast and afternoon hors d'oeuvres. At both hotels, children under 18 stay free. The Hyatt offers a supervised kids' activities program on Friday and Saturday evenings. Stouffer's has complimentary cable TV, including the Disney Channel.

Kids under 18 stay free in two conveniently located Holiday Inns: one in the downtown area (127 S. Cherry St., 919-725-8561) and one near the sprawling Hanes Mall (I-40 and Silas Creek Pkwy., 919-765-6670).

Also adjacent to Hanes Mall is a Days Inn (I-40 and 3330 Silas Creek Pkwy., 919-760-4770). In the same price range is the Hampton Inn (5719 University Pkwy., 919-767-9009) and the Comfort Inn (3111 University Pkwy., 919-727-1277). All three of these motels offer a free continental breakfast and kids under 18 stay free.

For an extended stay, you might want to choose the Residence Inn by Marriott (7835 N. Point Blvd., 919-759-0777), an all-suite property where children stay free and weekly rates are available. (See "Where to Stay" in TRAVELING WITH KIDS for a fuller description of Residence Inns.)

If you're looking for privacy, try the cabins at Tanglewood Park (in nearby Clemmons, 919-766-0591). There are just five of them and they're located in a secluded woodland overlooking a lake. The cabins have either two or three bedrooms, come with fully equipped kitchens and rent by the week. Tanglewood also offers bed-and-breakfast in the Manor House (a bit fancy for kids), plus rooms in the motor lodge, a plain, two-story accommodation. In addition, there are 100 family campground sites at the park, most with electric and water hookups.

WHERE TO EAT

The Old Salem Tavern in the heart of Old Salem (736 S. Main St., 919-748-8585) provides a unique dining experience—especially at night when candlelight enhances the feeling that you're back in another century. The small, simply furnished dining rooms were built in 1816 as an annex to the 1784 Tavern next door. Waiters and waitresses in Moravian costumes serve such dishes as chicken pie, ragout of beef and rack of lamb. Pumpkin muffins and Tavern-made ice cream are special treats. In the summer, you can eat in the outdoor arbor.

Also in Old Salem is Michael Casey's, next to the visitor center, a good place for a soup-and-sandwich lunch (919-723-0332).

Elsewhere in Winston-Salem, Annabelle's, in the Hanes Mall (Silas Creek Pkwy. exit off I-40), is lots of fun for family dining. One of a growing chain found in North and South Carolina, it's decorated with nostalgic items, including a painted hobby horse, a vintage Shell gasoline pump and an old jail. Kids are welcomed with a special menu and crayons for doodling while awaiting their food. The regular menu is varied and reasonably priced. You may have to stand in line, especially on weekends, but we found that it moved pretty fast and the wait was worth it.

A similar ambience is found at Darryl's, one of another popular chain. This one is on the site of an old 1837 cotton mill where material for Confederate uniforms was woven and dyed. Another area of the mill is now the Brookstown Inn (200 Brookstown Ave., 919-725-1120).

An interesting spot for an adults-only dinner is La Chaudière, located in the former boiler room of the Reynolds estate. The decor and cuisine are French country—pheasant, rabbit and veal are among the delicacies. It's closed Mondays and reservations are a good idea the rest of the time (on Reynolda Rd., 919-748-0269). Another good choice is the Quill in the Stouffer Winston Plaza Hotel (919-725-3500), where you can also get a nice Sunday brunch.

WHEN TO GO

Old Salem's restored buildings are open year-round except Thanksgiving Day, December 24 and 25, and Sundays and Mondays in January. Hours are 9:30 a.m.-4:30 p.m. Monday through Saturday, 1:30-4:30 p.m. Sunday—though you can stroll through the historic district any time. The area is particularly lovely in the spring, when the dogwood and cherry trees are in bloom, and in the early fall, when the leaves turn color.

FOR MORE INFORMATION

Contact:

Old Salem Inc.
Box F, Winston-Salem, NC 27108
(919-721-7300)

For information about Winston-Salem and its other attractions, contact the Convention and Visitor Bureau, c/o Greater Winston-Salem Chamber of Commerce, PO Box 1408, Winston-Salem, NC 27102 (919-725-2361 or, outside North Carolina, 800-331-7018).

ST. AUGUSTINE

Founded 42 years before the English colonized Jamestown and 55 years before the Pilgrims landed at Plymouth Rock, St. Augustine, on the northeast coast of Florida, is the oldest permanent settlement in the U.S. In the latter years of the 20th century, historic sites have been restored—giving the city the languid charm of the Spanish colony it was for so many years.

HISTORICAL BACKGROUND

St. Augustine's history is so long and includes so many separate chapters that it's hard to do it justice in a brief space.

It starts back in 1513, when Don Juan Ponce de Leon landed on the northeast coast of Florida and claimed the area for the king of Spain. Over the next half-century, the Spanish made various attempts to settle the new territory, but none was successful. Meanwhile, France—eager to get its own foothold in the New World—established a fort and colony near the mouth of the St. Johns River. Worried about this encroachment, King Phillip II of Spain appointed his most experienced admiral, Don Pedro Menendez de Aviles, as governor of Florida and sent him to drive out all settlers from other nations.

On Sept. 6, 1565, with ships' banners flying, trumpets sounding, artillery booming and 600 soldiers and settlers cheering, Menendez stepped ashore and proclaimed the area St. Augustine, in honor of the saint whose feast day it was when he first sighted land. With military skill and the help of a hurricane, Menendez did away with the French garrisons and set to work establishing a permanent colony.

Almost 100 years later, clashes with the British began, becoming more frequent after the English colonies were established in Georgia and the Carolinas. To protect the city's vulnerable position, a stone fortress now called Castillo de San Marcos was erected. It withstood a two-month siege by Governor James Moore of Carolina and a fierce attack by British General James Oglethorpe of Georgia.

NOTE

St. Augustine's founding and early days are vividly depicted in companion movies—*Dream of Empire* and *Struggle to Survive*—shown continuously at the Museum-Theater one block from the City Gate. Produced by the St. Augustine Foundation, Inc., there's a good deal of attention to authenticity. But be forewarned: The history is violent and that's reflected on the screen. Admission for children under 15 is nominal (5 Cordova St., 904-824-0339).

Spanish rule was interrupted between 1763 and 1783, when Florida was ceded to England, but it was returned to Spain after the Revolutionary War and remained a Spanish territory for another 37 years, until Spain sold Florida to the United States. In a colorful ceremony in 1821—256 years after Menendez founded St. Augustine—Spanish troops left the territory for good.

If you visit St. Augustine between mid-June and late-August, you can see "Cross and Sword" performed at the amphitheater at Anastasia State Park. This is another dramatic recounting of Menendez' coming— complete with simulated hurricane, booming cannons and music. The actors are from the Florida School of the Arts. To get good seats, purchase reserved tickets in advance (904-471-1965).

ABOUT THE TOUR

A visit to the historic district of St. Augustine should start at the visitor center at 10 Castillo Dr., where you can pick up maps and brochures and also view a film that gives you a brief overview of the city's history. From the visitor center, you can walk to the 300-year-old Castillo de San Marcos, located on Matanzas Bay at 1 Castillo Dr. The imposing structure has 13-foot-thick walls constructed of coquina, a soft limestone made of broken shells and coral. If you have young children, you may want to keep them firmly in hand until you're inside the fort—it's surrounded by a moat which has no guard rails or other restraints around it. The fort is maintained by the National Park Service and rangers give periodic talks. But if your timing isn't right for one of these, you can push buttons found in various locations within the fort for a brief taped explanation of what you're looking at. Be sure to climb to the upper level of the Castillo for a panoramic view of Matanzas Bay. Open daily starting at 8:30 a.m., with slightly extended closing hours in the summer. Children under 16 are admitted free and adult tickets are inexpensive.

St. George Street, a pedestrians-only path through the heart of the historic district, begins just across the street from the fort at the City Gate and continues for several long blocks. If you think that's too much to do on foot, you can buy a ticket for a narrated trolley tour of the city. The beauty of this is that you can get on and off the trolley at any of several stops and your ticket is good for the duration of your stay. Tickets can be purchased at the visitor information center or at 167 San Marco Ave. Other options include sightseeing trains (170 San Marco) and horse-drawn carriage tours. You'll find carriages lined up along the bay just outside the entrance to the Castillo. Also, if you want to explore the waterfront, the *Victory II* and *Victory III* scenic cruises (904-824-1806) offer a 1 1/4-hour tour of Matanzas Bay, departing from the Municipal Yacht Pier.

St. George Street and the side streets off it are lined with a variety of shops and historic attractions such as the Oldest Wooden Schoolhouse, the Oldest Store Museum and the Oldest House (separate admission charges for each). Be sure to see the Spanish Quarter, San Augustin Antiguo, a state-operated living history village where interpreters dressed in the costumes of the mid-1700s carry out such activities as black-smithing, candledipping, spinning and cooking. The entrance is at the Triay House, 29 St. George St. It's open daily and the family admission ticket is reasonably priced.

Curiosity propels many to visit the Fountain of Youth, as Ponce de Leon reportedly did. It's located in a complex at 155 Magnolia Ave., which also includes a planetarium. And, yes, you can take a sip from the spring if you wish.

THINGS TO DO NEARBY

St. Augustine Alligator Farm has been in operation since 1893 and continues to pack in tourists for the American Alligator Show, Snappin' Sam Show and Reptile Show (on A1A south just two miles from the Bridge of Lions, 904-824-3337).

At least drive by **Zorayda Castle**, a Moorish palace inspired by the Alhambra in Granada, Spain. One of St. Augustine's quirkier tourist spots, it was actually a private residence at one time. If you decide to pay the admission price, you'll see such oddities as a mummy's foot and a "sacred" rug made of prehistoric cat hair (83 King St., 904-824-3097). Right across the street is **Flagler College,** once a magnificent hotel built by Henry Flagler.

Speaking of oddities, you'll find plenty at **Ripley's Believe It or Not Museum.** Robert L. Ripley, the famous collector of the bizarre, reportedly traveled to more than 198 countries to gather 750 exhibits, ranging from a shrunken head to a grain of rice with the Lord's Prayer on it (19 San Marco Ave., 904-824-1606).

Potter's Wax Museum is the oldest wax museum in the U.S. You can gawk at more than 170 sculpted figures of famous and infamous people from the past and visit the wax works to watch craftsmen at work (17 King St., 904-829-9056).

Performing dolphins are the top attraction at **Marineland of Florida,** but they're by no means the only aquatic creatures found here—other denizens range from exotic tropical fish to penguins. There's also a 3-D movie, *Sea Dream,* and high-dive shows from June through Labor Day (located on A1A south, about 18 miles from St. Augustine, 904-471-1111).

WHERE TO STAY

Ponce de Leon Resort & Convention Center sits less than three miles north of the historic district. This popular resort has been around for quite a while—the original 50 rooms were built in the late Fifties; additional rooms and meeting space were added in 1970. Golf is a big attraction here, with an 18-hole Donald Ross course meandering through salt marshes, plus a putting green and an 18-hole putting course. But there are also lighted tennis courts and a huge clover-shaped swimming pool. If you prefer, you can stay in one of 33 villas on the property. Kids under 12 stay free and various packages are offered (on U.S. Hwy. 1 N., 904-824-2821, 800-824-2821 or, in Florida, 800-228-2821).

If you want to stay within walking distance of the historic area, we recommend the moderately priced Monterey, a two-story motel with some kitchen units that offers family rates. It's right on Matanzas Bay, close to the Castillo de San Marcos, and it has a pool and sundeck (16 Avenida Menendez, 904-824-4482). Farther away, but still in the downtown area, the Comfort Inn is also a good deal. It offers a shuttle to attractions and a free continental breakfast. Kids under 18 stay free (1111 Ponce de Leon Blvd., 904-824-5554).

Across the Bridge of Lions from the heart of town, you'll come across the Conch House Marina Resort on Anastasia Island. It's small—just 22 units—but more than half of these have kitchens. A tropical-style seafood restaurant and lounge are built on the dock over the water, and you can fish from the pier. Kids under 10 stay free (57 Comares Ave., 904-829-8646, 800-874-0853 or, in Florida, 800-432-6256).

If you want to stay right on the ocean, follow A1A south to St. Augustine Beach, where you'll find a number of accommodations, including the 144-room Anastasia Inn (904-471-2575) and the 150-room Holiday Inn Oceanfront (904-471-2555). Kids under 18 stay free at both places and the Anastasia Inn has a playground.

If you head north on A1A and drive for about a half-hour, you'll come to Ponte Vedra Beach, where you'll find the posh 4,800-acre Marriott at Sawgrass. The resort opened in the fall of 1987 and is bordered by 2 1/2 miles of beach on the east and the Intracoastal Waterway on the west. It boasts 99 holes of golf on five courses (plus driving ranges and putting greens) and a 10-court tennis island. Guests also have privileges at the Association of Tennis Professionals complex on the property, where there's a choice of 11 surfaces—including two Wimbledon-style grass courts and two cushioned hard courts à la Flushing Meadow. The resort's emerald-glassed hotel, surrounded by 15 acres of alligator-filled lagoons, has more than 400 rooms and suites and features a seven-story atrium. Golf and beachfront villas are also available. For the kids, the Sawgrass Grasshoppers Gang offers daily organized activities and evening pizza and movie parties. For additional entertainment, there's even a "Toyland" suite filled with giant tractors, Barbie Dreamland and big-screen television complete with Nintendo. And did we mention the four swimming pools and three restaurants, including the elegant Augustine Room? Open year-round; kids under 16 stay free (1000 TPC Blvd., 904-285-7777).

WHERE TO EAT

If you're looking for good seafood restaurants, St. Augustine has plenty. One of the best choices is Fiddler's Green, just north of the city in Vilano Beach, with big windows overlooking the ocean. Reservations are recommended (50 Anahma Dr., 904-824-8897).

Another excellent seafood place is Chimes, which has a second-floor dining area with a balcony overlooking Matanzas Bay. Breakfast and lunch are served as well as dinner (12 Avenida Menendez, 904-829-8141).

One of the most interesting restaurants in the historic district is Columbia, which features Spanish fare. A balcony surrounds a central interior courtyard and there's a bakery and ice cream parlor, too. A good place for Sunday brunch (98 St. George St., 904-824-3341 or 800-227-1905). We also like Mi Casa Cafe, where you can take a break from sightseeing and relax at a table on the outdoor terrace (69 St. George St., 904-824-9317).

Raintree is the place to go for a delightful adults-only dinner (though child's plates are available). You can sip a mint julep on the porch of this restored Victorian house before adjourning to a dinner of brandy pepper steak or grouper filets stuffed with crab mousse and baked in puff pastry. Reservations are a good idea (102 San Marco Ave., 904-829-5953 or 904-824-7211).

If Raintree is busy, try Le Pavillon just down the street. Located in a former home built in 1890, the specialties here are rack of lamb and bouillabaisse (45 San Marco Ave., 904-824-6202).

WHEN TO GO

All of the attractions in and around St. Augustine are open daily year-round, with occasional exceptions on Thanksgiving and Christmas Day. Similarly, festivals and special events are scheduled all the time, but especially in April, October and the summer months. We visited in the spring and found the weather absolutely gorgeous.

FOR MORE INFORMATION

Contact:

St. Augustine/St. John's County Chamber of Commerce
Drawer O, St. Augustine, FL 32085
(904-829-5681)

NATIONAL PARKS

▼ GREAT SMOKY MOUNTAINS

▼ SHENANDOAH

▼ MAMMOTH CAVE

▼ EVERGLADES

▼ BISCAYNE

NATIONAL PARKS

National parks offer visitors an opportunity to come in contact with a world far removed from our daily experience. And the national parks in the Southeast offer a wide variety of settings—the wooded hills of Shenandoah and Great Smoky Mountains, the dramatically lit tunnels of Mammoth Cave, the grassy marshes of Everglades and the sparkling undersea world of Biscayne.

Even if you don't think of yourselves as outdoor-types, your family can enjoy a national park trip because you can choose how much or how little you want to "rough it." You can stay in a motel (or even a resort) nearby and sample the park in small doses. Or you can pitch a tent in a park campground and get to know the place by night as well as by day.

Some campgrounds are big, developed areas, bustling with people and RVs. Though often crowded, these offer the advantages of proximity to camp stores, showers and laundry facilities, not to mention campfire programs and other activities which kids enjoy. If you want to get away from all that, you can head for a more remote area.

Another option—one we personally like—is to stay at one of the lodges or cottages which can be found at all but Biscayne. These can be pretty rustic (as in no TV—and sometimes no electricity), but at least you get a bed and four walls. Some of the lodges, of course, are fairly modern motel-type units with standard amenities. Check the where-to-stay listings with each park for a rundown of your choices.

We haven't gone into detail about how to get to the various national parks, though we've described their locations and noted nearby cities. Basically, these are all somewhat off the beaten path, so the best you can do, if traveling by plane or train, is to get close, then rent a car. A travel agent can help you work out the details and won't charge you anything for the service.

Admission to the parks is either free (Great Smoky Mountains, Biscayne, Mammoth Cave) or nominal ($5 per car per week at Shenandoah and Everglades in 1990). If you plan to visit several parks in the national system or one park repeatedly, you can save money by purchasing a $25 Golden Eagle pass, which provides unlimited access to any park for one year. It applies to entrance fees only.

Camping fees are usually charged for developed campgrounds. We've noted which are on a first-come, first-served basis and which take reservations. If you plan to stay at a campground that doesn't take reservations, show up early to make sure you get a good spot. For those that do take reservations, you can make them through the park or—as we've noted in some cases—through Ticketron outlets up to eight weeks in advance.

Fees are also charged for cave tours at Mammoth Cave, for tram tours at Everglades and for boat tours offered at several of the parks. Ranger-led hikes, campfire programs, slide shows, films and exhibits are usually free.

If you're visiting a park for the first time, talk to your kids about what the experience will be like. Present it as an adventure—which it undoubtedly will be. Go to the library and get books about trees, caves, fish or whatever you expect to see on your trip. This will not only enhance their interest, but can also give you a chance to allay any fears or apprehensions they might have.

NOTE

If you're visiting a park for the first time:
❏ Talk to your kids about what the experience will be like
❏ Present it as an adventure—which it undoubtedly will be
❏ Go to the library and get books about trees, caves, fish or whatever you expect to see on your trip

While you want to keep preparations for the trip upbeat, you do need to reinforce a few safety tips:

Don't feed or touch wildlife. That means raccoons and chipmunks, too—not just bears and alligators.

Don't drink water that doesn't come from a drinking tap. A stream may look clear and inviting, but it can harbor a protozoan that causes severe diarrhea. Water from it should be boiled or chemically treated before drinking.

Stay on trails. All the time. First, so no one gets lost and second, to lessen the chances of picking up a disease-carrying tick from foliage or underbrush.

A visit to a national park is an especially good opportunity for children to learn about the environment and how people help or hurt it. These days you'll hear park rangers talking about various kinds of pollution that threaten even these protected settings. Don't contribute to the problem by leaving trash behind when you camp or picnic. And leave those interesting rocks and flowers where they are, so those who come after you can enjoy them, too. Remember that our parks are popular places—we don't want to love them to death.

GREAT SMOKY MOUNTAINS NATIONAL PARK

Great Smoky Mountains National Park offers more than a half-million acres of wilderness laced with miles of scenic roadway. Located along the Tennessee-North Carolina border, it is the most popular national park in the United States, with more than eight million visitors per year. In peak months, cars stack up bumper-to-bumper on the Newfound Gap Road which bisects the park between Gatlinburg, Tenn., and Cherokee, N.C.

Incredibly, many visitors view the spectacular scenery only through their car windshields. According to park figures, 20 percent of the visitors drive right through; fewer than one-third hike the 900 miles of maintained trails. What this means is that it's possible to escape the crowds with just a little effort.

ABOUT THE PARK

Great Smoky Mountains National Park was officially dedicated by President Franklin D. Roosevelt in 1940. The land was purchased by the states of Tennessee and North Carolina from logging companies and private owners, then donated to the United States. Schoolchildren helped raise some of the money and John D. Rockefeller kicked in a crucial $5 million.

Before the logging companies arrived on the scene, pioneer settlements existed in the mountain coves. And before the settlers, the Cherokees, the largest Indian tribe in the Southeast, considered the Smokies part of their empire. When the government forced the tribe to relocate to the West in 1838, some escaped into the mountains. The Western Cherokees disbanded in the early 1900s; thus the Eastern Cherokees, who still live in this area, are the last of the tribe.

The Smokies are among the oldest mountains on earth. They get their name from the filmy bluish haze that hangs over them, which is caused by the water and hydrocarbons exuded by the close-packed trees and brush. In recent years, air pollution has contributed to the effect.

> **NOTE**
>
> ■ There are some 500 black bears in the park, but you're not too likely to run into one. Since 1968, the use of bear-proof garbage cans with heavy iron lids has cut the number of bear "incidents" dramatically. If a bear does begin to frequent a developed area, it is tranquilized and relocated to the backcountry.
>
> ■ Should you happen to spot a bear, give it a wide berth. The place to see bears up close is the Black Bear Habitat at Ober Gatlinburg.

The park is noted for its matchless variety of flowering plants—some found only here—and for its ancient forests. Because it contains so many types of vegetation, the area has been designated an International Biosphere Reserve. In 1983, it was also named a World Heritage Site.

Unhappily, the park is not immune to environmental damage. Insects and acid rain are taking their toll on the red spruce and Frasier firs found along the mountaintops.

THINGS TO DO IN THE PARK

Hiking—The many trails in the park vary in length and difficulty; you can take a leisurely stroll on a paved path or a challenging hike in rugged backcountry. The easiest paths are the park's 21 Quiet Walkways, short trails 1/4- to 1/2-mile long. These are marked along park roads. The next-easiest paths are the 11 Self-Guided Nature Trails scattered along roadsides and leading from campgrounds, visitor centers and picnic areas. At the start of these trails, which usually form a loop of a mile or less, you can get a brochure which explains the trail's features.

If your children are old enough and everyone is fit enough, you might want to tackle a longer hike. But before you start on a trail, make sure you know just how long and how difficult it is. You'll find some relatively short, flat trails near the campgrounds and visitor centers—ask for advice.

If you'd rather not be on your own, join one of the many ranger-led walks offered in the spring, summer and fall, some of which are for children only. Check at visitor centers for a schedule.

Biking—Most of the park is too steep for biking, but an ideal area is the Cades Cove Loop Road. If you get up early Saturday mornings in the summer, you can ride without having to worry about cars—they're not allowed on the road until 10 a.m. Bikes can be rented from the campground store in Cades Cove.

Fishing—You'll find game fish and many smaller species in the park's 625 miles of fishable waters. Brook trout, which are native, are protected and must be released if caught. Anyone aged 16-65 needs a Tennessee or North Carolina fishing license.

Horseback riding—There are many miles of horse trails in the park. Stables at several locations offer rides at an hourly rate and provide guides as well. You can also bring your own horse and keep it at one of the five horse camps in the park.

Historic areas—Scattered throughout the park you'll find traces of the homesteads and logging towns found in this area before the park was created. For kids, the two most interesting areas are Cades Cove and the Oconaluftee Pioneer Farmstead. The Cades Cove Historic District, which includes cabins and churches built in the early 1800s, is located in a picturesque valley where cattle and horses still graze. The Pioneer Farmstead, adjacent to the Oconaluftee Visitor Center, is a working farm with crops, animals and craft demonstrations. Mills at both locations grind corn in the summer; sorghum molasses is made in the fall.

Camping—The Park Service maintains 10 developed campgrounds in the park with tent sites, some trailer and RV spaces, restrooms, water fountains, tables and fireplaces. You won't find showers or electrical or water hookups, however. Reservations for the three biggest campgrounds—Cades Cove, Elkmont and Smokemount—can be made up to eight weeks in advance through Ticketron outlets. Each of these campgrounds has an amphitheater where programs are offered in the spring, summer and fall, and Cades Cove has a camp store.

> **NOTE**
>
> Kids ages 8-12 can earn an official Junior Ranger badge by completing a series of activities such as walking one of the Self-Guided Nature Trails, visiting one of the historic areas, completing a workbook and collecting a bag of litter. Get info at the visitor centers or campgrounds.

THINGS TO DO NEARBY

Tennessee side

You'll find miniature golf, water slides and an array of kitschy stuff like the Elvis Museum all along the strip from Pigeon Forge to Gatlinburg. The major attractions are **Dollywood** (see THEME PARKS chapter) and **Ober Gatlinburg.** The latter, as its name implies, is on a mountain above Gatlinburg. You can drive there or take a cable car. In the winter, this is a ski area, but it's worth a visit in summer. Our kids loved riding the chair lift, trying the alpine slide and visiting the **Black Bear Habitat.** And there's more: a good-sized ice skating rink, snack bars, a sit-down restaurant and shops.

North Carolina side

Cherokee, at the entrance to the park, has one souvenir shop after another with items ranging from mocassins to Day-Glo war bonnets. For a more authentic view of Indian culture, visit the **Oconaluftee Indian Village** and the **Museum of the Cherokee Indian.** From mid-June to late August, the outdoor drama "Unto These Hills" recreates the history of the Cherokees. It's shown at night in the Mountainside Theater and kids old enough to stay awake for the entire production are likely to be impressed. Bring a sweater or sweatshirt and insect repellent.

WHERE TO STAY

In the park

If you're not into camping, there are two choices for lodgings: LeConte Lodge and Wonderland Hotel.

LeConte Lodge is truly unique. It's located just below the peak of Mt. LeConte, one of the highest mountains in the Smokies, and the only way to get to it is on foot or horseback. Supplies are hauled up by llamas (their hooves do less damage to the trails than horses' or mules').

There are five trails to the lodge, and the easiest way up is to follow the pack animals on the Trillium Gap Trail, which takes about five hours with breaks along the way. The most popular route is the Alum Cave Trail. This is not for the faint-hearted, because it's steep and narrow in places. The Park Service has installed hand cables to help with the tricky spots.

Once you get to the top, you'll find seven one-room cabins in a line above the main lodge, which was built in 1926 and actually predates the park. Each cabin has a massive double bunk bed that sleeps four. Three larger cabins, which can sleep 10-13 people, are also available. There is no electricity, but kerosene lamps are provided. Family-style breakfasts and suppers are served in the lodge.

Most visitors stay two or three nights, taking a day or two to explore the forest and numerous trails and catch a brilliant sunset.

Obviously, this isn't an adventure everyone would relish. But a measure of its popularity is the fact that reservations must be booked six months to a year in advance. The lodge is open from late March to mid-November. To make reservations, contact: LeConte Lodge, PO Box 350, Gatlinburg, TN 37738 (615-436-4473).

Wonderland Hotel, built in 1912, is also rustic. Located near the entrance to the Elkmont campground, it's open May-October and includes a restaurant. For reservations, contact: Wonderland Hotel, Rte. 2, Gatlinburg, TN 37738 (615-436-5490).

Outside the park—Tennessee side

Gatlinburg and Pigeon Forge, which sit next to each other on the main route into the park, are the obvious choices. Both are very tourist-oriented, with hundreds of shops, motels, restaurants and attractions. On summer days, crowds are thick on the sidewalks.

You'll find lots of "mom-n-pop" type motels, plus several chains in the area. Or you can stay in mountain chalets or condo-style accommodations, which offer kitchens and other amenities. For info, contact: Gatlinburg Chamber of Commerce, 520 Parkway, Gatlinburg, TN 37738 (615-436-4178 or 800-822-1998) or Pigeon Forge Dept. of Tourism,

11159 N. Parkway, Pigeon Forge, TN 37863 (615-453-8574 or 800-251-9100).

Outside the park—North Carolina side

There's a Holiday Inn and some smaller motels in Cherokee, but if you're willing to venture farther from the main entrance to the park, you'll find more interesting possibilities.

Along the southwest border of the park is 30-mile-long Lake Fontana, created by the highest dam in the eastern United States. Fontana Village, a family resort dating back to the 1940s, has cottages, a rustic lodge and a modern inn, plus boat rentals, tennis, golf, swimming pool and more. In 1987, Peppertree Resorts took over the operation and spent some $10 million on renovations. The place offers a friendly, camp-like environment with softball games and fishing tournaments among the regularly scheduled activities. Kids of all ages will enjoy it. Contact: Peppertree Fontana Village, Fontana Dam, NC 28733 (704-498-2211 or 800-438-8080).

Northeast of Cherokee is Maggie Valley, which—along with Waynesville and other neighboring communities—is promoting itself as a "gateway" to the Smokies, since it offers access to the park's least-visited area. Taking a cue from Gatlinburg and Pigeon Forge, the area is trying to lure tourists with such attractions as Ghost Town in the Sky, a cowboy theme park that you get to via incline railway or double chair lift, and the Stompin' Ground, a huge dance hall billed as the World's Capital of Clogging. For more info, contact: Maggie Valley Chamber of Commerce, PO Box 87, Maggie Valley, NC 28751 (704-926-1686 or 800-334-9036).

Just outside Maggie Valley, you'll find Cataloochee Ranch, a family-owned dude ranch with a handful of cabins, plus rooms in the main ranch house and the Silverbell Lodge. It's a laid-back place where you can ride horses, fish or pitch horseshoes. Children must be over 6. Contact: Cataloochee Ranch, Rte. 1, Box 500 Maggie Valley, NC 28751 (704-926-1401 or 800-868-1401).

WHERE TO EAT

Everything is so informal and family-oriented in this area that you can take the kids practically anywhere. You'll find lots of country cookin'—which usually means bountiful meals, simply prepared. Local specialties are trout, quail and country ham. The largest collection of restaurants is on the Tennessee side of the park where popular places include the Burning Bush, Smoky Mountain Trout House and Ogle's Buffet (Gatlinburg), plus Cole's Mill House, Green Valley and Apple Tree Inn restaurants (Pigeon Forge).

WHEN TO GO

The park is open year-round, but many programs and activities are seasonal. Summer is when you'll find the most things to see and do; it's also when motels and campgrounds are most likely to be full, so reservations are a must. Early June is less crowded than July and August. In October, another peak month, the foliage is spectacular, but that's when the Newfound Gap Road through the park is most congested. If you drive it then, try very early in the morning or late in the day.

Keep in mind that it rains a lot in the Smokies, especially in the spring and summer. It's wise to come prepared for afternoon thunderstorms. Also, remember that temperatures drop several degrees as the elevation rises.

FOR MORE INFORMATION

Contact:

Great Smoky Mountains National Park
Gatlinburg, TN 37738
(615-436-1200)

SHENANDOAH NATIONAL PARK

This long, narrow park deep in the Blue Ridge Mountains of Virginia is one of the most popular in the nation, drawing two million visitors a year. The scenic Skyline Drive runs the 80-mile length of the park, crisscrossed at several points by the famous Appalachian Trail.

ABOUT THE PARK

Shenandoah National Park was a Christmas gift to the nation from the people of Virginia. On Dec. 26, 1935, during the depths of the Depression, the state presented the Secretary of the Interior with deeds to nearly 200,000 acres of land for the establishment of the park. Nine years earlier, Congress had approved legislation to create the park but had stipulated that no federal funds could be spent to acquire land. The necessary money came from the Virginia Legislature and a statewide fundraising campaign.

The deeded land had been privately owned by mountain people who scraped a meager living from farming and logging operations. Today, the marks of human use are disappearing as the forests make a slow, steady return to their pristine state.

Within the park are 60 mountain peaks, ranging in elevation from 2,000 to more than 4,000 feet. The Skyline Drive runs along the mountain crests, providing a lofty (and sometimes scary) vantage point for viewing the scenery. The speed limit on the drive is 35 mph, but holiday and weekend crowds can slow traffic even further. Be sure to provide the kids with something to keep them occupied in the car.

Shenandoah can be enjoyed on a day trip or an extended stay. It is a good place for birdwatching, with more than 200 species found there at one time or another during the year. Wildflowers also abound.

The park has four entrances: Front Royal at the northern end, Rockfish to the south, and Thornton Gap and Swift Run Gap at intervals in between. The Dickey Ridge Visitor Center, near the north entrance, is open daily from late March through November. The Byrd Visitor Center, near the middle of the park, is open daily March through December and Friday through Monday in January and February. Both centers provide information and exhibits to acquaint you with the park and its facilities.

THINGS TO DO IN THE PARK

Hiking—Shenandoah's 500 miles of trails vary in length and difficulty and include a 94-mile portion of the Appalachian Trail, which can be hiked in large or small measures. You can reach trails by parking your car on an overlook along the Skyline Drive or by setting out from one of the developed areas in the park, such as Skyland or Big Meadows. Guided hikes are conducted daily from mid-June to Labor Day to major points of interest like Bearfence Mountain, which offers a spectacular 360-degree view.

Fishing—You can fish for native brook trout in more than 100 miles of streams within park borders. A Virginia license is needed and can be obtained at any major concession facility. The Rapidan and Staunton rivers are fishing-for-fun only: artificial lures with barbless hooks are required and if you catch anything, you have to put it back.

Horseback riding—Horses can be rented at Skyland for an hour, a half-day or all-day. A guide accompanies each trip and the horses are gentle enough for children. Still, you'll get the feel of a real wilderness trail ride.

Camping—There are five campgrounds in the park with tent and RV sites, but no hookups. The most popular campground is Big Meadows, which is open March through December. Reservations, available through Ticketron, are a good idea from Memorial Day weekend through October. The rest of the campgrounds—except for the Dundo Group Campground—are on a first-come, first-served basis. Both Big Meadows and Loft Mountain have camp stores, pay showers and coin laundries. Kids will enjoy another special offering at Big Meadows: a ride in a horse-drawn wagon.

THINGS TO DO NEARBY

Luray Caverns is a network of tunnels and chambers that covers 64 underground acres in Luray, Va., just nine miles west of the Skyline Drive (from the Thornton Gap Entrance Station). Among the wonders of the caverns is a "stalacpipe organ" which uses reverberating stalactites rather than conventional pipes to produce music that surrounds visitors to the Cathedral Room. Guided one-hour tours start about every 20 minutes (703-743-6551).

The **Museum of American Frontier Culture** is located in Staunton, about 30 miles west of the southern entrance to the park. For more information, see HISTORY PLACES.

Also at the southern end of the park, you can pick up the **Blue Ridge Parkway,** a National Park Service highway which runs between Shenandoah and Great Smoky Mountains national parks.

WHERE TO STAY

Accommodations are available in the park at Big Meadows, Skyland

and Lewis Mountain. At Big Meadows, choices include a lodge, a motel and cabins, which are open May through October. At Skyland, there's a lodge and 10 rustic cabins, open April through mid-December. At both locations, children under 16 stay free and there are playgrounds and planned activities. Lewis Mountain has seven cabins open May through October. For reservations, contact ARA Virginia Sky-Line Company, Box 727, Luray, VA 22835 (703-999-2221 or 703-743-5108).

Near the north entrance to Shenandoah, in Front Royal, is a Quality Inn with 107 rooms. Kids under 16 stay free (703-635-3161).

At the southern end of the park, in Waynesboro, there's a Comfort Inn (703-942-1171) and a Holiday Inn (703-942-5201). Charlottesville, about 20 miles east of Waynesboro, is the closest city to Shenandoah National Park and offers a broader range of accommodations. For information, contact the Thomas Jefferson Visitors Bureau, PO Box 161, Charlottesville, VA 22902 (804-293-6789 or 804-977-1783).

> **TRAVEL TIP**
>
> ■ Wintergreen, a wonderful family-oriented resort in the Charlottesville area, makes a good base for a day trip to Shenandoah, providing you can drag your family away from the many things to do there.
>
> ■ Known primarily as a ski resort, Wintergreen is open year-round and offers an excellent children's activity program in the summer. Accommodations include rental homes and condominiums ranging in size from studios to six bedrooms.
> Contact: Wintergreen, Wintergreen, VA 22958 (804-325-2200 or 800-325-2200)

WHERE TO EAT

You'll find restaurants in the park at Skyland, Big Meadows, Panorama and Loft Mountain. If you want to go on a picnic, you can pick up a light lunch at Skyland or Elkwallow or buy groceries at Loft Mountain or Big Meadows Wayside.

WHEN TO GO

The park is open year-round, but snow or ice may temporarily close the Skyline Drive in winter. Summer is a good time to visit because temperatures are pleasant and seasonal activities are in full swing. But because it's a peak period for visitors, reservations are a must if you'll be staying in the park. Try to time your visit for midweek, which is considerably less crowded than weekends. The same is true for September and October, when lots of tourists come for the fall foliage show.

FOR MORE INFORMATION

Contact:

Shenandoah National Park
Rte. 4, PO Box 348, Luray, VA 22835
(703-999-2243)
For recorded information, call 703-999-2266.

Mammoth Cave National Park

Mammoth Cave National Park is located along I-65 about halfway between Louisville, Ky., and Nashville, Tenn. The above-ground portion of the park consists of some 52,000 scenic acres. But the main attraction is underground: the largest cave system in the world, with more than 300 miles of chartered passages.

ABOUT THE PARK

Mammoth Cave was discovered sometime before 1799 and was already a tourist draw in the 19th century, when visitors brought whale-oil lamps to explore "the greatest cave that ever was." How large it really is, no one knows.

The cave's intertwining passages were formed by mildly acidic rainwater seeping into the ground and slowly dissolving layers of limestone beneath the surface, eventually creating an underground river system. As the streams cut deeper and deeper into the lower depths, the upper levels were drained and rocks fell from the ceilings, enlarging the caverns. After the upper levels filled with air, the continued seepage of water dissolved and redeposited the limestone to form travertine (cave onyx) in intricate patterns. This process has been underway for thousands of years and continues today to form new caves and enhance the beauty of older ones.

Some unusual creatures have made the caves their home—such as the colorless, eyeless crayfish that have adapted to survive their entire lives in the park's underground rivers. But while Mammoth Cave may seem like a world of its own, it's not. Water pollution on the surface—even outside park boundaries—poses a threat to the ecosystem below.

The history of Mammoth Cave, which became a national park in 1941, is recounted in an interesting 14-minute film, *Voices of the Cave*, shown throughout the day in the visitor center auditorium. The visitor center is also where you sign up for cave tours, for which a fee is charged. The only way to see the cave is to take one of these guided tours. About a half-million people, including families with young children, do so each year.

Strollers are not permitted in the cave, since there are numerous stairs to negotiate and passageways are narrow. If you're going to attempt to carry a small one in an over-the-shoulder backpack, be cautious about low ceilings.

Cameras are allowed in the cave, but getting a good photo is tricky—especially in the large caverns where the light dissipates. For best results, use fast-speed film and a flash.

THINGS TO DO IN THE PARK

Cave tours—A variety of tours ranging in length from a quarter-mile to five miles is offered. They are rated easy, strenuous or very strenuous, and if you have doubts about which to try, ask the rangers at the visitor center for advice. The easiest is a self-guided tour of the Rotunda, one of the largest known rooms in the cave, which takes about 30 minutes. The most difficult is the six-hour Wild Cave Tour, whose participants must be at least 16 years old and physically fit. An in-between possibility is the Historic Tour, which is two miles long and takes two hours.

In recent years, a special tour for children ages 8 to 12 has been offered in the summer months twice daily at 9 a.m. and 2 p.m. No adults are allowed other than the guides. The tour lasts about 2 1/2 hours and youngsters are furnished with hard hats with lights, just like real cave explorers.

Participants on all tours should wear sturdy shoes (no sandals). Trail surfaces are primarily hard-packed dirt and can be rough or uneven. Dripping or seeping water can make them slippery as well. Keep in mind, too, that cave temperatures are cool (54 degrees) even when it's hot above ground; dress accordingly.

You can make tour reservations through Ticketron outlets or at the visitor center. Tickets for kids under 16 are half of the adult price; children under 6 are admitted free.

> **NOTE**
>
> Kids ages 6-13 are eligible to become Junior Rangers (earning a patch and a certificate) after they participate in a variety of park programs and fill out an activity book with puzzles and questions about Mammoth Cave. Even if you won't be staying long enough to complete all the requirements, get a copy of the free activity book from the desk at the visitor center—it will keep the kids occupied while you wait for a tour to start.

Riverboat cruise—The *Miss Green River II* seats 122 for a scenic, one-hour cruise along the Green River, which runs through the park. Tickets should be purchased in advance at the visitor center. (Reservations: April-October, 502-758-2243.)

Nature trails—There are some 70 miles of above-ground trails at Mammoth Cave National Park, ranging from short walks to dayhikes and backpacking trails. Ask at the visitor center desk for maps and information. Ranger-led nature walks on the Green River Bluffs Trail are offered every afternoon in the summer. The Joppa Ridge Motor Nature Trail can be viewed from your car, and wayside exhibits are located throughout the park along roads and trails.

Camping—The park has four campgrounds: a 110-site Headquarters Campground located a quarter-mile from the visitor center; two small, free camping areas next to ferry crossings on the Green River, and a remote group campground for which reservations are required (502-758-2251). All campgrounds have picnic tables and fire grates, and restrooms or chemical toilets. Except for the group campground, campsites are available on a first-come, first-served basis. A camp store, laundry facilities and a service station are adjacent to the Headquarters Campground. During the summer, rangers conduct nightly campfire programs.

THINGS TO DO NEARBY

Want to see a herd of buffalo? **Kentucky Buffalo Park** at the Horse Cave interchange of I-65 is a working farm where travelers may observe the animals free of charge. **Mammoth Onyx Cave** (one-hour tour) is just across the road (502-786-2634).

Guntown Mountain in Cave City is a re-created Wild West town accessible via a chair lift that takes you up 1,360 feet. Here you'll find gunfights and stunt shows, a haunted house and various amusement park rides. Open daily from Memorial Day to Labor Day; weekends only from Easter to Memorial Day and Labor Day to October (502-773-3530).

At **Kentucky Action Park** near the I-65 Cave City interchange, you can take a chair lift up a mountain and then slide down a quarter-mile on an alpine sled (don't worry, it has brakes). The park also features go-karts, bumper boats and a water slide. Open daily from Memorial Day to Labor Day; weekends only from Easter to Memorial Day and Labor Day to October (502-773-2636).

The only **Corvette assembly plant** in the world is found in Bowling Green off I-65 at exit 78 just north of town. Free tours are offered Monday-Friday at 9 a.m. and 1 p.m. (502-745-8419).

WHERE TO STAY

On park property, there's a concessionaire-operated hotel and motor lodge, both open year-round, and two sets of cottages, open seasonally. All are serviceable and reasonably priced. The Woodland Cottages offer the most rustic accommodations—no TV or air-conditioning. Tennis and shuffleboard courts are adjacent to the hotel. For rates and reservations, contact: National Park Concessions, Inc., Mammoth Cave Hotel, Mammoth Cave, KY 42259-0027 (502-758-2225).

If you're interested in more amenities, there are two nice resorts in the area—both quite affordable. The closest is Best Western Park Mammoth Resort in Park City (502-749-4101). A two-story facility with 101 rooms, it offers 18-hole and mini golf, lighted tennis, shuffleboard, an indoor-outdoor pool and a playground. Special on-property features are a miniature train ride, horseback riding and tours of a cave which was the reputed hideout of outlaw Jesse James. Kids under 18 stay free.

Further away, but still an easy drive, is Barren River Lake State Resort Park, one of the excellent Kentucky state parks. Don't let the name fool you, for the setting is anything but barren; the resort sits on a beautiful lake surrounded by wooded hills. A 51-room lodge and 12 cottages are open year-round. At the marina, you can rent fishing boats, houseboats and pontoons. Recreational facilities include a nine-hole golf course, a game room and playground, and tennis, volleyball and handball courts. If that's not enough to keep you busy, a recreation program is offered, along with horseback riding and bike rentals. Contact: Barren River Lake State Resort Park, Route 1, Box 191, Lucas, KY 42156-9709 (800-325-0057; lodge: 502-646-2151, marina: 502-646-2357).

Bowling Green, a 30-minute drive from Mammoth Cave, offers a variety of motels and restaurants. Good bets include the Holiday Inn or the Best Western Motor Inn, both at exit 22 off I-65, or the Ramada Inn on Scottsville Rd. For additional information, contact: Bowling Green-Warren County Chamber of Commerce, 812 State St. (PO Box 51), Bowling Green, KY 42101 (502-781-3200).

WHERE TO EAT

A restaurant (open all year) and a snack bar (open seasonally) are located in the park across a footbridge from the visitor center.

A good place to eat in Park City is the Park Mammoth restaurant at Best Western Park Mammoth Resort. The setting is pretty and child's plates are offered. The dinner specialty is prime rib.

In Bowling Green, you'll find the usual chain offerings that populate most sizable interstate exits. Popular local places include Andrew's (2019 Scottsville Rd., 502-781-7680) and Briarpatch (956 Fairview, 502-781-2045), both of the steak-seafood-salad bar genre.

WHEN TO GO

The cave is open every day of the year except Christmas and can be enjoyed in winter or summer since the temperature below the surface is always 54 degrees. However, some of the tours—including the special kids-only one—are seasonal (June through Labor Day).

FOR MORE INFORMATION

Contact:

Mammoth Cave National Park
Mammoth Cave, KY 42259
(502-758-2328)

EVERGLADES NATIONAL PARK

Everglades National Park, on the southwestern tip of Florida, is the second largest national park (after Yellowstone) in the continental U.S. The park attracts about a million visitors a year, who come to see its ecological wonders. Nowhere else on the planet will you find the combination of animals and vegetation that lives in the Everglades.

ABOUT THE PARK

Although Congress voted to establish an Everglades National Park in 1934, it was another dozen years before enough money was raised to purchase private lands in the area. The park was actually dedicated in 1947.

The 1.4-million-acre park encompasses just a portion of the area known as the Everglades—a vast subtropical wilderness which runs from Lake Okeechobee to Florida Bay. The Indian name for the Everglades is pa-hay-okee, or "grassy waters." It's an appropriate description, because during the wet season, the area is fed by a slow-flowing river inches deep and miles wide. Unfortunately, as south Florida is built up, water is being increasingly diverted to land developments and agribusinesses. As a result, the Everglades is shrinking and its unique mix of animal and plant life is being threatened.

The park is home to more than 300 species of birds and such endangered creatures as the North American crocodile and the Florida panther. So rare are the park's biological resources that it is one of a handful of areas in the world designated as both a World Heritage Site and an International Biosphere Reserve.

The main visitor center is at the entrance to the park near Homestead. Here you can get oriented by viewing a short film and checking the schedule of ranger-led hikes and concessionaire-operated boat tours. The main park road takes you past the Royal Palm Visitor Center, just beyond the entrance, to the Flamingo Visitor Center, about 40 miles away on Florida Bay. Along the way are short, self-guided trails and roadside exhibits. You can see more of the Everglades by taking a tram tour at Flamingo or at Shark Valley, on the northern border of the park on a portion of the Tamiami Trail. You'll find commercial airboat rides offered along this strip, but they are not allowed within park boundaries since they disturb wildlife and tear up vegetation.

Excursion boat tours originate at Flamingo and are also offered at the Gulf Coast Ranger Station near Everglades City at the northwest corner of the park.

THINGS TO DO IN THE PARK

Nature walks and talks—While you can walk trails on your own, you're more likely to spot wildlife if you've got a ranger along to guide you—plus you'll learn all kinds of interesting facts about the plants and animals that you see. Check at visitor centers for schedules. If your kids want to look at alligators, a good spot is the half-mile Anhinga Trail (an elevated boardwalk) near the Royal Palm Visitor Center.

Boat tours—You can sign up for pontoon boat tours in the marina ticket office near the Flamingo Visitor Center. Choices include a 90-minute cruise on Florida Bay or a two-hour backcountry tour. On the bay cruise you'll get an up-close look at bird nesting areas; on the backcountry tour, keep an eye out for crocodiles sunning themselves on the banks of the waterway. Phone ahead for the day's schedule and make reservations (305-253-2241 or 813-695-3101).

Boat tours from the Gulf Coast Ranger Station near Everglades City take you through the Ten Thousand Islands region of the park. Along the way, bottle-nosed dolphins and manatees may pop up alongside your boat. Phone for schedule (813-695-2591 or, in Florida, 800-445-7724).

Tram tours—Two-hour, narrated tram tours are offered at both Flamingo and Shark Valley. The latter takes you to an observation tower from which you can view the "river of grass" that seems to go on forever. Sometimes on the way back passengers are given the choice of walking the last half-mile along a stretch of road used as a nature trail. Those who do are likely to see alligators. Call for schedule and reservations (305-221-8455). For Flamingo tram tours, use the same phone number as for boat tours.

Camping—Campgrounds are located at Flamingo and at Long Pine Key (six miles from the park entrance). Tent and RV sites are available on a first-come, first-served basis, so you need to arrive early to get a good spot. There's no electricity, but Flamingo offers cold showers.

THINGS TO DO NEARBY

Near the Shark Valley entrance on the park's northern border, the Miccosukee tribe operates an **Indian village** as a tourist attraction. You can see an alligator-wrestling demonstration and watch Indian women make baskets and do beadwork. From here you can also take a 30-minute airboat ride to another Indian camp on an island in the Everglades (outside park boundaries). The village is open daily from 9 a.m. to 5 p.m. (305-223-8388).

If you stay in or drive through Homestead, it's worth stopping at an unusual fruit stand called **Robert Is Here.** Robert grows and sells exotic tropical fruits like Monstera deliciosa, which looks like a giant green ear of corn and tastes like banana and pineapple. Try one of his fruit shakes or homemade key lime pies. Open daily 8 a.m.-7 p.m. (19200 SW 344th St., 305-246-1592).

From Homestead, **Biscayne National Park** is practically next door; see the entry in this chapter for details. Miami is about an hour away by car; read about things to do there in the CITIES section.

WHERE TO STAY

You can stay in the park at Flamingo, where the choice of rustic, concessionaire-operated accommodations includes a lodge (with some suites) and kitchenette cottages. Kids 12 and under stay free. For reservations, contact: Flamingo Lodge, PO Box 428, Flamingo, FL 33030 (305-253-2241 or 813-695-3101).

Homestead is a gateway to both Everglades and Key Biscayne national parks. On Homestead Boulevard, the main drag, there's a Days Inn (with a playground) and a Holiday Inn, each with 100 or more rooms. A good-sized Knights Inn opened in 1987 in nearby Florida City. Toll-free numbers for these chains are listed in the appendix and all three offer kids-stay-free programs. For information on the smaller motels in the area, contact the Homestead/Florida City Chamber of Commerce, 160 US Hwy. 1, Florida City, FL 33034 (305-247-2332).

If you prefer a more upscale, resort-type atmosphere, try one of the Florida keys (see the entry for Biscayne National Park) or Marco Island, the northernmost and largest of the Ten Thousand Islands off the western shore of the park. You'll find deluxe accommodations and excellent restaurants on Marco Island, including a Radisson resort—an all-suite beachfront hotel with a supervised activity program for kids ages 3-12 (600 S. Collier Blvd., 813-394-4100). For more information, contact: Marco Island Area Chamber of Commerce, PO Box 913, Marco Island, FL 33937 (813-394-7549).

WHERE TO EAT

There's a restaurant in the park on the second floor of the Flamingo Visitor Center with picture windows overlooking Florida Bay. The seafood is fresh, the conch chowder tasty and they'll even cook fish you catch, if you have it cleaned at the marina. Closed early May to mid-October. Reservations are required for dinner (305-253-2241 or 813-695-3101).

In the Florida City-Homestead area, recommended eateries include Richard Accursio's Capri Restaurant (great Caesar salad, pizza and local specialties), Captain Bob's and the Seafood Feast House (seafood), El Toro Taco (Mexican) and Potlikker's (Southern country-style cooking). All are informal and reasonably priced.

If you travel the Tamiami Trail along the northern border of the park, try the Miccosukee restaurant near the Shark Valley entrance for a taste of American Indian cuisine—including variations on tacos and burgers.

WHEN TO GO

The park is open daily year-round, but we don't recommend a visit between mid-April and mid-December: too many mosquitos. During the rest of the year you'll still need insect repellent.

FOR MORE INFORMATION

Contact:

Everglades National Park
PO Box 279, Homestead, FL 33030
(305-247-6211)

BISCAYNE NATIONAL PARK

Of the 181,000 acres that comprise this unique park along Florida's southeast coast, only about four percent is land—a narrow mangrove shoreline and about 45 small barrier islands. The rest of the park is underwater. You can view what's below on a glass-bottom boat cruise or by snorkeling in the shallow waters.

ABOUT THE PARK

Biscayne is a relatively new national park—established in 1980. A dozen years before that, much of the area had been designated a national monument in order to save it from developers who were making plans to build resorts and subdivisions on Florida's northern keys, the string of islands that protects Biscayne Bay. A bulldozed tract on Elliott Key is a silent reminder of the narrowness of the escape.

But conservationists prevailed, and the rich breeding ground beneath the tranquil surface of the bay was preserved. In these clear waters you can see coral reefs—part of the only living ones in the continental U.S.—plus hundreds of varieties of brightly hued tropical fish.

NOTE

The living animals that form and build coral reefs are polyps that feed on plankton. They have a life span of centuries, but grow very slowly. Before marine sanctuaries were established and federal and state laws passed, commercial collectors dynamited reefs for coral and even removed it with crowbars. Today, all species of coral are protected all along the Keys' reef tract.

THINGS TO DO IN THE PARK

Reef cruises—Reef cruises aboard 53-foot glass-bottom boats are run by a concessionaire and leave from Convoy Point, where park headquarters is located. Some of the cruises stop at Adams Key, seven miles from shore, where rangers point out the remains of sunken ships. For information and reservations, contact: Biscayne Aqua-Center, Box 1270, Homestead, FL 33030 (305-247-2400).

Snorkeling—Anyone who can swim at all can enjoy snorkeling in the warm, shallow waters of the park. Since everyone wears flotation devices, it's easy to paddle around on the surface—even young children do it. You can sign up for a snorkeling cruise (and rent equipment) at Convoy Point. Scuba diving is an option for the more adventurous.

Canoe trips—Park rangers lead canoe trips into the mangrove tidal creeks along the shore. The mangroves attract birds, including—on rare occasions—the peregrine falcon and bald eagle, two of the 13 endangered animal species that are monitored by park naturalists. At the trees' half-submerged roots you'll see barnacles, fish and other sea creatures. If you're lucky, you might even spot a manatee, or "sea cow," in these waterways.

Camping—The park has two primitive campgrounds—on Elliott Key and Boca Chita Key—which you can only get to by boat. They're open all year on a first-come, first-served basis and there is no fee. Elliott Key has restrooms, cold showers and a group campground, for which reservations are required. The visitor center there displays coral, sponges and sea-turtle shells on a "touching table."

THINGS TO DO NEARBY

John Pennekamp Coral Reef State Park, the first underseas park in the continental U.S., lies directly south. Here you'll find more glass-bottom boat cruises and snorkeling. There are two small beaches on park grounds and in the shallow waters of one of them the state has reconstructed a galleon wreck. There's a campground on the shore.

Everglades National Park is 30 minutes west. See the listing in this chapter for details.

To the north, about an hour away, is **Miami.** Read about things to do there in the CITIES section.

WHERE TO STAY

Since there are no lodgings in the park, the closest you can get—unless you're planning to camp on Elliott Key—is Homestead or Florida City, about 15 miles from the park entrance. Either place also makes a good starting point for a trip to Everglades National Park (see that entry for more details).

If you want a wider selection of accommodations, you can stay in Miami and make a visit to the park a day trip (see the CITIES section). Another possibility is to stay on one of the nearby keys—Biscayne to the north, Largo to the south. Two deluxe resorts on Key Biscayne are the Sheraton Royal Biscayne Beach Resort and Racquet Club (555 Ocean Dr., 305-361-5775) and the Sonesta Beach (350 Ocean Dr., 305-361-2021 or 800-343-7170). The Sheraton offers some suites and kitchen units, and kids under 18 stay free. At the Sonesta Beach, kids under 12 stay free and there's a free supervised activity program called "Just Us Kids."

On Key Largo, the Sheraton-Key Largo Resort offers free kids' activities (May-September) and kids under 17 stay free (97000 Overseas Hwy., 305-852-5553 or 800-826-1006).

WHERE TO EAT

See the Everglades National Park section for recommendations of places to eat in the Florida City-Homestead area. If you get to Key Biscayne, don't miss Two Dragons at the Sonesta Beach Hotel. This is really two restaurants in one—Chinese and Japanese. On the Chinese side, you can sit in an intimate booth behind a curtain of hanging beads or at an open table overlooking an outdoor Oriental garden. On the Japanese side, food is prepared at a cooking table. Whichever you choose, you'll undoubtedly be pleased.

WHEN TO GO

The park is open year-round, but the time to visit is from mid-December to mid-April, which is the dry season in subtropical Florida. Hotel and motel rates are highest then, but you won't be bothered by the mosquitoes and fast-moving thunderstorms that plague the area in the summer.

FOR MORE INFORMATION

Contact:

Biscayne National Park
PO Box 1369, Homestead, FL 33090
(305-247-7275)

RESORTS

♠ AMELIA ISLAND PLANTATION

♠ CALLAWAY GARDENS

♠ GROVE PARK INN

♠ KIAWAH ISLAND INN AND VILLAS

♠ MARRIOTT BAY POINT RESORT

♠ SADDLEBROOK

♠ SOUTH SEAS PLANTATION

RESORTS

With the pace of modern life grinding away at us, and TV and print ads constantly reminding us that we deserve time off in sumptuous surroundings, who wouldn't want to escape for a week to a luxury resort?

But you're going to pay dearly for that luxury. As we go to press, the per-night cost of a hotel room at one of the inns in this chapter ranges from $80 to $160 (double occupancy), and the range for a two-bedroom villa or condominium is much greater: $110 to $445, depending on location, what you can see out your window and the time of year.

Resort packages can reduce these costs significantly, in some cases providing free rounds of golf, free tennis time and no-charge meals for kids. But those packages rarely include air fare, and even if you drive you're looking at a $1,000 mimimum for a week's vacation for a family of four. And it could easily be twice that, depending on how expensive your tastes are. That's why you can't afford to make a mistake and choose a resort that you and your family won't like.

To help you avoid guesswork, we visited seven top-flight resorts in the Southeast. To cover a range of preferences, we picked two on the Gulf (Marriott Bay Point and South Seas Plantation), two on the Atlantic (Amelia Island and Kiawah Island), a mountain hideaway (Callaway Gardens), a grand old hotel (Grove Park Inn) and a modern golf/tennis center (Saddlebrook).

In the process, we paid return visits to some of the most vibrant cities in the Southeast—Asheville, Charleston, Jacksonville and Tampa—and we interviewed some of the most dedicated and innovative children's recreation directors in the country.

When you're considering where to go on vacation, try to decide ahead of time whether you want to enroll your kids in a resort recreational program. (And take it from our daughter, who was 11 when she started in kids' rec activities, "They can really be fun!") To help you decide, note the appropriate sections where we discuss the nature of these programs and what months of the year, days of the week and hours of the day they're operational. Expect to pay anywhere from $15 to $30 per child for a single day and roughly $90 for a full week.

If this sounds high, consider what it costs to send a child to a good camp these days, and realize that a resort rec program is a comparable experience—perhaps even a bit nicer than the average day camp back home.

Kids under the age of 6 aren't eligible for some resort rec programs. So if you want some free time for golf or shopping or other adult activities, you'll need to arrange for a baby-sitter—which is much more expensive for you and not nearly as much fun for your child. That's another reason to choose your resort rec program carefully.

TRAVEL TIP

When you're considering where to go on vacation, try to decide ahead of time whether you want to enroll your kids in a resort recreational program.

Oddly enough, teenagers—though often reluctant to join a rec group function—may have it best. Every teen activity we heard about sounded terrific, and at Kiawah Island the four-hour-a-day teen program is free.

Once your kids are enrolled in a rec program, make sure they show up for the day's activities with all the necessary clothing and paraphernalia (bathing suit, towel, visor, sneakers, flip-flops, etc.). And assume nothing. South Seas' brochure assured us that rec staffers would have suntan lotion, but when we dropped off our daughter, they didn't; our supply was back in the room, so we had to walk to the general store and buy a bottle.

Most resorts offer a variety of activities for families, and we've noted them in the "Sports" and "Family Fun" sections of this chapter. And be sure to read "Shopping/Nearby Fun" so you don't miss out on special off-property attractions.

With the exception of the Grove Park Inn, every resort in this chapter has villa/condominium accommodations which include fully equipped kitchens. And if you plan to prepare some of your own meals, it's wise to do your grocery shopping before you get to the resort. Actually, we were surprised that the prices weren't even higher at the on-site food marts and general stores, but the selection is limited and why pay more for peanut butter and apple juice when you're already spending a bundle?

If your kids are as addicted to frozen dinners and quick snacks as ours are, be sure to request a villa that has a microwave. (They're even more handy when you're on vacation and don't want to make dinner from scratch.)

Keep in mind that most of today's top resorts operate on a no-cash basis; you show your resort passport/ID and sign for everything, then pay one lump sum when you leave. This is convenient, but it also makes it easy to say yes to extra activities and expenses.

AMELIA ISLAND PLANTATION

Amelia Island Plantation is located 29 miles northeast of the Jacksonville, Fla. airport, just south of the Georgia-Florida border (take I-95 to the Fernandina Beach/Callahan exit, turn east on U.S. A1A and follow the signs). The 1,250-acre resort has been honored for nearly every phase of its operation: golf, tennis, beach, youth recreation, landscape architecture, environmental consciousness—even its pastry.

ABOUT THE RESORT

Amelia Island is the northernmost of Florida's barrier islands, and the southernmost of the "Golden Isles" chain which begins off the North Carolina coast. Nestled between the Intercoastal Waterway and the Atlantic, this 13.5-mile sliver of sand, marshland and forest was once a haven for the vilest pirates ever to sail the Seven Seas; Blackbeard, the Lafittes and Captain Kidd are among those rumored to have left buried treasure here.

The island was settled by the Spanish in 1566, and it is the only U.S. location to have had eight different flags flown over her shores. The island was named by the governor of Georgia, James Oglethorpe, who toured it in 1735, thinking it might be a good site for an English fort to be used against Spanish St. Augustine. "Amelia" was Princess Amelia, daughter of King George II of England.

Amelia Island Plantation opened on July 4, 1974. The property was once fated for strip mining when it was owned by Union Carbide. Fortunately, that didn't happen, and the resort has done a superb job of blending man-made beauty with nature's own. Roadways tunnel through thickets of palmetto, pine and towering live oaks strewn with moss. Portions of the Amelia Links and Long Point golf courses hug the beach, yet they're scarcely visible to sunbathers because of the 60-foot sand dunes. The 13 miles of public beach are gorgeous, but until an ordinance is passed prohibiting jeeps, 4-by-4's and other vehicles from cruising the beach, the island's relationship with nature won't be perfect. On the other hand, you'll never confuse Amelia's beach traffic with Daytona's.

ACCOMMODATIONS

Amelia handles high occupancy as gracefully as any resort we've visited. The resort has roughly 550 rental units—nearly as many as South Seas Plantation, which is reviewed later in this chapter. But Amelia is nearly four times the size of South Seas, which accounts for the tranquility of this beautiful resort. Those 550 units are divided into 170 beachside hotel rooms (some at the Amelia Inn and some at courtside) and 380 villas located along the beach, golf courses, marshlands and secluded forests.

The most expensive lodging is found at the Dunes Club and Windsong villas; a mimimum three-night's stay is required at Windsong, where tennis star Chris Evert used to own a villa. If there's another family (or even two) you like to vacation with, you could share a four-bedroom villa here and find it surprisingly affordable.

The least expensive are Fairway Oaks and the Lagoon and Club villas. For the best combination of price and location, you might consider staying where we did—at the Beachwood villas, which are within easy walking distance of the kids' rec headquarters (Beach Club) and equidistant from two important areas: the reception center, where you can eat, shop and rent bikes; and Racquet Park, where you can eat, play tennis and use the fitness center. These owner-maintained units have some years on them (our patio furniture was terribly rusted), but they're spacious and well-equipped, including a laundry room.

SPORTS

Golf, Golf Digest and *Golfweek* have all sung the praises of the plantation's golf courses. The original 27-hole Amelia Links course (each nine has a name: Oysterbay, Oakmarsh, Oceanside) was designed by Pete Dye. What the three nines lack in distance, they more than make up for in difficulty; players have to contend with overhanging trees, narrow fairways and small greens perched along the sand marsh or tucked behind sand dunes. The Long Point Club opened in 1987, and architect Tom Fazio routed his 18-hole layout through marshes, woods and sand dunes. The course also features elevated fairways and large bodies of water.

Both *Tennis* and *World Tennis* have raved about Amelia's tennis facilities. The resort features 25 courts, most of which are scattered among the oaks at Racquet Park. Three courts are lighted for night play, and the predominant surface is Har-Tru, a granular, composition surface which is easy on the legs. Which is more than we can say for the gnats.

We played a lot of tennis at Amelia during spring break, and we were bothered by small swarms of "no-see-ums"—as locals call them. They were a real nuisance, and they bite, too! Local remedy: Coat yourself with Skin So Soft hand and body lotion; no-see-ums hate the stuff.

Racquet Park is also the site of Amelia's health and fitness center, which features Universal, Keiser and Hydra exercise equipment, aerobic programs, steamrooms, sauna, whirlpool, indoor-outdoor lap pool and racquetball courts.

Amelia has lots of swimming pools, and the ocean surf is so strong that several members of the resort's rec staff spend their off-hours ridin' waves.

Actor David Hartman is among those who bring their kids to Amelia

Island to fish. On one trip, the Hartman family landed 20 bass in one day. The next day, Hartman's 9-year-old daughter caught a 9 1/2-pound large-mouth bass. Most of Amelia's freshwater lagoons are strictly catch-and-release fishing areas, and live bait isn't allowed because fish can die if they swallow live-bait hooks. If you want to take your catch home and eat it,

the saltwater fishing is good at Walker's Creek (red fish, sea trout, black drum, flounder, whiting) or you just stand in the surf at the south end of the island and catch lunch or dinner. To rent tackle or charter a boat, check with the Amelia Angler (at the Beach Club).

FAMILY FUN

Bicycles, paddleboats and Island Hoppers (four-passenger golf carts) are a great way to see the island. Rent them at Wheels 'N' Keels directly behind the reception center.

Every spring, Amelia hosts the Bausch & Lomb championships, a regular stop on the women's pro tennis tour. For ticket information, call the resort (see "For More Information").

Sea Horse Stables, located two miles south of the plantation, offers horseback riding on the beach. Dial ext. 75244 and the resort will shuttle you there, but the stable does not accept the Amelia charge card. Reservations are required (904-261-4878).

> **NOTE**
>
> One note of warning for ocean users: Keep an eye out for jellyfish, which can be a problem—particularly in the month of August. Something else to keep an eye out for, although they're not a problem, are the pelicans which come zooming in over the waves—six or seven of them strung out in single file. The brown ones will plunge-dive from 20 to 50 feet in the air to nab a fish; white ones merely submerge their heads and scoop up fish in their wide, flat bills.

Two sightseeing areas appeal to families: **Fort Clinch,** which was built by the U.S. in 1847 when Florida was still a territory, and the island's century-old **Indian mounds.** Fort Clinch is now a state park, and it's located on the northern tip of the island; take your car and head north on A1A. The Indian mounds are located at Walker's Landing within the plantation; you can reach them via bikes/Island Hopper.

The Amelia Island Museum of History features artifacts from two Spanish mission sites unearthed in the 1980s (233 S. 3rd St., in Fernandina Beach, 803-261-7378).

KIDS' PROGRAMS

Amelia used to have off-property day care, but the current on-site program—one of the best we've seen—has been in place since 1982. It operates from mid-March to late April, Memorial Day to Labor Day, plus Thanksgiving weekend. There are usually no more than 25-30 kids enrolled (70 during peak periods) and the resort claims that the ratio of day campers to counselors is never more than 6:1.

The programs are divided into three main age groups:
▲ **Children (Ages 3-5)**
   Activities include beach, fishing, crabbing and crafts (Monday-Saturday/8:30 a.m.-1 p.m.).
▲ **Youth (Ages 6-8)**
   Activities are the same as for 3-5-year-olds, plus field trips. Parents can choose half- or full-day programs. (Monday-Friday/8:30-4, Saturday/8:30-1).
▲ **Pre-teens (Ages 9-12)**
   Activities include tubing in the ocean, arts and crafts, tennis and golf lessons, plus day trips to places like the Jacksonville zoo. (Monday-Friday/ 8:30-4, Saturday/8:30-1).

The rec program also caters to teens (volleyball, DJ parties, bonfires, videogame tournaments) and the 18-and-over crowd (casino night, shopping trips, dinner theater, dog races in nearby Jacksonville).

The rec center is well-equipped for indoor fun with lots of board games, and your kids can take part in talent shows, make their own ice cream or decorate balloons. Hikes to Drummond Park are great because there's a tree house there, plus a basketball court and a playscape.

What we liked best about Amelia's rec program was the people. From the director to the counselors, they seem to like their work—and the kids in their care—as much or more than any rec team we've come across.

WHERE TO EAT

At the resort

Overlooking center court at Racquet Park, The Verandah is your best bet for a family sit-down dinner. The night we ate there (following a six-hour drive), it was crowded, noisy and a bit slow in the service department. But the seafood was fresh, and kids get crayons to color their menus while they wait for their food.

Another idea—if your kids are older and a bit adventuresome —is the cook-your-own "Hot Rocks" dinner at the Beach Club Restaurant (seasonal). A superheated (550 degrees) block of granite is brought to your table, along with a selection of meats, poultry, seafood and vegetables. You cook the food to your tastes, then top it off with a selection of sauces: teriyaki, sweet-and-sour, herb, barbecue or cajun.

The Dune Side Club (Amelia Inn) should be reserved for an adults-only dinner. The decor is plush, the menu is extravagant and a solo pianist adds to the romantic mood. Jackets are required. They also serve a whale of a Sunday brunch here.

As you might expect, there are lots of places around the island where you can get breakfast and lunch, including the Coop, a lagoon-side eatery behind the reception center which serves up terrific sandwiches; we recommend the grilled calypso chicken, which you can eat indoors or out on the deck. We also recommend the Beach Club Lounge, where the seafood salad, shrimp salad on croissant and key lime pie are all first-rate.

And remember this special deal: For each adult guest who orders an entrée from the regular menu at one of the resort's restaurants, one child eats free from the kids' menu.

Off property

Fernandina Beach, a 15-minute drive from the resort (but still on the island), has a quaint, 50-block downtown area which is listed on the National Register of Historic Places. It also has a wharf-side restaurant, Brett's Waterway Cafe, which is located on the site of the old welcome center. The food was just okay the night we were there, but there was lots of it—and it's a great spot to watch shrimp boats and sunsets. Afterward, you'll want to stroll up Centre Street, where the Bradford pear trees sparkle with miniature white lights year-round. The kids will be intrigued by Faith Wick's World of Little People, which features Wizard of Oz characters in music boxes. The 19th century hardware store is now Fantastic Fudge, and Ship's Lantern, a sea-faring shop, features brightly colored fish and turtles in a mini sidewalk pond. If you've left the kids back at the resort and the night is still young, check out the old Palace Saloon (opened in 1903) where the live music is loud and the beer is cold.

SHOPPING/NEARBY FUN

Amelia shopping is limited to t-shirts/souvenir hunting at the general store, sportswear purchases at the tennis/golf pro shops and clothes hunting at the health and fitness center. If you're serious about shopping, try downtown **Fernandina Beach** or make the drive into Jacksonville and stop at **Jacksonville Landing,** a shopping and entertainment complex that's all under one roof (904-353-1188).

Jacksonville is located on the St. Johns River, which is one of the few rivers that flow from south to north. The biggest event of the year in this city is the annual Georgia-Florida college football clash in early November, but tickets are hard to come by unless you know someone from the competing schools.

Other seasonal activities include the **Riverwalk Arts & Crafts Festival** (Mother's Day weekend, 904-396-4900); the **Jacksonville Jazz Festival** (October, 904-353-7770); the **Jacksonville Agricultural Fair** (October, 904-353-0535); and the Gator Bowl college football game (New Year's holidays, 904-396-1800).

The Jacksonville Zoo covers 61 acres and features more than 700 animals from all over the world (8605 Zoo Rd., 904-757-4466).

For more information, contact: Jacksonville Convention & Visitors Bureau (3 Independent Dr., Jacksonville, FL 32202, 904-353-9736).

WHEN TO GO

Amelia's high season runs from early March to early May. Rates are slightly cheaper the rest of the year.

An important factor to weigh is the north Florida weather, which is slightly cooler than Orlando's, for example. Amelia's mid-day highs average 65, 68 and 67 degrees in January, February and December, compared to 70, 72 and 72 in Orlando during those same months. Mid-day highs reach 73 and 74 during March and November; it's 80s and 90s the rest of the year. The Atlantic is almost too chilly to swim in from January through March (57, 59, 62) and again in December (60); from April through November, it's 72-80.

If you visit Amelia on the Fourth of July—the resort's anniversary, as well as our country's—you'll be treated to air shows, fireworks and all sorts of holiday fun. Christmas is also a festive time of year: The resort puts up a huge tent which resembles a winter wonderland inside.

FOR MORE INFORMATION

Contact:

Amelia Island Plantation
Amelia Island, FL 32034
(904-261-6161 or 800-874-6878)

CALLAWAY GARDENS

Callaway Gardens is located in the foothills of the Appalachian Mountains 70 miles southwest of Atlanta on U.S. 27 in Pine Mountain, Ga. The 2,500-acre resort features woodlands, lakes and gardens, and offers practically every kind of vacation experience imaginable. Elevation: 1,000 feet.

ABOUT THE RESORT

Callaway Gardens was conceived by textile industrialist Cason J. Callaway, who happened on the southwest Georgia area known as Blue Spring while on a summer outing in 1930. His wife, Virginia, was a lover of wildflowers, so when Callaway returned home that day he brought her a sprig of reddish-orange blossoms from one of the shrubs that dotted the hillside. The shrub turned out to be a Prunifolia azalea, a rare species which is only found naturally within a 100-mile radius of that area. Callaway felt a responsibiity to preserve this beautiful species, which is commonly known as the "plumleaf azalea," so he purchased the land, and thus Callaway Gardens was born.

Callaway originally planned to create a private retreat, complete with lakeside homes, fishing and golf. But after work began in 1940 he changed his mind. "Every child ought to see something beautiful before he is six years old," said Callaway, explaining why he chose to open his sanctuary to the public.

Callaway Gardens isn't merely a public resort; it's an educational, horticultural and charitable organization, and as such, it's not set up to benefit any individual. The resort is owned and operated by the non-profit Ida Cason Callaway Foundation, named for its founder's mother. After-tax profits go to the foundation to support and maintain the gardens and the 11,500 acres of undisturbed wilderness which surround it.

To say that the resort provides every kind of vacation experience imaginable is not an overstatement. Most golf resorts don't have nearly as many holes as Callaway does (63) and most tennis resorts don't have 16 lighted courts, as Callaway does. And there's so much more: a 65-acre lake, man-made beach, water skiing shows, swimming pools, sailing, fishing, racquetball, hunting and skeet shooting, nature activities, kids' playgrounds, miniature golf, outdoor music and theater, circus performances, a five-acre horticultural center. There's even a butterfly conservatory.

But beyond its multitude of offerings, Callaway succeeds because of its warm-hearted approach to families on vacation. We've visited many times, and we always come away with the feeling that Callaway is a first-rate country club with no entrance requirements; anyone and everyone can come and enjoy it, which is the way Mr. Callaway intended it.

ACCOMMODATIONS

Callaway Gardens has three types of lodging, but no matter where you stay you're going to be surrounded by lush, green Southern forest.

The Inn at Callaway Gardens has 350 rooms, junior suites and one- and two-bedroom roof garden suites in a traditional motel-like setting.

Mountain Creek villas are available in one- to four-bedroom configurations. The exact number of villas available for rent varies because most are privately owned, and they're bought and sold on a regular basis. But each unit has a living room/dining room area, fully equipped kitchen, separate baths for each bedroom, fireplace, plus screened porches, patios or sundecks.

Our favorite place to stay at Callaway is the Country Cottages area at the north end of the resort. There are 155 cottages and they're spacious and modern, with complete kitchens, roomy bedrooms with private baths, fireplaces and screened porches where you can play cards, party or talk when the kids are in bed. The swimming pool complex can be a bit of a hike, depending on which group of cottages you're staying in, but it's an attractive, indoor-outdoor facility.

From early June to late August, the Country Cottages are available only to people on the Family Summer Recreation Program, an eight-day, seven-night plan which puts you in a two-bedroom cottage for considerably less than you'd pay for seven nights at the regular daily rate. You can then purchase a family pass, which is good for seven recreational activities. Your choices include: a round of golf, use of a golf cart, an hour and a half of tennis/racquetball for up to four people, a day of fishing (three persons maximum), two hours of sailing and five rounds of skeet/trap shooting. Considering that the cost of the family pass isn't too much more than a round of golf, it's a good deal.

SPORTS

Callaway Gardens has three 18-hole golf courses of varying difficulty. Mountain View is by far the toughest (four water holes, 24 fairway bunkers, 41 sand traps guarding the greens). Lake View is short (6,006 yards from the regular tees) but tricky; a friend of ours put seven balls in the water from the island tee at No. 5. He should've played the Gardens View course, which has such wide fairways it's almost impossible to lose a ball. The best place for a family golf outing is Callaway's nine-hole Sky View course, which measures only 2,096 yards from the back tees. No matter which course you play, be sure to call ahead to reserve a tee time (800-282-8181).

Callaway's tennis center was named a five-star tennis resort by *Tennis* magazine. Located in a beautiful, wooded section of the resort, the complex includes 10 courts (8 clay, 2 hard). Racquetball is always in season at a pair of indoor courts, located behind the tennis center, which are climate-controlled for year-round comfort.

If you're looking for crystal-clear water to swim in, man-made Robin Lake isn't it. The water's dark, the bottom's a bit mucky and the roped-off swimming area is rather small. But the mile-long white sand beach is fine, and waterskiing thrill shows are presented on weekday evenings and weekend afternoons throughout the summer. There are pools at the Inn, the Mountain Creek Villas and the Country Cottages.

Fishing boats and sailboats are available for rent at the boathouse on Mountain Creek Lake, adjacent to the Gardens/Veranda restaurants. The hunting preserve and the steeplechase track are located off property, but within easy driving distance.

Callaway has a fitness center, located at The Inn, which features nautilus-type equipment and free weights. There's also a sauna and men's and women's dressing rooms.

FAMILY FUN

Florida State University's Flying High Circus has made Callaway Gardens its summer headquarters since 1961, and when you and your kids take your seats under the Big Top tent next to Robin Lake you'll see tricks that are more difficult than those performed at some professional circuses: for example, triple somersaults on the flying trapeze and seven-man pyramids on the high wire. The circus is dark one day a week (Wednesday, as a rule), so make sure to check ahead of time before you plan to attend. Admission is free to those staying at Callaway, and there are afternoon and evening performances.

In similar fashion, the **LaGrange College drama department** has made Callaway its summer home since 1966. The company usually numbers about 20, and there's usually something specifically geared to kids in its family-oriented summer repertoire. Plays are presented at the Old Soap Opera House in the Country Cottage area.

Callaway Gardens' **Day Butterfly Center** is a 7,000-square-foot conservatory filled with 800 to 1,000 tropical butterflies and more than 50 species of tropical plants. In general, this is a delightful experience, but be forewarned that when you walk into the conservatory lots of beautiful, winged lepidoptera may flutter about your face. Our daughter was put off by this at first, but soon readjusted and when it came time, could barely be persuaded to leave (open 10 a.m.-4 p.m., Monday-Friday).

When was the last time you just went walking with your kids? Callaway Gardens has miles and miles of trails. Pick up a hiking brochure and go exploring; the trails are well-marked and you can spend as little as 10 minutes or as much as three hours. The kids can look for white-tailed deer, ducks, herons, turtles and squirrels, while you admire 700 varieties of azaleas, 400-500 varieties of holly, plus dogwood, rhododendron and all kinds of wildflowers. Make a stop at **Mr. Cason's Vegetable Garden,** which was created in 1961 with 15,000 yards of bottom land silt loam. You'll find 400 varieties of vegetables, herbs and fruits in this 7.5-acre plot.

Even if your kids aren't flower lovers, take them to the **John A. Sibley Horticultural Center,** an indoor-outdoor botanical garden complete with a 22-foot waterfall and gorgeous flowers. There's something therapeutic about the experience, and all ages should enjoy it. Keep your eyes peeled for the topiary animals—and don't forget your camera (open May-November).

There are more than seven miles of **bike trails** at Callaway; our favorite route starts at the Mountain Creek Lake boathouse, the best of the three bike rental sites. The trail winds through lakes, woods and streams past the Sibley Center, the Ida Cason Memorial Chapel and an authentic log cabin, crossing 18 wooden bridges along the way. The trail ends on the opposite side of Mountain Creek Lake from where you started. How do you get back? By boarding a little ferry. Now isn't that nice?

KIDS' PROGRAMS

Callaway has the oldest children's recreation program in the country. It was created in 1961, and one facet which distinguishes it from most resorts is that it puts young kids on golf courses and tennis courts and gives them professional instruction on how to play. At most resorts, those courses and courts are too crowded for recreation program use. But Callaway's staff believes that kids deserve access to these facilities.

There's another plus to the Callaway rec program: Some of the counselors are performers from the FSU circus. You're not likely to find another resort rec program where kids can learn circus tricks in the morning and watch their counselors perform under the Big Top in the afternoon. The children's center is located adjacent to both Robin Lake beach and the circus tent. It includes a large outdoor playground. Nearby you'll find a riverboat ride, paddleboats, mini golf and a train ride.

At a nature center like Callaway, the educational programs are wide-ranging; Turtles Are Terrific, Butterfly Basics, Vegetable Scavenger Hunt, Nature Canoeing, Snakes Are Snazzy, Wild Mammals and Bats! Bats! Bats! are among the offerings. Sessions usually last about an hour.

Callaway's rec program operates Monday-Friday and is divided into five different age divisions: 3-6, 7-12, 13-15, 16-18 and adult (19 and up).

The schedule/sample of activities is as follows:

▲ **(Ages 3-6)**
Flexible time schedule. Typical activites include music, art, swimming, puppet shows and a trip to the butterfly center.

▲ **(Ages 7-12)**
9 a.m.-3 p.m. Circus activities, beach games, water skiing, vegetable garden hike.

▲ **(Ages 13-15)**
9-3 three days a week, 9-4:30 p.m. two days a week, plus a 7:30-8:30 p.m. discovery program which is open to anyone—and it's free. Sailing, bike hike, Sky View golf tournament, tennis mixer.

▲ **(Ages 16-18)**
Hours are similar to but slightly longer than the 13-15 group. Activities are similar.

▲ **(Ages 19 and up)**
Hours are longer still. Activities and athletic instruction become more specialized. There's an early-morning Fun Run (5,000 meters).

WHERE TO EAT

At the resort

The truth is, you don't go to Callaway for the food; not that the food is bad—just undistinguished. We had dinner at the Gardens Restaurant overlooking the Lake View golf course, and we probably enjoyed the college kids' musical revue as much as the food—which is to say, sort of. But it is a sit-down restaurant where you can take older children. Downstairs from the Gardens is the Veranda restaurant, which used to be more romantic. But prices have been lowered to encourage family business—and kids can eat spaghetti here free. Callaway's most elegant dining spot is The Georgia Room, which specializes in fresh seafood and steaks. Jackets are required.

The best places to take kids to eat are The Plantation Room, where you can eat buffet-style or order from the menu, and—an even better choice—The Flower Mill, a re-creation of an old-fashioned soda fountain. The juke box can be loud, but we liked the food (burgers, chicken sandwiches, pizza, shakes). Depending on the weather, you also have the option of eating outside. The Country Store serves breakfast and lunch, but its best feature is its view of Pine Mountain.

There's also a food pavilion at Robin Lake beach which serves hot dogs/hamburgers all day. And three nights a week, Callaway puts on themed beach night buffets there, complete with live entertainment. Be sure to ask, because the staff also stages mini-carnivals (ring toss, dart games, etc.) for kids.

Off property

The Victorian Tea Room specializes in Southern cooking (Broad St., in Warm Springs, 404-655-2319). Even closer is the Oak Tree Victorian Restaurant (Highway 27, in Hamilton, GA, 404-628-4218), which features French continental cuisine. Another good choice for continental fare is In Clover (205 Broad St., in Lagrange, GA, 404-882-0883).

SHOPPING/NEARBY FUN

There's a small shopping center just north of the resort on U.S. 27, which is handy for those who are staying in the Country Cottages or the Mountain Creek villas and need to stock their refrigerators. Food products, horticultural/decorative items and clothing are available at eight stores on the property.

Franklin D. Roosevelt's modest country retreat, **The Little White House,** is located just 18 miles east of Callaway Gardens in Warm Springs, Ga. President Roosevelt first visited Warm Springs in 1924, hoping that the warm, buoyant spring water would help him recover from the effects of infantile paralysis. Maintained substantially as it was when FDR died there on April 12, 1945, The Little White House contains FDR's collection of ship models and a portrait that was being painted when he died. You can also see FDR's 1938 Ford convertible, which was fitted with hand controls that enabled him to drive. A 12-minute film, *FDR in Georgia,* is shown at the Franklin D. Roosevelt museum (on Hwy. 85W, 404-655-3511).

WHEN TO GO

Callaway Gardens is not located quite far enough South to be a true retreat from winter weather. Daily highs range from 52 degrees in January to 88 in July.

Callaway's high season runs from early March through Thanksgiving weekend. Rates are significantly lower from late November to early March. Certain kinds of accommodations—for example, junior suites and roof garden suites at the Inn—have year-round rates which do not change with the season.

Waterskiing fans flock to Callaway in late May for the Masters Water Ski Tournament, a three-day international event with $100,000 in prize money.

Callaway is always peaceful. But occupancy is usually a bit low the first two weeks of June, so that's a particularly good time to go.

If you're interested in seeing the plumleaf azalea at its fiery-colored peak, July through late August is the time to visit. In particular, it's fun to be at Callaway on Prunifolia Day in late July when costumed characters, puppeteers, balloon sculptors and clowns provide special entertainment for kids.

FOR MORE INFORMATION

Contact:

Callaway Gardens
Pine Mountain, GA 31822
(404-663- 2281 or 800-282-8181)

Grove Park Inn and Country Club

The Grove Park Inn is located on Sunset Mountain, two miles from downtown Asheville, N.C. (exit 5B/Charlotte Street, off I-240). The 140-acre resort is listed in the National Register of Historic Places. It features a main lodge constructed from stone and sweeping views of the Blue Ridge Mountains.

ABOUT THE RESORT

The Grove Park Inn and Country Club is named for Edwin W. Grove, a pharmaceutical entrepreneur from St. Louis who visited Asheville in the summers to improve his health and eventually bought land here. The idea of building a unique resort overlooking the Blue Ridge Moutains was a long-time dream of his, but he couldn't find an architect who shared his vision. Eventually, Grove turned to his son-in-law, Fred L. Seely, who was—of all things—a newspaperman. Influenced by Frank Lloyd Wright and by the Old Faithful Inn at Yellowstone National Park, Seely designed the Grove Park as an example of naturalistic architecture. Built of boulders from Sunset Mountain, it was immediately hailed as one of the finest resort hotels in the world when it opened on July 12, 1913. It has granite walls, a distinctive red clay roof and a superstructure of steel; if anything, it is even more of a marvel today.

The Grove Park Inn's opening was considered such a momentous occasion that no less an orator than William Jennings Bryan (then U.S. Secretary of State) delivered the official address. Over the years, eight U.S. presidents have stayed here.

For nearly three-quarters of a century, Grove Park was a seasonal resort. Originally, it was a haven for the rich and famous: Thomas Edison, Harvey Firestone, Henry Ford and Woodrow Wilson were among the first wave of guests. F. Scott Fitzgerald actually lived at the hotel in 1935 and 1936, when he was struggling with alcoholism and tuberculosis, and his wife was institutionalized in an Asheville hospital. You can stay in Fitzgerald's room (No. 441 in the 1913 wing), but you won't have to observe the archaic rules which were in place during his days at the Inn: Only low tones and whispers were permitted after 10:30 p.m., and slamming doors was strictly forbidden. Not surprisingly, children's presence was discouraged.

Fortunately, that's all changed. In 1984, Grove Park became a year-round resort and management now considers kids to be important guests, as evidenced by the new children's recreation program. Don't be put off by that mammoth stone facade which greets you when you drive into the large brick parking lot, or by Grove Park's "grand resort" reputation; the place is actually quite relaxed, the staff is friendly and whatever haughtiness once existed is now just a memory.

ACCOMMODATIONS

Grove Park has 510 guest rooms—142 in the 1913 Wing, 202 in the Sammons Wing (1984) and 166 in the Vanderbilt Wing (1988). Among those 510 rooms, you'll find 19 suites and, on the Club Floor, 28 oversized guest rooms with jacuzzis, terrycloth robes and all sorts of complimentaries: flowers, pressing service, continental breakfast and late afternoon cocktail service and hors d'oeuvres.

The 1913 wing is a delight for those with a sense of history. The rooms have high ceilings and rustic mission oak furnishings, nearly all of which are original. It's doubtful that you'll ever need to turn on the AC—even in July and August—because the highland air is so invigorating and stone walls block out the heat of the sun. Think about it: When was the last time you spent a summer evening in a hotel where the windows opened and the night breezes made your room seem fresh and comfortable instead of hot and sultry?

The lobby, or Great Hall, will bowl you over the first time you see it. As stunning as any Hyatt atrium, the Great Hall is 120 feet long, 80 feet wide and has a pair of massive, walk-in fireplaces which are large enough to burn 12-foot logs. To get to the upper floors in this wing, you enter a cave-like elevator which runs straight up through the chimney shaft.

To keep pace with other resorts, Grove Park embarked on an extensive renovation campaign in 1982. By 1988, $75 million had been spent to refurbish and enlarge the property into a full-scale, year-round resort. In our view, management could've done a better job of making the new wings look more compatible with the main lodge. Grafted onto the 1913 Wing to form a U-shaped complex, the new wings are big and blocky and the exterior walls don't blend well with the stone facade which makes the old wing so distinctive. We also regret the decision to sacrifice a large expanse of sloping front lawn in order to install two more tennis courts. Granted, it's now a beautiful setting in which to play tennis, but it can't compare with the look of the original lawn.

Do not shy away from the newer wings just because of their less-than-perfect exteriors. On the inside, management has maintained the 1913 look by using authentic Arts and Crafts period furniture and lighting fixtures, or, when necessary, modern reproductions.

To appeal to families who travel with their kids, Grove Park allows children to stay free in their parents' room—and management recently expanded that policy by changing the definition of a child from "under 12" to "under 17."

SPORTS

Grove Park's 18-hole golf course sits in a beautiful valley beneath the resort. The course dates back to 1909, when it was known as the Asheville Country Club. The Inn purchased the course, pool and clubhouse in 1976, and a major renovation was completed in 1989. The back nine was redesigned and updated, the greens were rebuilt and 700 trees (maples, birches, oaks, sycamores, mountain ash, sweet gum, white pine and European white birch) were planted. Rock gardens with perennial grasses were also added. The course isn't long (6,301 yards from the back tees), but the fairways are rolling, the greens are fast and the par threes are a real test (particularly No. 7). And beware of those mountain vistas; they're enough to distract you from your shot-making.

The resort has nine tennis courts—six outdoors and three at the indoor sports center, where you'll also find racquetball and squash courts, Nautilus equipment, aerobics classes, jacuzzis and saunas.

There's a large indoor swimming pool at the main lodge and an outdoor pool at the country club.

FAMILY FUN

Grove Park is located in a quaint old neighborhood with winding streets, beautiful Tudor-style homes and the Blue Ridge Mountains in the background.

Your kids will enjoy the **antique car museum** which is located in a separate building just a short walk from the lobby.

Considering that Grove Park is an inland resort without access to a lake, that's about it in the on-site family fun department. But don't underestimate how good it feels just to be at the Grove Park Inn; it's a one-of-a-kind place, and there are lots of things to do in **Asheville** and the surrounding area (see "Shopping/Nearby Fun").

KIDS' PROGRAMS

Grove Park's children's recreation program runs May 21-September 2, Monday-Saturday, 9:30 a.m.-4:30 p.m., with evening sessions (6-10:30 p.m.) on Friday and Saturday. The program is divided into two principal age groups—Teddy Bear Club (3-5) and Operation "Kid Nap" (6-11)—but teen activities are also offered.

Activities include arts and crafts, board games, nature hikes, tennis, badminton, swimming, ping-pong, playground fun, walking tours of the grounds and, during the summer months, cookouts and picnics. On Friday nights, kids enjoy pizza and movie parties.

The playground is located near the sports center. The seven-level playscape features a corkscrew slide and a swing.

The playroom is adjacent to the indoor pool, and kids will also find video games there.

WHERE TO EAT

At the resort

When it comes to food, Grove Park falls into the same general category as Callaway Gardens: good, but nothing to rave about. Grove Park's newest restaurant is Horizons, located in the Sammons Wing. The menu features "innovative classic cuisine" such as breast of duck with smoked scallops and endive. Coat and tie are required, and this restaurant is really not suitable for kids.

Located atop the Vanderbilt Wing, the Blue Ridge Dining Room and Terrace features both buffet and à la carte dining. You might want to try the Friday night seafood buffet or Sunday brunch. The Carolina Cafe is on the ground floor between the main lodge and the Sammons Wing, and it serves breakfast, lunch and dinner. Both restaurants are open year-round, while the resort's two outdoor restaurants, the Sunset Terrace and Pool Cabana, are seasonal. The Sunset Terrace serves lunch and dinner, and offers a picture-perfect view of Asheville and the mountains. The Pool Cabana is a sandwich and lunch spot which overlooks the golf course. Jackets are required for dinner at the Blue Ridge and the Sunset Terrace. But the former is a large restaurant with plenty of noise, so don't take that to mean you can't bring your kids.

Off property

Bill Stanley's Barbecue and Blue Grass (20 S. Spruce St., 704-253-4871) features oodles of southern mountain food at moderate prices. But the real fun here is the foot-stompin' country music which crowds the dance floor with cloggers, square dancers and anybody who wants to shake a tail feather.

Our favorite Sunday brunch spot is Stone Soup (50 Broadway, 704-255-7687), which has a Sixties coffee house feel to it. Typically, the menu includes eggs benedict, fresh fruit and a variety of pastries. You can get *The New York Times* here and the spacious, arty, brick-walled atmosphere encourages diners to linger. Stone Soup has a smaller location (8 Wall St., 704-255-7687) and both spots are perfect for lunch.

For an elegant adults-only dinner (Grove Park does offer baby-sitting in addition to the kids' Friday-Saturday evening program) we recommend Gabrielle's at Richmond Hill, a century-old mansion which has been transformed into a handsome, wood-paneled inn (87 Richmond Hill Dr., 704-252-7313).

SHOPPING/NEARBY FUN

Grove Park has several boutiques, including the **Gallery of the Mountains,** which features native crafts. But visitors to Grove Park shouldn't become so enamored with the resort that they don't sample the many pleasures of Asheville.

In 1983, Rand McNally's Places Rated Almanac ranked **Asheville** (pop. 61,000) No. 1 among America's small cities in terms of quality of life, and nothing has happened in the intervening years to alter that distinction. In a city where even the local minor league baseball team is nicknamed the Tourists, the problem isn't what to do—it's how to fit everything in. We've visited again and again, and never seem to get our fill.

Surrounded by the Blue Ridge Mountains on one side and the Great Smoky Mountains on the other, Asheville (elevation: 2,500 feet) is the hub of tourist activity in western North Carolina—and it starts in the heart of the city.

Downtown Asheville has undergone a major facelift in recent years, and our family enjoyed browsing the **Wall Street walking mall** which connects Otis Street to Battery Park Avenue. The Book Store on Wall Street has a special children's reading area and a story hour on Saturday mornings. Asheville's oldest store, T.S. Morrison, has been in business so long (since 1891) that the original proprietor sold wagons to the Grove Park Inn when it was being built. Hard candy is stowed in century-old bins, an old Coke cooler contains ice-cold bottles of sarsaparilla and cream soda, and you'll find plenty of antique toys amidst the museum-like clutter (39 N. Lexington, 704-253-2348). A few doors away is Tops for Shoes, which draws footwear shoppers from all over the South (27 N. Lexington, 704-254-6721).

Asheville's new cultural hub is **Pack Place,** an art and science center scheduled to open sometime in 1992 (intersection of Biltmore and Patton Avenues).

In general, we don't consider touring a famous author's home a children's activity. But if you have teenagers or younger children who love to read and are interested in history, take them with you when you visit the **Thomas Wolfe Memorial** (48 Spruce St., 704-253-8304). Wolfe's most famous novel, *Look Homeward Angel,*draws heavily on the years he spent in this boarding house, and the guided tour does an excellent job of tying the house and its former inhabitants to incidents and characters in the book. We also recommend a trip to **Connemara,** which was Carl Sandburg's home for the last 22 years of his life. During the summer, performers from the Flat Rock Playhouse present "The World of Carl Sandburg," based on the author's poetry, humor and philosophy, plus the "Rootabaga Stories," Sandburg's tales for children. Located in nearby Flat

Rock, N.C., three miles south of Hendersonville off I-26 (704-693-4178), Connemara is open daily except Christmas.

If you've never visited the **Biltmore Estate**—George W. Vanderbilt's homage to French Renaissance chateaus—you must go at least once. Granted, this doesn't seem like an ideal kids' activity either, but our two were as fascinated by the excess as we were. It took 1,000 men five years (1890-95) to build this 250-room mansion, which is known as the "largest private home in America." Call it "a castle" and your kids may consider it an adventure. A behind-the-scenes tour is now offered, but we don't recommend it. It's basically a tour of turn-of-the-century heating systems and rooms of unrestored furniture. You can also visit the Biltmore winery and gardens, and the grounds—8,000 acres worth—are covered with wildflowers. The admission price is steep, but children 11 and under are free. The Biltmore Estate is located just north of exits 50 or 50B off I-40. For more information, contact: Biltmore Estate, One North Park Square, Asheville, NC 28801 (704-255-1715 or 800-543-2961). Closed on Thanksgiving.

Adjacent to the entrance of the estate is **Biltmore Village,** a neighborhood of English-style houses which have been turned into shops and galleries. We've always had fun wandering around here, and you'll find gifts/souvenirs for your kids (kites, books, dolls, educational toys/games) which you won't find at your local mall.

For more information on Asheville, contact: Asheville Convention and Visitors Bureau (P.O. Box 1010/151 Hayward St., Asheville, NC 28802, 704-258-6104, 800-257-1300, or, in North Carolina, 800-548-1300).

To lose your cares completely, take a ride on the **Blue Ridge Parkway,** where you'll be treated to some of the most beautiful scenery in the Southeast. Be sure to visit the **Folk Art Center,** which is located at Milepost 382 on the parkway, just east of Asheville. Here you'll find handmade quilts, pottery, wooden toys, jewelry and sculpture. It's all produced by members of the Southern Highland Handicraft Guild, which celebrated its 60th birthday in 1990 (704-298-7928).

Take the parkway south from the Folk Arts Center and have lunch at the Pisgah Inn (704-235-8228), which is located at one of the highest points on the parkway. But beware of dense ground fog; the 20-mile trip is like going from North Georgia to Canada in terms of the changes that take place in climate and horticulture from the base of Mt. Pisgah to the top (elevation: 5,749). Pisgah Inn guests sleep with blankets all summer, and in a real heat wave the daytime high may reach 78 degrees. Along the way, you'll see more than 100 species of trees and, depending on the time of year, 1,500 varieties of flowering plants—more than the entire continent of Europe.

Great Smoky Mountains National Park—the nation's most popular national park—is less than an hour's drive west of Asheville (for information, see the NATIONAL PARKS chapter).

Southern skiers flock to the **Maggie Valley** and **Banner Elk** areas for surprisingly good snow and après-ski activities. Maggie Vally is just 35 minutes west of Asheville on I-40, and the best slopes are at the Cataloochee Ski Area (704-926-0285). For the best skiing in North Carolina, take the Blue Ridge Parkway east to Banner Elk, where you'll find Ski Beech (704-387-2011) and Sugar Mountain Resort (704-898-4521). A word of caution about skiing in the South: Never head to the slopes without first calling to inquire about conditions; it could be raining, or sunny and 70 degrees.

WHEN TO GO

Grove Park's high season extends from April 1 to mid-November, although rates are slightly lower during the weeks leading up to and including Memorial Day, Fourth of July and Labor Day. Rates are lowest from January 1 to March 31. If you plan to enjoy outdoor activities, we recommend that you go in the middle of the summer, when Grove Park can offer sweet relief from the heat but the temperature is still warm enough for golf, tennis and swimming.

FOR MORE INFORMATION

Contact:

Grove Park Inn
290 Macon Ave., Asheville, NC 28804
(704-252-2711 or 800-438-5800)

KIAWAH ISLAND INN & VILLAS

Kiawah Island Inn & Villas is located 21 miles south of Charleston, S.C. (take U.S. 17 south, turn left on Main Road, which becomes Bohicket Road, and follow the signs). The island is 10 miles long, but only 1.5 miles wide, and its 10,000 acres are largely undeveloped. The resort features 10 miles of unspoiled beach, plus superb golf and tennis facilities.

ABOUT THE RESORT

Kiawah Island is named for the Kiawah Indians. But as you'll learn from one of the Kiawah nature guides, that tribe never lived on this particular island. The story of how Kiawah became a resort is also curious. The Vanderhorst family of Charleston owned the island from colonial times until 1952, and during that time they grew cotton and indigo here. The next owner made the ill-advised decision to grow pine trees on Kiawah, which is a barrier island—not a natural habitat for pines. At one point, a company from—of all places—Kuwait held the deed. Nowadays, Kiawah is owned by a California-based hotel chain which has properties in such ultra-chic locations as West Palm Beach, Fla., and LaQuinta, Calif.

To cut down on traffic, the resort is divided into two principal areas— West Beach Village (opened in 1976), which includes the Kiawah Inn, and East Beach Village (1981), which includes a conference center, a retail center and Night Heron Park. Both areas feature lodging, dining, sports, shopping and meeting facilities, allowing guests to do as little or as much as they want without needing their car. But East Beach won't be finished until the mid-1990s when two additional beachfront hotels, a 40,000-square-foot health spa and a 50,000-square-foot retail village are built.

One of those new hotels will be an all-suites facility. Plans call for each of the 200 suites to have views of both the ocean and the marshes. Each unit will have two balconies with a hot tub on one of them. The second hotel, an 800-room facility, will include ocean views from every room, plus conference facilities and the retail village.

If this sounds like a lot of commotion, forget it; Kiawah is so quiet, it's almost eerie—and with 10,000 acres to play with, there's room for a little more development.

ACCOMMODATIONS

Kiawah has 150 newly remodeled rooms at the Kiawah Inn, plus 260-300 villas, depending on how many of these privately owned residences are being used as rental properties at a given time.

The Kiawah Inn is a four-lodge complex; all guest rooms include private balconies with views of either the ocean, sand dunes or tropical forests.

The villas are one- to four-bedroom units, and they're sprinkled throughout the island. They feature a living room/dining area, fully equipped kitchens and washer/dryer. Four price ranges are available: ocean view, oceanside, fairway/tennis and scenic. If you're looking for something really special, ask for the Turtle Cove villas which overlook the ocean and the 17th and 18th fairways of the Turtle Point golf course.

SPORTS

Kiawah has even more holes of golf (72) than Callaway Gardens, and its newest course—The Pete Dye-designed Ocean Course—will be the site of the 1991 Ryder Cup matches between the United States and Great Britain/Europe. With 2.5 miles of oceanfront property to work with, Dye (who also designed one of the courses at Amelia Island) found room for 10 seaside holes—more than any other golf course in the Northern Hemisphere. All 18 holes feature views of the ocean, and what's especially nice about the course layout is that there's no surrounding real estate development. Kiawah has three other courses, and all have impressive pedigrees: Marsh Point, a Gary Player design, opened in 1976 (6,250 yards); Turtle Point, a Jack Nicklaus design, opened in 1981 (6,889 yards); and Osprey Point, designed by Tom Fazio, opened in 1988 (6,678 yards). Like Dye, Fazio also designed one of the courses at Amelia Island. Located at West Beach, Marsh Point is a bayside course with water hazards on 13 holes. Osprey Point, which meanders through the island's tropical forests, has water on 15 holes. Turtle Point, at East Beach, features three oceanside holes and long, tight fairways. For reservations, call 803-768-2121.

When it comes to tennis, Kiawah is extremely well-endowed. The resort has 28 courts—16 at the West Beach Racquet Club (14 clay, 2 hard) and 12 at the East Beach Tennis Club (9 clay, 3 hard), but only two (at West Beach) are lighted. Of particular interest to those who want to work on fundamentals is the fully automated practice court at East Beach, where players work with ball machines which refill themselves.

Nearby Bohicket Marina charters boats for fishing, or you can grab a net, take off your shoes and socks and go shrimping, oystering or crabbing.

There are several swimming pools on the island. At the Inn, you'll find a family pool, a wading pool and an adults-only pool with a lane for swimming laps. The Turtle Point pool is adjacent to the Turtle Point Golf Shop, and Night Heron Park has a 25-meter pool.

FAMILY FUN

Kiawah has 14 miles of bike trails, and the sand is hard enough to ride the 10 miles of beach.

You can also arrange to go on various nature excursions offered through a program known as "Kiawah College." Those programs include: a two-mile island walk, a marsh biking safari, bird watching and loggerhead turtle tours, canoe trips, gator gawks and a unique ocean seining experience. Taking its name from a kind of fisherman's net, the seining program enables guests to join hands with a biologist and pull a 40-foot net through the ocean surf. The marine animals which are trapped in the net are then transferred to portable aquariums on the beach, and a lecture plus question-and-answer session ensues. Children are welcome, but they must be accompanied by an adult; Kiawah College is not a supervised children's program.

NOTE
Kiawah Island is home to 18 species of mammals, 30 species of reptiles and amphibians, and more than 140 species of birds. Out of respect for one of those species, no overhead lights shine on Kiawah's roads at night. Why? Because nesting loggerhead turtles are disturbed by light.

If you like watersports, you can rent sailboats and windsurfers at the Inn or in front of the Mariners Watch villas.

As an adjunct to its children's recreation program, Kiawah hosts family cookouts and volleyball games on Saturday nights at Night Heron Park during the summer. But don't wait until Saturday to take your kids to this 21-acre expanse, which includes large playing fields, a special play area for small children, picnic sites, a lake with a fishing dock, a swimming pool, a bike rental shop, a recreation pavilion and an ocean-access point with an observation deck and a bathhouse nearby.

KIDS' PROGRAMS

Kiawah's children's recreation program was started in 1975, and in the beginning it was nothing more than a bike rental operation with a few activities thrown in for good measure. The program has since been expanded to include a wide variety of activities for 3-year-olds to teens. The average daily enrollment is 60, but on peak days in August as many as 100 kids may show up.

The Monday-Friday program runs from Memorial Day through Labor Day and is divided into four age groups: 3-5, 6-8, 9-12 and teenagers:

▲ **(Ages 3-5)**

This half-day program gives parents the option of enrolling their kids for either a morning (9 a.m.-12:30 p.m.) or afternoon (1-4:30 p.m.) session. Activities include shelling, scavenger hunts, nature hikes and sand-castle building.

▲ **(Ages 6-8)**
This full-day program (9-4:30) includes crabbing, water sports and ice-cream making. Lunch is provided for a nominal fee.

▲ **(Ages 9-12)**
Same hours as the 6-8 group. Activities include bike hikes and an unusual Kiawah version of Scrabble, where ping-pong balls with letters painted on them are tossed into the surf. Object of the game: Retrieve them in such a way that they form words.

▲ **(Teens)**
Kiawah's teen program (4-6 p.m./9-11 p.m.) is unique in that it's absolutely free. Exceptions: the cost of a t-shirt if the activity is tie-dyeing and a cover charge for the non-alcoholic specialty drinks served at volleyball and cabana parties. Other activities include soccer, ultimate frisbee, cookouts and TGIF dances.

Kiawah's kids' rec program is available to anyone who is staying on the island, but resort guests get a preferred rate. If you want to save money, consider either the three-day or the weekly rate.

WHERE TO EAT

At the resort

Kiawah features lowcountry cooking: fresh seafood, locally grown vegetables, herbs and spices. And with the exception of the Vintner's Dinner, a special four- to five-course gourmet meal with limited seating at the Inn, kids are never out of place.

The Jasmine Porch, an indoor-outdoor restaurant located at the Kiawah Inn, gives diners a scenic view of the ocean; the menu features not only seafood but continental favorites, as well. Sunday brunch includes 20 kinds of salad, 11 hot dishes and Belgian waffles. The Indigo House, located across the street from the East Beach Tennis Club, specializes in buffets. Jonah's at the Straw Mart features soups, salad and seafood at lunch and dinner. For poolside burgers, french fries and snacks, try Sundancer's at the Inn.

The dining experience at Kiawah isn't limited to restaurant settings. Theme dinners and cookouts are offered throughout the year at special prices and locations. We enjoyed the oyster roast and barbecue at Mingo Point next to the Kiawah River, and the Vintner's Dinner, which includes wine specially chosen for each course.

Jilich's, located at Night Heron Park, is a casual spot where you can get sandwiches for lunch and seafood for dinner.

Off property

Charleston, S.C., is best known for its elegant restaurants, but there are lots of good places to take the family. For starters, there's the Variety Store, which is located in an unpainted, wooden house on stilts at the edge of the Ashley River, next to the Charleston city marina (803-723-6325).

If you've been to Patriots Point (see "Shopping/Nearby Fun") try R.B.'s Rusty Pelican (on Shem Creek, in Mt. Pleasant, 803-881-0466). A.W. Shucks is a good place for a casual seafood lunch or dinner (70 State St., in the old city market area, 803-723-1151).

Or try the Privateer, a seafood restaurant located at Bohicket Marina near the entrance to the resort.

SHOPPING/NEARBY FUN

The Straw Market, located next to the Inn, has seven shops: two women's boutiques, a men's boutique, two gift shops, a jewelry store and a children's shop.

Like Asheville, its distant neighbor to the north, **Charleston** has also been named No. 1 in the U.S. in terms of quality of life. In Charleston's case, that honor came in 1986 and it was bestowed on the city by the U.S. Conference of Mayors. Some of the things that make Charleston special—its reverence for art, architecture and, most of all, history— won't delight young children. But as kids get older, parents want them to be exposed to something besides MTV. And when families go on vacation, sometimes the adults get to pick what they want to do.

Our advice, if you're spending more than a weekend at Kiawah, is to visit Charleston—but brief the kids ahead of time so they'll know you plan to mix adult activities with ones they'll like.

The Visitor Information Center (85 Calhoun St., 803-722-5225) is a good place to familiarize yourself with what the city has to offer. After you've picked up a pile of brochures and asked a lot of questions, head for the **Adventure Theatre,** where you'll enjoy *The Charleston Adventure*, a 38-minute color film shown on a 40-foot screen. The theater is located just behind the information center, and the admission fee is nominal.

There's no more joyous time in Charleston than spring— particularly late May to early June, when the city hosts the **Spoleto Arts Festival,** which was patterned after the world-famous Spoleto, Italy, festival. Spoleto USA is a 17-day civic extravaganza which includes more than 100 performances: theater, symphonies, ballets, jazz and the visual arts (803-722-2764). If the main festival is too highbrow for your kids, try **Piccolo Spoleto,** a spirited companion festival which showcases the best local and regional talent. Roughly half of these 700 performances are free, and the rest are offered for a nominal admission fee. There's also a day-long **Children's Festival,** which could include everything from puppet shows to fireworks (803-724-7305).

Founded in 1773, the **Charleston Museum** is the oldest museum in the U.S. This is a $6 million complex, and kids should like the wildlife dioramas, the life-sized replica of the Confederate States' submarine and the hands-on activities in the Discover Me Room (360 Meeting St., 803-722-2996). Open daily, 9 a.m.-5 p.m., except Sunday, 1-5 p.m.

Waterfront Park is a great place to plop down in a swing or to spread out a picnic and gaze across Charleston Harbor. City planners added an extra-nice touch: They built fountains which are designed for hot, cranky kids to run through on steamy summer days.

If your family is interested in American/military history, take a boat ride out to **Fort Sumter,** where the first shot of the Civil War was aimed. Boats leave from the city Marina at 9:30 a.m., noon and 2:30 p.m. The trip takes a little more than two hours, with a one-hour stop at the fort. Children under 6 are free (803-722-1691).

You can also visit **Patriots Point** in nearby Mt. Pleasant, S.C. Patriots Point has the world's largest naval and maritime museum. Moored here are the famed aircraft carrier *Yorktown,* the nuclear merchant ship *Savannah* and a World War II submarine—all of which you can board and tour (803-8845-2727). Oh, yes, there's an 18-hole public golf course right next door.

Everyone enjoys the **old city market,** located in a series of low-slung sheds which used to house fish and produce markets. If you're cooking for yourself in a Kiawah villa, check out the vegetable and fruit vendors. We got a kick out of rummaging through the picture frames, palmetto-leaf baskets and other knicknacks on sale here. You'll also find fruit and vegetable stands along Bohicket Road near the entrance to the resort.

WHEN TO GO

Kiawah is located at almost the same latitude as Callaway Gardens, and while it doesn't have Callaway's altitude to help cool people off, it does have refreshing ocean breezes. As a result, visitors can expect mid-day highs in spring and summer to reach the 80s and, occasionally, the 90s. Mid-day highs in the fall range from the 80s to the 60s, depending on how late in the season it is. Winters are chilly (highs range from 60s to 30s) but the island seldom gets any snow—and as we Georgia residents can attest, there's always the possibility of a 70-degree day in the middle of winter.

Kiawah's high season runs from mid-March to the end of October, and despite what we said about the possibility of mild mid-winter weather, that's when we would go. August is Kiawah's busiest month, but if you want to swim in the ocean, that's when it's at its warmest.

FOR MORE INFORMATION

Contact:

Kiawah Island Inn & Villas
PO Box 12357, Charleston, SC 29412
(803-768-2121 or 800-654-2924)

MARRIOTT BAY POINT RESORT

The Marriott Bay Point Resort is located in Panama City Beach, Fla. (take U.S. 98 to Thomas Drive, turn south and follow the signs). Set amidst a 1,100-acre wildlife sanctuary, the resort is home to the largest private yacht marina on the Gulf Coast and to one of America's most difficult golf courses.

ABOUT THE RESORT

This property was a residential yacht community and country club for 15 years before Marriott spent $40 million to transform it into a Gulf Coast resort in 1985. But is it a Gulf Coast resort? Well, yes and no. The property is located on a private peninsula between Grand Lagoon and St. Andrews Bay; you can see the Gulf from the resort, but it's not actually on the Gulf—which sounds like a real drawback for those who want to frolic in the surf and sunbathe by the sea. But Bay Point turned a potential negative into a positive by purchasing a Mississippi River paddlewheeler to take its guests out to Shell Island, an uninhabited barrier island where there's powdery-white sand, beautiful emerald-colored sea and decent surf. It takes the *Island Queen* 45 minutes to get to Shell Island, and if you stay on-deck you may see Atlantic bottle-nose dolphins jumpin' waves. To help pass the time, the crew serves hot dogs, sandwiches, beer and specialty drinks. One drawback: Shell Island (which is owned by the state) has no bath house and no potties. If you need to make a pit stop while you're there, you have to walk a considerable distance back to the dock to use the riverboat's facilities. Warning: Do not, under any circumstances, attempt to make that trek barefoot; one of us did, and he found the wooden walkway hotter than the grill at Benihana.

ACCOMMODATIONS

The resort has 386 guest rooms, suites and villas. The ones we saw were in excellent condition, and Marriott refurbished all 200 rooms in the main hotel building in 1990.

Loch Legend Village features one- and two-bedroom suites, which are located between fairways on the Legends golf course. There are seven buildings in all, and each one is named for a famous golf course: Winged Foot, St. Andrews, Muirfield, Merion, Seminole, Firestone, Augusta. Helpful hint: Seminole is the only one of the seven buildings with a pool; if you get a first-floor suite, as we did, your kids can hop in and out with ease. The Loch Legend suites are nicely appointed, but our one-bedroom unit was cramped for a family of four. We squeezed in a rollaway next to the fold-out couch in the living room, but it left little room to maneuver.

Lagoon Towers/Harbour Villas feature one- and two-bedroom villas, which are located on St. Andrews Bay.

SPORTS

Bay Point has two 18-hole golf courses: the Club Meadows course, which opened in 1971, and the Lagoon Legend, which opened in 1985. Club Meadows is a long, but traditional 6,913-yard layout with wide fairways. The 7,080-yard Legend is known as "The Dragon" and it's anything but traditional. The course has been molded from Southern marshes and topography which is unusual for Florida: rolling hills. You may have to carry your drive over sand dunes and sea oats just to reach the start of the fairway. Water comes into play on all but two holes, and on No. 18, you have to shoot over the Grand Lagoon not once but twice in order to reach the green. How tough is the Legend? Second-toughest course in the U.S., according to *Golf Digest*. The PGA tour has used the course for its qualifying school. Saving grace: Hole-by-hole hints on how to tame the Legend are available on an instructional video. For reservations, call 904-234-3307 or 800-874-7105.

Golf gets a lot of attention at Bay Point, but the resort's tennis center is quite nice. It features 12 Har-Tru courts (four are lighted) and a small pro shop.

The resort has two workout complexes—one in the hotel and another at the nearby 19th Hole sports complex.

Bay Point has five swimming pools (one indoors), and there is a narrow beach out at Alligator Point. But it's a hike out there via the boardwalk, so make sure you've got everything you need— sun lotion, towels, frisbees, etc.—before you start out. Redeeming feature: You can't get to Alligator Point without passing by Teddy Tucker's (see the "Where to Eat" section).

Alligator Point is Bay Point's watersports center. You can rent sailboats, catamarans, windsurfers, jet-skis or fishing equipment. You can also book passage on the *Hoot Mon II* for deep-sea fishing or off-shore sailing. Our family had a blast driving and riding the two-passenger Wave Runner, which is a sit-down version of the jet-ski. Guests also can take advantage of free daily scuba and windsurfing clinics.

FAMILY FUN

To enhance its family recreation/entertainment programs, the resort has opened a sports park that's just a few minutes away by car or shuttle bus. **The Bay Point Sports Park** features 36 holes of miniature golf, six baseball batting cages, a PGA-certified driving range, a 25,000-square-foot putting area, a bumper boat pond (where we got totally soaked!), a fishing lagoon, a cafe/bar and a golf pro shop (1703 Thomas Dr., 904-233-0145).

Both kids and adults are intrigued by the carved-wood parlor games (chess, miniature box hockey, bumper pool, marble football) which are found in the hotel lobby.

Thinking of buying a boat or motor yacht? You can window shop at Bay Point's 12-acre, 145-slip marina, where on a given day $45 million worth of merchandise could be tied up at the docks.

If you can't afford one of those 100-foot beauties, climb aboard the *Island Queen* for a moonlight cruise.

KIDS' PROGRAMS

The Alligator Point Gang (ages 5 to 12) has only been in operation since 1988, but it's a pretty good program—although we thought a couple of the counselors on duty when we were there needed a shot of enthusiasm.

The program has a three-part operating schedule, which is more extensive than most:

March through May—Weekends, holidays and special occasions.

June through August—Seven days a week, and nights too (Thursday through Saturday, plus holidays and special occasions).

September through February—Selected weeks.

For more information on schedules, call the activities director at 904-234-3307, ext. 1806.

On an average day, the Alligator Point gang will start with a nature walk, which includes a shell safari. Games, a snack and water Olympics might come next, followed by lunch. Afternoon activities can include kite flying, sand-castle building, arts and crafts, and a splash party. Other activities: trips to amusement parks, croquet on the front lawn, fishing on the dock.

WHERE TO EAT

At the resort

If you count the *Island Queen*, Bay Point has 11 restaurants and lounges which serve food—and everything we sampled was good.

We ate dinner at Stormy's Restaurant and Olde Fashion Ice Cream Parlor, which is advertised as a family place even though it's located in the same building as the Legends pro shop. The food (burgers, grilled chicken sandwiches, etc.) was tasty, but our waitress was short on patience when our kids changed their minds while ordering.

Both Fiddler's Green (Bay Point Resort Hotel) and The Terrace Court (overlooks the marina) should be reserved for adults-only dinners. We ate several meals at Fiddler's Green, which is fine for families at both breakfast (buffet-style or menu) and lunch. But at dinner, the fine china and linen are brought out. The menu features American fare; the fish and fowl is grilled slowly over an oak wood hearth, although you can ask the chef to broil or blacken it instead.

Teddy Tucker's boardwalk cafe would be a perfect set for a Jimmy Buffett video. Feast on raw oysters, burgers or grilled chicken sandwiches and toast the sunset with a margarita.

Please note: If you've purchased a special Bay Point travel package, kids under 12 eat free at Stormy's or Fiddler's Green when accompanied by a paying adult.

Off property

See "Where to Eat" in the Panama City Beach section of the BEACHES chapter.

SHOPPING/NEARBY FUN

Bay Point's Bay Town shopping village features an array of specialty shops. The hotel boutique features Ralph Lauren designs and an assortment of colorful t-shirts at reasonable prices. The t-shirts at the tennis pro shop were so nice, we each bought one. For more information, see "Shopping/Nearby Fun" in the Panama City Beach section of the BEACHES chapter.

WHEN TO GO

Marriott Bay Point's high season runs from mid-March to mid-August. Rates are slightly lower from early February to mid-March, and the least expensive time to visit is early November to early February.

People who work at the resort say that April, May and June are the best months, weatherwise. July and August are hot and muggy, but Gulf breezes help cool you off.

If you're really into fishing—to the extent that you like watching how the pros do it—you may want to visit the resort during the second week in July, when it hosts the Bay Point Billfish Invitational. Total purse is $300,000, making it the richest billfish tournament in the continental U.S. Competitors have to ante up $10,000 just to enter.

Do your kids like to fish? If so, they can compete for more than $3,500 in savings bonds at the AmSouth/Bay Point Junior Angler's Tournament held every summer. A couple hundred kids aged 7-14 try to catch snapper, grouper and other bottom fish, vying for savings bonds and ribbons for biggest fish caught, as well as smallest and ugliest fish caught. The tournament is usually held in late August. Unlike the Billfish Invitational, the entry fee is nominal. Call the resort for schedule.

Tennis fans interested in getting a peek at some of tomorrow's male and female stars will enjoy the Du Pont National Intercollegiate Clay Court Championships, which are held at Bay Point in mid-November.

FOR MORE INFORMATION
Contact:
Marriott Bay Point Resort
100 Delwood Beach Rd., Panama City Beach, FL 32411
(904-234-3307 or 800-874-7105)

SADDLEBROOK GOLF AND TENNIS RESORT

Saddlebrook is located 15 miles north of Tampa in Wesley Chapel, Fla. (one mile east of I-75 on State Road 54/exit 58). The 480-acre resort is home to two Arnold Palmer golf courses and the Harry Hopman/Saddlebrook International Tennis academy.

ABOUT THE RESORT

Saddlebrook was developed in 1974 as a residential golf and country club community. Its conversion to a resort began when a new owner purchased the property in 1979. Saddlebrook is an inland resort, and its biggest selling point is its golf and tennis—both of which feed its sizable convention business. When we were there in late summer, most guests seemed to be going back and forth between workshops and the golf course.

Unlike most resorts, Saddlebrook was designed as a "walking village," meaning you leave your car in a lot outside the main entrance when you check in. To get around the resort, you either hoof it or hail a bellman who will give you a ride on one of the resort's stretch golf carts. For the most part, this is a good idea—encourages people to walk, reduces noise, creates a nice overall atmosphere, etc. The down side occurs when you need to make a quick grocery run, especially late at night. It took us at least 10 minutes to get from our condo to a darkened parking lot, another 10 minutes to locate our car and get off the property—well, you get the picture. With the closest grocery store located within a mile of the resort's front gate, it took us nearly an hour to get back to our room with breakfast cereal and microwave popcorn.

ACCOMMODATIONS

Saddlebrook has nearly 400 one- and two-bedroom condominiums and 123 hotel rooms located in 10 two-story clusters around the property. Every hotel room has two double beds and a private balcony or patio. Every condo has a living room/dining room area, a fully equipped kitchen with serving bar and a patio or balcony. Our two-bedroom unit overlooked a small pool and whirlpool in the restaurant/pro shop area, and it was roomy enough for us to have spent a considerable amount of time there. Laundry facilities are available elsewhere in the two-story unit. Some of the wooden landings outside the entryways have seen their share of golf spikes and weather over the years, but it's nothing a fresh coat of paint couldn't cure.

If you plan to stay at least seven nights and you're willing to sacrifice a little bit of convenience and ambience, you can save money by staying at Saddlebrook's Lakeside Village, which is located along the entry road to the resort. This is a particularly good idea if you have a large family (or plan to travel with another family) because three-bedroom suites are available at what you'd pay for a two-bedroom condo closer to the action. Plus, you can park your car right outside your door.

SPORTS

Saddlebrook features two 18-hole golf courses designed and built by Arnold Palmer—and they get plenty of use. The 6,469-yard Palmer course was cut from an orange grove, and water comes into play on seven of the holes. The 6,603-yard Saddlebrook layout is flatter, but water is still a nemesis on six holes.

Saddlebrook's tennis program was created by the late Harry Hopman, an immortal tennis figure who captained 21 Australian Davis Cup teams, 16 of which won the Davis Cup title. Hopman helped develop all the great Aussie players of the Fifties, Sixties and Seventies—Rod Laver, Ken Rosewall and John Newcombe, to name a few. And a number of top-ranked players have trained at the Saddlebrook/Hopman school since it opened in 1976. Those players include John McEnroe, Andres Gomez and, most recently, Jennifer Capriati, who lives just down the street from the tennis center. Saddlebrook has 37 courts; 27 are Har-Tru composition, 10 are hard courts and five of those 37 are lighted for night play. Low fences help prevent balls from straying onto other courts, and there's a cabana (table, chairs, drinking fountain) for every two courts. The ratio of players to instructor is never more than 4:1.

The half-million gallon Superpool is a hub of activity, both in and out of the water. In: swimming (there's a lap lane), water basketball and water volleyball. Out: ping-pong, live bands and snacking. There's a tots' playground too, but it's so small you might miss it.

Saddlebrook's many lakes are filled with bass and bream, and the resort can arrange sailing or deep-sea fishing excursions in the Gulf.

The fitness center includes a nautilus workout room, plus sauna, steamroom and whirlpool. Aerobics programs are available, and the Health Services staff can give you a complete fitness makeover, which includes fitness analysis and training tips, a nutrition profile, a computerized wellness appraisal and tips on stress management.

FAMILY FUN

Sports is the basic medium for family fun at Saddlebrook. You can also rent bicycles, and the summer themed weekends may be something older kids will enjoy. In June, there's a Western hoedown with square dancing at poolside. In July, Saddlebrook goes Hawaiian; you can do the limbo, watch a fire dancer or take a hula lesson. August is Summer Safari month; activities include scavenger hunts, campfires and nature walks.

KIDS' PROGRAMS

Saddlebrook's children's recreation program is not quite as extensive as other resort programs reviewed in this chapter, and the age range (6-12) is narrower. (Children under 6 can be watched by a private sitter, which you arrange through housekeeping.) The rec program operates five days a week (Wednesday-Sunday), but there's a special Friday night Movie Madness session (7 p.m.-midnight) in the Centre Club where you check in.

WHERE TO EAT

At the resort

Located next to the tennis/golf pro shops, the Little Club sounds like a snack bar. But it's a full-service restaurant/bar with nice atmosphere. We ate dinner there and recommend the New York-cut sirloin with bernaise sauce. The Little Club Patio serves outdoor breakfasts and lunches. The Cypress Room is a good choice if your kids enjoy a grownup meal now and then. Specialties here include pasta and fresh Florida seafood.

Off property

Tampa offers lots of family dining choices, and one of the best places to start is the Harbour Island Market, a waterfront complex featuring food, shopping and entertainment. It's located on Harbour Island in Tampa Bay directly across from downtown Tampa. Take Franklin Street south and you can't miss it.

Bern's Steak House is famous for its steaks, but the superlatives don't stop there. The wine list is endless, and there are 42 dessert rooms where you can enjoy sublime post-meal treats (1208 S. Howard Ave., 813-251-2421).

SHOPPING/NEARBY FUN

Tampa offers lots of shopping opportunities. **Olde Hyde Park Village** is the place to go for upscale shopping and fine dining (712 S. Oregon Ave., 813-251-3500).

Ybor Square is located in a converted cigar store which has been transformed into a unique specialty mall (1901 13th St., in the heart of Tampa's historic **Latin Quarter,** 813-247-4497).

The Shops on Harbor Island are particularly dazzling when lit up at night (601 S. Harbor Island Blvd., 813-228-7807).

If you visit Saddlebrook in March, that's the height of **Major League Baseball's spring training** season and nine Major League teams are head-quartered within easy driving distance. Those teams include the Boston Red Sox in Winter Haven (813-293-3900), the Baltimore Orioles and Chicago White Sox in Sarasota (813-365-0753/813-953-3388), the Cincinnati Reds in Plant City (813-752-7337), the Detroit Tigers in Lakeland (813-682-1401), the Philadelphia Phillies in Clearwater (813-442-8496), the Pittsburgh Pirates in Bradenton (813-748-4610), the St. Louis Cardinals in St. Petersburg (813-894-4773) and the Toronto Blue Jays in Dunedin (813-733-0429).

A lot of families vacation in August, and that's **pre-season NFL football** time for the Tampa Bay Buccaneers (813-879-BUCS). College football's Hall of Fame Bowl is usually played on New Year's Day (813-874-BOWL).

The **Senior PGA tour** (Lee Trevino, Arnold Palmer, Chi Chi Rodriguez) makes a winter tour stop in Tampa. The **GTE Suncoast Classic** is played at the Tampa Palms and Country Club (813-971-1726).

The Tampa Bay Rowdies play their **North American Soccer League** games from April through August at Tampa Stadium (813-877-7800).

For information on **Busch Gardens/The Dark Continent,** see the THEME PARKS chapter—where you'll also find several other fun things to do in the "Nearby Fun" section. For information on **Adventure Island,** see the "Best of the Rest" section in WATERPARKS.

For more information, contact: Tampa/Hillsborough Convention & Visitors Assoc., 111 Madison St., Suite 1010, Tampa, FL 33602-4706, 813-223-1111 or 800-826-8358).

WHEN TO GO

Saddlebrook's high season runs from January 15 to April 30. Rates are slightly lower from May 1-25 and from September 16 to January 14. Summer rates (roughly half-price) are in effect from May 25 to September 15, and that's our recommendation.

FOR MORE INFORMATION

Contact:

Saddlebrook Golf and Tennis Resort
100 Saddlebrook Way, Wesley Chapel, FL. 34249
(813-973-1111 or 800-729-8383)

SOUTH SEAS PLANTATION

South Seas Plantation is located on the northern tip of Captiva Island, a tiny, four-mile stretch of sand near Fort Myers on Florida's Gulf Coast. The 330-acre resort opened in 1972 and is known for its tranquility, its beautiful flora and its water sports.

ABOUT THE RESORT

TV personality Willard Scott narrates the in-house TV tour of South Seas Plantation, noting that a visit to this Gulf Coast hideaway is "a chance to take off your watch, put it in your pocket and do things on island time."

Scott ought to know because he and his family have been vacationing on Captiva Island for more than 20 years. And while South Seas is a little hard to get to—the drive from Fort Myers took us 45 minutes—that also accounts for the quiet, leisurely pace of life. Hence the phrase "island time."

"Even when we're full, you can't tell anybody's here," says Suzanne Willis, who vacationed at South Seas as a kid and later went to work in the resort's PR office. "You look down the beach and you hardly see anyone."

Like Amelia Island, Captiva Island was once a sanctuary for pirates. During the late 1700s and early 1800s, these buccaneers are said to have harbored their ships in the island's many coves and hidden bays. The name, Captiva, apparently came about because a pirate named José Gaspar kept his captives on the island.

In 1900, Clarence Chadwick, inventor of the checkwriting machine, acquired all of Captiva and the north end of its larger neighbor, Sanibel Island. Chadwick turned Captiva into a key lime plantation. But in the 1920s, a hurricane destroyed most of the buildings and dumped so much salt water on the land that growing limes was out of the question. Coconuts were grown here for a time, and the island was accessible only by boat until 1962. With the completion of the Sanibel Causeway in 1968, cars gained free and easy access to the island for the first time; South Seas opened four years later.

Unless you're leaving the island to visit Sanibel or Fort Myers, you can get along very nicely without your car. For one thing, South Seas is small enough that you can walk to a lot of places. Another pleasant way to get around is to hop on one of the resort's trolleys; catch them at regular stops or just flag one down.

The island's one main roadway is lined with natural vegetation which is so thick and green it obscures your view of the bay and the Gulf. However, the coconut palms and mangrove swamps provide little tree cover and shade—which gives South Seas a different look than Amelia Island Plantation.

ACCOMMODATIONS

South Seas celebrated its 15th anniversary in 1987, and since then most guest villas have been refurbished. The resort has 600 lodging units and no building is more than three stories high.

Perched on the northern tip of the island, the Land's End villas are South Seas' most expensive/luxurious accommodations. Built in 1986, these two-bedroom suites feature wrap-around terraces, skylights and jacuzzis (some indoors, some outdoors on the deck) plus excellent views of the Gulf and of South Seas' nine-hole golf course.

Beach homes are almost as expensive as Land's End. Located on the two-mile stretch of sand between the north and south ends of the island, each cluster of two-, three- or four-bedroom homes shares a pool and tennis court.

Harbourside villas are the least expensive, but these hotel rooms—even those with two queen-sized beds—are not the way a family of four should experience South Seas.

For economy, choose from tennis or bayside villas (south end) or marina villas (north end). We stayed in the one- and two- bedroom tennis villas which overlook the tennis center near the main entrance. Built in the 1970s, the concrete landings and stairways, as well as the elevators, are a bit spartan. But the rooms are modern (we had a loft bedroom) and our third-floor porch afforded us a nice view of both the swimming pool and the courts.

You can also cut down on expenses by doing some of your own cooking; all but the Harbourside villas have kitchens.

SPORTS

South Seas has 22 tennis courts, seven at the tennis center and 15 more sprinkled throughout the island. The nine-hole golf course was closed for refurbishing when we visited in the summer of 1990 but it's finished now. Guests may also play golf at The Dunes, an 18-hole course on Sanibel Island.

South Seas has 18 fresh-water pools and one salt-water ocean. And if you're interested in chartering a boat for fishing (tarpon, snook, grouper, redfish), head for the bayside marina. That's also where you'll find Holiday Water Sports, South Seas' waterskiing center. Holiday Sports conducts waterskiing clinics for both kids and adults, and if you're brave enough to like parasailing (it's like hang-gliding except you're being pulled by a boat) Holiday's parasailing captains and crew are licensed by the Coast Guard, and there's a second location on the north end of the island adjacent to the Harbor side villas.

The Pieces of Eight Dive Center offers both full- and half-day charters. You can dive with scuba gear, go spear fishing or enjoy underwater photography. The dive center also rents equipment.

Sailboats, Hobie Cats, paddleboats, canoes, 18- to 25-foot powerboats, sunfish, windsurfers—Club Nautico will rent you almost any kind of boat you can name. You can also take sailing lessons at Steve Colgate's Offshore Sailing School, which drew rave reviews in *Sports Illustrated*. And if your kids are at least 16, they're old enough to ride jet-skis.

You also have to be 16 to use the resort's fitness center, The Island Club, which is adjacent to the children's recreation area. That's a good location because it allows parents to work out while their kids are busy. The fitness center is staffed by an exercise physiologist and features nautilus-type machines, chrome dumbbells, Air-Dyne exercise bikes and the Stairmaster 4000. Complete aerobics programs are available.

FAMILY FUN

Bingo/casino nights, crab races, ping-pong, cookouts, bonfires, nature walks and cane pole fishing are typical family activities at South Seas.

The *Fort Dearborn*, South Seas' party/excursion boat, is another source of family fun. Sign up for breakfast, lunch or dinner cruises to Cabbage Key or Useppa Island, or for sightseeing cruises to Cayo Coast (a state park) or Boca Grande island (site of some of the best tarpon fishing in the world).

Experts say neighboring Sanibel Island ranks among the top three in the world (along with Jeffreys Bay in Africa and the Sulu Islands in the Southwest Pacific) as a source of exotic shells. More than 400 species can be found here, from the common clam and sand dollar to the exotic paper fig shell and the rare brown-speckled, twisted Junonia. Shelling fever is so rampant some hunters don miner's helmets with lights and continue searching after sunset. But the best times to go scavenging are when the tide's going out or just after a storm.

KIDS' PROGRAMS

Founded in 1982, South Seas' children's recreation program is unusual in that a) it's a year-round program, and b) it offers activities for two-year-olds and teens, as well as ages in between.

▲ **Totally Two (age 2)**
One-hour story time where toddlers can bang on drum sets and feel totally secure because either Mom or Dad is there, too. One hour picnic with teddy bears and tea party sets. Mom-and-tots swim program.

▲ **Pelican Pals (ages 3-5)**
For kids who are potty trained. Activities: crafts, storytelling, shelling, swimming, puppet play, games. A snack is provided, and there's a new beachside playground adjacent to the rec center (9:30 a.m.-noon).

▲ **Captiva Kids (ages 6-8)**
Pelican Pals activities, plus picnics, crafts and sand play. Lunch is provided (9:30-2 p.m.).

▲ **Castaway Club (ages 9-12)**
Activities include bike hikes, canoeing, crafts, water fun. Lunch is provided (9:30-2 p.m.).

▲ **Tropical Adventure (ages 13-19)**
Low-key approach at work here so teens don't think they're being babied. If a counselor clicks with a group, he/she may stay with them all week. Activities: sunset parasailing, jet-skiing, snorkeling, pool parties in Fort Myers, cookouts, beach and water volleyball, casino nights (everybody wins something) and photo scavenger hunts where teens have to shoot Polaroids of pelicans, couples kissing, etc. South Seas also prides itself on having the country's top video games in its gameroom.

When South Seas kids go swimming, blow-up float animals add to the fun. When they dig in the sand, they may be looking for buried treasure. (Little kids even get to dress like pirates!) Crafts class may include making shell jewelry or tie-dyed t-shirts.

Two counselors per group is a minimum in the kids' rec program, which is busiest from February to April and June to August. Counselors are college students (or graduates) majoring in recreation; they must also be 21 or older. South Seas started the 1990s with more than 30 people on its summer rec staff; in high season, 80 kids may be enrolled in the program.

South Seas schedules special children's activities throughout the year, so check to see what's going on during your visit. The Vagabond Marionettes sometimes draw 350 kids and parents for a performance of "Pinocchio" and there are all sorts of fun things tied to holidays: The Easter bunny arrives by boat for a huge egg hunt, Santa Claus delivers stockings filled with goodies at Christmas and Mister Rogers' TV buddy, Chef Brockett, pays a Christmas visit, too.

WHERE TO EAT

At the resort

If your family visits South Seas during the summer, don't miss the "All American Family Food Fest" at Chadwick's on Wednesday nights. Part carnival, part pig-out—but in a restaurant setting—the food fest was a delight. Though they weren't included in the price of the buffet, we started with specialty drinks (golden margaritas for the adults, virgin strawberry daquiris for the kids). Then we tackled the never-ending buffet: hot dogs, pizza, chili, fish, chicken, salad, ice cream, strawberry shortcake and the kitchen sink. What makes the All American so special is that while you eat, magicians visit your table. And they're good! Even better were the guys who made balloon animals.

Cap'n Al's pub is a light and breezy spot for breakfast, lunch or dinner, and the King's Crown—once the commissary for the old Chadwick key lime plantation—is a good place for a quiet, adult dinner (jackets sometimes required).

Off property

One food critic said The Bubble Room looks like a house where the kids never picked up their toys. The walls of this labyrinthian restaurant are covered with postcards, Hollywood press photos and other cultural debris. Every table is a glass-topped shadowbox filled with old baseball cards, kewpie dolls and the like. There's even a toy train that runs along a track near the ceiling. The amount of food is just as excessive: pork chops as big as bricks and two-pound slabs of roast beef. We were wasted by dessert time, and could only nibble. Mercifully, there is a children's menu: fried fish, chicken strips, Gulf shrimp, steak patty, ravioli (15001 Captiva Rd., just outside the main entrance to South Seas, 813-472-5558—but they don't take reservations).

Both the Mucky Duck (Andy Rosse Ln., 813-472-3434) and Bellini's (11521 Andy Rosse Ln., 813-472-6866) are located just outside the entrance to the resort.

On Sanibel, Truffles features fresh seafood, salads and pasta in an island mansion setting (2255 West Gulf Dr., 813-472-9200). Another popular seafood spot is the Jacaranda Restaurant (1223 Periwinkle Way, 813-472-1771).

You might consider making the 10 a.m. to 2 p.m. *Fort Dearborn* lunch cruise to Cabbage Key, an adults-only activity. If your kids are old enough to stay for the rec program lunch, they'll be busy while you munch at the inn on Cabbage Key; Jimmy Buffett made the place semi-famous in his song, "Cheeseburger in Paradise."

SHOPPING/NEARBY FUN

We enjoyed **South Seas' Chadwick Square** shopping area, which runs the gamut from t-shirt shops to boutiques featuring unique women's casual clothing. And the prices were reasonable for a resort.

The J.N. "Ding" Darling National Wildlife Refuge (named for a conservation-minded political cartoonist) is located on Sanibel Island. The 5,000-acre animal refuge is home to some 290 species of birds, 50 types of reptiles and a variety of mammals. You can walk, drive, bike or canoe through this unspoiled land where rare and endangered species such as white pelicans, manatees and bald eagles coexist with alligators, falcons, ospreys, herons and loggerhead turtles. There's a visitor center and an observation tower. Admission is a nominal fee per car (813-472-1100).

Thomas Edison maintained a winter home in Fort Myers, where he worked on the phonograph, teletype and other inventions. He also had a green thumb, collecting thousands of species of plants from all over the world. The home and gardens are now a museum (2350 McGregor Blvd., 813-334-3614). Next door is the newly renovated home of Edison's good friend, **Henry Ford,** who spent 29 winters here from 1916 to 1945. You can save money by purchasing a combined tour ticket for both homes (813-334-3614).

WHEN TO GO

South Seas' rates are highest during Christmas vacation; February through spring break is also expensive. Summer is the most affordable time of year, and the Gulf breezes help temper the heat. If you don't mind regular late-afternoon thunderstorms, we recommend it.

FOR MORE INFORMATION

Contact:

South Seas Plantation
South Sea Plantation Rd., Captiva, FL 33924
(813-472-5111 or 800-237-3102)

THEME PARKS
AMUSEMENT PARKS

✦ Walt Disney World

✦ Universal Studios

✦ Sea World

✦ Busch Gardens/The Dark Continent

✦ Busch Gardens/The Old Country

✦ Carowinds

✦ Dollywood

✦ King's Dominion

✦ Opryland

✦ Six Flags Over Georgia

THEME PARKS
AMUSEMENT PARKS

America's love affair with theme parks and amusement parks is more fervent than ever; 250 million people visit them annually, which is equivalent to one admission ticket for every man, woman and child in the U.S.

Those 250 million people spend $4 billion annually at some 600 parks across the U.S., and with competition fiercer than ever for tourist dollars, parks are adding new rides and attractions at a feverish clip, hoping to offer something for every taste and age group. It's hard to find a major amusement park which hasn't added one or more of the following themed attractions—water slides, dolphin/sea lion show, musical revue, wild animal safari or concert stage—to satisfy its intergenerational audience. Theme parks, meanwhile, are looking for thrill rides which will appeal to teenagers, who are apt to get restless if they have to tour too many make-believe foreign countries or sit through too many animatronic-actor attractions.

A case in point is the new flight-simulator technology which is the creative force behind four new rides you'll read about in this chapter: Body Wars (EPCOT Center), Star Tours (Disney-MGM Studios), the Funtastic World of Hanna-Barbera (Universal Studios) and Questor (Busch Gardens/The Old Country).

With so much going on in the industry and admission prices spiraling higher and higher, it's more important than ever for parents to choose a park which fits their family's interests and entertainment needs. But that can be tricky, especially for families with children of significantly different ages—because they seldom like the same rides.

With that in mind, we have written this chapter so parents can gauge which rides and attractions are suitable for young children (up to the age of 7, let's say), which have enough thrills and chills for teenagers and which are suitable for the entire family. (Given these parameters, it's up to you to decide about 8- to 12-year-olds.) When in doubt, we erred on the side of being too cautionary in our assessments. We did so even with the knowledge that today's 7-year-olds have, as a rule, seen and done more than their parents did at the same age—which means they probably have more nerve when it comes to scary rides and attractions.

But are they old enough to separate illusion from reality? That question came up when we toured the Magic Kingdom at Walt Disney World with good friends whose son, Aleks, was 6. Aleks loved Space Mountain, scary as it is to some of us adults. But his eyes widened at the Haunted Mansion, where he saw holographic images of spooks dancing madly around a dinner table. When the ride ended, Aleks took his mother's arm, looked her straight in the eye and said, "Now do you believe in ghosts?"

Speaking of traveling with another family, we highly recommend it—assuming you get along well enough to watch each other's kids. If you do, that allows each couple the freedom to go off on their own for a few brief hours of adults-only fun and sanity—which can help everybody have a better time on a theme park/amusement park vacation. Grandparents can provide the same kind of relief, provided they have the stamina and enthusiasm for this kind of trip.

We also recommend at least one adults-only dinner if you're on an extended theme park/amusement park vacation. One way to get free, if you're not traveling with friends or family, is to hire a baby-sitter. Also, many major hotels are now offering kids' programs, which frequently include evening activities. Of course, if you have teenagers, you could consider leaving them in your hotel room with pizza and a movie and instructions to keep the door locked and stay put.

> **TRAVEL TIP**
>
> With so much going on in the industry and admission prices spiraling higher and higher, it's more important than ever for parents to choose a park which fits their family's interests and entertainment needs—but that can be tricky.

Because of the kind of weather we enjoy in the Southeast, most theme park/amusement park vacations will take place when temperatures are either warm or hot. And since a lot of today's parks present ways for you to get wet—raft ride, water slides, killer whale/dolphin show—you should wear light clothing which will dry quickly. If you're staying after dark you may want to pack a sweatshirt. (We forgot and ended up spending $60 on Disney sweatshirts at EPCOT one night.) Wear comfortable shoes with good support because you're going to do a lot of walking. It's best to travel light; you'll get very tired of lugging excess paraphernalia around. But be prepared with whatever essentials you think you'll need: stroller, ponchos, etc., although most parks have those items on hand for rent or purchase.

Operating schedules quoted in this chapter are purposely general because park managers frequently change their minds. Instead of giving you dates and times which could change and thus mislead you, we strongly suggest that you call or write the park of your choice for specific information before making travel plans.

As for admission prices, you'll pay the most at Walt Disney World and Universal Studios (1991 one-day rates: $32.75 for adults, $26.40 for children at WDW and $30.74/$24.38 at Universal). Dollywood is the least expensive ($17.99 for adults, $12.99 for children). The rest of the parks profiled in this chapter fall somewhere in the middle, except for Sea World ($27 for adults, $23 for children, tax included).

This chapter begins with the five Orlando-area parks; the other seven are listed alphabetically.

Walt Disney World
Magic Kingdom

The Magic Kingdom is located 20 miles southwest of Orlando, Fla., off I-4 and U.S. 192. The park features 45 rides and attractions on a 100-acre site.

ABOUT THE PARK

Walt Disney World is the granddaddy of all theme parks. Disneyland is older, having turned 35 in 1990, but in terms of popularity, 30 million people visit WDW every year—more than twice as many as visit Disneyland. All this Central Florida tourism magic started with the first of the WDW theme parks, the Magic Kingdom, which opened on Oct. 1, 1971.

A park that old is bound to have some things that need updating; in the Magic Kingdom's case, it's Tomorrowland, which hasn't been futuristic for some time now—and which won't be for some time to come. Disney CEO Michael Eisner has announced plans for wide-scale expansion of all the WDW theme parks during the "Disney Decade" of the 1990s, but a new Tomorrowland isn't slated to open until 1996, when a George Lucas adventure, Alien Encounter, will premiere. Several new shows are in store for the Magic Kingdom before then, and the first new attraction, a Circle Vision 360 film having to do with Western culture, is slated for 1992. Disney publicity says the attraction will feature "sophisticated audio-animatronic characters" which will "disappear into the film at key points, thereby blurring the line between fantasy and reality." Splash Mountain, an elevated log flume imported from Disneyland, is scheduled to open in 1993. No date has been set for the debut of the Little Mermaid adventure ride, which will be the first addition to Fantasyland since the park opened.

The Magic Kingdom is divided into seven areas (clockwise from the main entrance): Main Street U.S.A., Adventureland, Frontierland, Liberty Square, Fantasyland, Mickey's Starland (formerly Mickey's Birthdayland) and Tomorrowland.

With the exception of Space Mountain (Tomorrowland), there are no high-voltage thrills and chills at the Magic Kingdom. On the other hand, parents with very young or easily frightened children need to be aware that Big Thunder Mountain Railroad (Frontierland) is more than just a kids' coaster. Clue to that effect: the number of teens and adults without little ones who are standing in line. And some of the so-called "baby rides" such as Snow White's Adventures and Mr. Toad's Wild Ride (Fantasyland) can be scary too because they take place in semidarkness and things jump out at you—a witch, for example. In any case, there are still lots of milder choices in Fantasyland: Peter Pan's Flight, 20,000 Leagues Under the Sea, It's A Small World, the Mad Tea Party and a carousel. Peter Pan is just plain wonderful, 20,000 Leagues isn't worth a long wait and It's a Small World has to be seen—if only for the distinctive doll clothes and the air-conditioning.

To save wear and tear on your feet, keep in mind that the Disney railroad makes stops at the main entrance, Mickey's Starland and Frontierland. You may also want to use the railroad for sightseeing; the 1.5-mile journey around the entire park takes 14 minutes. The Disney Skyway, which connects Tomorrowland and Fantasyland, is also fun if you're not afraid of heights.

If you're wondering which mode of transportation gets you from the parking lot to the Magic Kingdom faster—monorail or ferry—they both take about five minutes. We prefer the ferry because the breeze feels great and you get a terrific view of the entire Magic Kingdom area. For variety, take the monorail in the morning and ride the ferry at night, when you can stand on deck and marvel at all the lights.

Disney research shows that, on the average, Magic Kingdom guests can count on visiting no more than seven or eight attractions per day, so start out early (9 a.m. is normally when the park opens) and plan ahead so you don't end up hop-scotching from one area to another; that wastes time and it's hard on your feet.

Most people arrive at the Magic Kingdom between 9:30 and 11:30; if you're one of them, the roads approaching the Auto Plaza and the parking lot are going to be jammed. If you're visiting at spring break, Christmas or in the summer, try to arrive before 8:30 a.m. If you plan to stay until closing time at night, you'd be well-advised to leave in the middle of the day (remember to get your hand stamped!) and do something else: swim or take a nap. We've pulled lots of 13-hour marathons at Disney and without a mid-day break, we either run out of gas around 9 p.m. or can barely drag ourselves out of bed the next morning.

Please note: A one-day ticket to WDW is good for only one of the three theme parks. If you want to visit the Magic Kingdom, EPCOT Center and Disney-MGM Studios, you must buy a four- or five-day passport. And a separate admission is required for Typhoon Lagoon and River Country, the Disney water fun areas; Discovery Island, the nature area; and Pleasure Island, the nighttime entertainment area.

If for some reason you should have to leave without using up all the park days you're allotted, hang onto the ticket; it's good forever.

ABOUT THE RIDES/ATTRACTIONS
Thrills and Chills
Space Mountain
A brilliantly conceived coaster which darts and dives through its eerie blue-black world as though it were a great space serpent trying to shake off the humans who cling for dear life to its back. Years pass, but unlike the rest of Tomorrowland, Space Mountain still seems futuristic. Lines are bad, but few people—even those who aren't wild about roller coasters—come away from this 2-minute-and-38-second ride disappointed. Disney requires children to be 3 years old to ride Space Mountain, but it's hard for us to imagine any 3-year-old capable of handling this spine-rattling journey; children under 7 or less than 44 inches tall must be accompanied by an adult. One saving grace is that kids sit virtually in their parent's lap in Space Mountain's pod-shaped cars.

Haunted Mansion
The epitome of "it's fun to be scared"—from the mysterious entry room which takes you to your appointment with the after-life to the uninvited holographic spook which inhabits your ghost buggy at the end of the ride. The haunted dinner party is a classic, and Disney's imagineers somehow manage to keep the whole thing surprisingly wry and upbeat. The narrator is perfect and so are the audio-visual effects. No age/height restrictions.

The Most Fun
Big Thunder Mountain Railroad
Always a blast because of its Wild West scenery, its tight turns and its energetic, little-coaster-that-could demeanor. Height restriction: Kids must be at least 4'2".

Pirates of the Caribbean
The ship-to-shore cannon battle is imaginatively staged and so is the plundered village, where a variety of criminal acts occur on a non-stop basis. This is also a great place to seek refuge from the heat because lines form within a great hulking fortress where it's always cool.

Best Bets for the Younger Set
Peter Pan's Flight
A sentimental favorite of ours, and a cut above the rest of its Fantasyland neighbors because your mini pirate ship takes you right through Jane and Michael Banks' bedroom window and on to Never-

Never Land. The sets are splendid—particularly the moonlit London cityscape below you—and so is the music. Everyone has to grow up, but this ride will remind you what it was like to be a kid.

It's a Small World
Originally created for the 1964 New York World's Fair, Small World should, ideally, be seen shortly before you leave—otherwise, its saccharine theme song will be locked in your head for the rest of the day; some people who visited the ride in the Seventies still haven't gotten rid of it.

Jungle Cruise
The tour guides are so corny you have to laugh, and young kids won't mind that the wild animals which threaten your boat are only moderately realistic. Drawback: Lines can be an hour long, but the ride takes only 10 minutes.

Mickey's Starland
A petting zoo is a highlight of this area, where your kids can also visit Mickey's House and get their picture taken with a costumed Mickey figure.

WHERE TO EAT
Expect standard theme park food at the Magic Kingdom, which has five full-service restaurants: Tony's Town Square Cafe and the Plaza Restaurant (Main Street U.S.A.), The Diamond Horseshoe (Frontierland), the Liberty Tree Tavern (Liberty Square) and King Stefan's Banquet Hall (Fantasyland). King Stefan's is located on the second floor of Cinderella's castle, and reservations are required both there and at the Diamond Horseshoe. The Crystal Palace (Main Street U.S.A.) is a cafeteria which even serves full breakfasts. And no matter where you are in the Magic Kingdom, fast-food restaurants and refreshment stands are always handy.

NEARBY FUN
Universal Studios, Sea World and **Wet 'n Wild** are all nearby. For more information on Orlando attractions, see the CITIES and WATERPARKS chapters.

WHERE TO STAY
In 1980, Disney had seven hotels on-property, which provided roughly 4,500 rooms. Ten years later, the number of hotels had increased

to 13 and the number of rooms to more than 11,000, counting vacation villas. By 1993, Disney expects to have 18 hotels up and running, providing more than 17,000 rooms.

Here are some basic characteristics of the various on-property hotels, plus an idea of what's on the drawing board:

The largest and most affordable is the Caribbean Beach Resort (2,112 rooms).

The smallest and quietest is the Disney Inn (284 rooms), which is located between two Joe Lee-designed golf courses, the Magnolia and the Palm.

The newest are two hotels scheduled to open in late 1990, Disney's Yacht Club Resort (634 rooms) and Disney's Beach Club Resort (580 rooms), and two which opened in 1989, the Walt Disney World Dolphin (1,509 rooms) and the Walt Disney World Swan (758 rooms). The Yacht Club and Beach Club resorts share a 2.5-acre water-recreation area which includes water slides and a snorkeling lagoon.

Scheduled to open sometime in 1991 is the Port Orleans Resort (1,008 rooms); slated for 1992 is the Dixie Landings Resort (2,048 rooms), which will rival the Caribbean Beach Resort in size.

Five more resorts are in the design and development stage, based on the following themes/styles: Mediterranean/Greek islands, wilderness lodge, Wild West town, Atlantic City/circa 1900 and a luxury suite companion facility to the Contemporary Resort.

The oldest are the Contemporary Resort (1,052 rooms) and the Polynesian Resort (855 rooms).

The closest to the Magic Kingdom are the Contemporary Resort, the Polynesian Resort and the Grand Floridian Beach Resort (900 rooms); all three are just a monorail ride from the main entrance. But in being close, you pay a price; both the Contemporary Resort and the Grand Floridian bustle with people and activity. Staying there doesn't afford as much relief from the crowds as other WDW hotels or something completely off Disney property.

The most popular, according to Disney's return-visit research, is the recently remodeled Polynesian Resort; 60 percent of the guests have stayed there before.

Located at the Disney Village Plaza, near the Village Marketplace, are seven hotels which Disney doesn't own, but which are designated as "official" hotels. Guests at these hotels enjoy privileges similar to those of guests at WDW-owned hotels, including bus service to all three Disney theme parks and use of tennis and golf facilities at the Village Clubhouse. These seven hotels are: the Buena Vista Palace, Grosvenor Inn, the Hilton, Howard Johnson's Resort Hotel, Pickett Suite Resort, Hotel

Royal Plaza and Travelodge Hotel. We spent two nights at the Buena Vista Palace and we give it high marks (see "Where to Stay" in the Orlando section of the CITIES chapter).

Disney's Fort Wilderness campground nestles amidst 730 acres of pine and cypress forest and has 785 campsites for RVs and tents. More than 400 additional sites are occupied by permanent "suite-trailers" which are available for nightly rental. Every necessary convenience is provided, and the recreational perks include tennis courts, swimming pools and a nightly dinner show.

For more information on Disney-property hotels, call the WDW central reservations line (407-934-7639).

For information on where to stay off the Disney property, see "Where to Stay" in the Orlando section of the CITIES chapter.

KIDS PROGRAMS

Both the Contemporary Resort and the Grand Floridian Beach Resort feature a Mousketeer Clubhouse program for kids ages 3-9. Hours are 4:30 p.m.-midnight, seven days a week. Kids listen to records/stories, watch TV, play games and are treated to refreshments. At the Contemporary, there's a four-hour minimum stay, and reservations may be made up to 30 days in advance. The Grand Floridian has a four-hour maximum stay. The Contemporary's program can be used by any family staying on the Disney property; the Grand Floridian's is for GF hotel guests only. For more information, call 407-824-3737 (Contemporary Resort) or 407-824-2945 (Grand Floridian Resort).

The Contemporary Resort also has a Fiesta Fun Center where kids can watch Disney movies. Starting times are 7 and 9 p.m., seven nights week. Admission is nominal and children under 7 must be accompanied by a resort guest 13 or older.

The Grand Floridian also has a loosely structured afternoon program which operates during the summer. Kids play volleyball on the beach, take swim lessons, go for a ride on a float boat and play outdoor games such as horseshoes. For information, call the Grand Floridian marina (407-824-2438).

The Polynesian Resort has a Neverland Club program for kids ages 3-12. Hours are 5 p.m.-midnight, seven nights a week. Kids eat a buffet dinner (fried chicken, hot dogs, peanut butter and jelly sandwiches) between 5:30 and 8 p.m., then watch Disney movies. A bird show and a visit from a Disney character are included. There's a three-hour minimum stay, but some package deals include this service at no extra cost. And unlike the Contemporary/Grand Floridian programs, the Polynesian's is open to anyone, no matter where they're staying. For more information, call 407-824-2170.

The Polynesian also has a video game room, Moana Mickey's Fun Hut, which is open 8 a.m.-midnight.

You won't find kids' activity programs at the Caribbean Beach Resort, the Disney Inn or the Dolphin/Swan resorts. Guests at those hotels have to rely on the Contemporary and Polynesian programs. However, the new Yacht Club and and Beach Club resorts are expected to have their own kids' programs.

Fort Wilderness doesn't have a kids' activities program per se, but there's lots for kids to do there, including evening canoe trips and marshmallow roasts (ages 3 and over), horseback riding, pony rides (ages 2 and over) and hay rides. A great source of family fun is the nightly Hoop-Dee-Doo "western vaudeville dinner show." Seatings are at 5, 7:30 and 10 p.m. For more information, call 407-824-2900.

If all you need is baby-sitting, Disney has an arrangement with KinderCare, which will provide in-room sitting—or you can drop off your kids at either of two nearby KinderCare locations (407-827-5444).

Another kids' program worth investigating is "Disney's Wonders of the World," which is tied to the theme parks. This program offers classes in either art, entertainment/show-biz magic or nature for ages 10-15. When we went to press, the cost for each of the three classes was $75. The art class is offered 8:45 a.m.-2:45 p.m., Monday, Wednesday and Friday, and the $75 includes books, materials, lunch and admission to Disney/MGM Studios, where kids take the Disney animation tour, talk to Disney animators and learn to draw Disney characters. The entertainment/show-biz magic class is offered 9:30 a.m.-3:30 p.m., Monday-Thursday. It includes tours of both Disney/MGM and the Magic Kingdom; kids visit the MGM makeup, wardrobe and wig departments. The nature class is offered 8:45 a.m.-2:45 p.m., Tuesday and Thursday. It includes a tour of the Living Seas pavilion at EPCOT and visits to both Discovery Island zoological park and Disney's nature preserve on Highway 192.

WHEN TO GO

The Magic Kingdom is open 365 days a year. Specials include annual passes. And here are Disney's suggestions for park visitation strategy:

Most Crowded

Avoid Mondays, Tuesdays and Wednesdays because—with the exception of holidays and holiday weekends—those are the most crowded days of the week at all three Disney theme parks. The most crowded times of the year are mid-February (President's Week), the second and third weeks of April (spring break), the second week of June through the third week of August (summer vacation) and Christmas break through New Year's Day.

At peak times (11 a.m. to 5 p.m.) on busy days, the following attractions may not be so packed: Walt Disney World Railroad and Main Street Cinema (Main Street U.S.A.), Pirates of the Caribbean (Adventureland), Liberty Square Riverboats (Liberty Square), all of Tomorrowland except Space Mountain and the Grand Prix Raceway, and It's a Small World (Fantasyland).

Least Crowded

Sunday morning is the least crowded time of the week and Fridays are a close second. The least crowded times of the year are the second week of January through the first week of February, the week after Labor Day until Thanksgiving, and the week after Thanksgiving through the week before Christmas.

And remember, occasionally—during busy periods—Disney parks may open early and/or close later than scheduled. Call 407-824-4321 for up-to-date information.

FOR MORE INFORMATION

Contact:

Walt Disney World
PO Box 10,040, Lake Buena Vista, FL 32830-0040
(407-824-4321)

Walt Disney World
EPCOT Center

EPCOT Center is located 20 miles southwest of Orlando, Fla., off I-4 and U.S. 192. The park, which Disney terms an "international exposition," covers 260 acres.

ABOUT THE PARK

EPCOT Center debuted on Oct. 1, 1982—11 years to the day after the Magic Kingdom opened its gates. And, in many ways, it's a magic kingdom for adults. Which is not to say that kids won't find things to like at EPCOT—in particular, the new Wonders of Life pavilion. But the park has only two rides (Body Wars and Maelstrom) and its two principal areas—Future World, which focuses on science and technology, and World Showcase, which features international culture—are more attuned to adult tastes.

EPCOT was conceived back in the 1950s by Walt Disney, who envisioned it as a "community of tomorrow which will never be completed, but will always be introducing and testing and demonstrating new materials and systems." Hence, the acronym, EPCOT, which stands for "Experimental Prototype Community of Tomorrow." What has evolved from Walt Disney's noble vision is something less, sad to say. Some say EPCOT is a paean to industry and technology—past and present, primarily—and to an international brotherhood of nations which may or may not exist. But so are World's Fairs, which is what EPCOT is patterned after. If nothing else, EPCOT makes us feel good and reminds us that almost anything is possible—if we set our hearts and minds to it.

Future World is an oval-shaped area divided into eight large pavilions, each one devoted to a specific sphere of human life; all but two are sponsored by an American industrial giant which does business in that sphere. The Future World skyline is dominated by the distinctive 171-foot silver geosphere of Spaceship Earth (information, AT&T). The other seven pavilions are (clockwise from Spaceship Earth): Universe of Energy (Exxon), Wonders of Life (Met Life insurance), Horizons (technology/General Electric), World of Motion (General Motors), Journey into Imagination (no sponsor), The Land (foodstuffs/Kraft) and The Living Seas (no sponsor). Lines tend to move quickly at all but Spaceship Earth, mainly because it's the first pavilion you come to when you enter the park; that huge silver dome just looks so extraordinary, people can't wait to see what's inside. Actually, all eight pavilions are interesting enough to visit over and over again, so avoid Spaceship Earth if the lines are long and see what else Future World has to offer. Try Spaceship Earth again late in the day and you can probably walk right in.

We advise doing all of Future World with your kids, plus two stops at the World Showcase: They'll enjoy the Maelstrom ride at the Norway pavilion, and you may want to do some souvenir shopping with them at Mexico. But we recommend doing the rest of World Showcase without them. You'll want to linger in the shops (Morocco's jewelry is particularly interesting) and enjoy the movies at the French, Chinese and Canadian pavilions; chances are, they won't. So if you can make other arrangements such as grandparents or traveling companions, do it.

At the World Showcase, 11 different countries have seemingly been transported to EPCOT's lagoon area. The countries are: Mexico, Norway, China, Germany, Italy, United States, Japan, Morocco, France, United Kingdom and Canada. Of course, these 11 countries are presented in condensed, set-like form—an entire nation's architecture, culture and people reduced to an area about the size of a city block. Too much of that small area is allotted to shopping, but the look is right—in part because scaled-down replicas of the Eiffel Tower, a Mayan temple and a Japanese pagoda give the World Showcase the proper backdrop. It is possible, however, to learn more about France, China and Canada by viewing the films which are presented at those pavilions.

Impressions de France is shown in a beautiful, ornate theater, and the film is lush and romantic, owing to gorgeous photography and the timeless music of Debussy and other French masters. (On your way out of the theater, stop for French pastry at Au Petit Cafe.) Both *O Canada!* and *Wonders of China* have a majestic sweep to them because they're presented in Circle Vision 360, which makes you feel like you're part of the film. It can also make you a bit dizzy, and our kids (yes, we took them— once) fussed at us about it. They ended up sitting/lying on the floor of the stand-up theaters throughout the films, each of which lasts about 20 minutes. The U.S. pavilion also has a multimedia show, *The American Adventure*, which uses animatronic narrators—Ben Franklin and Mark Twain—and a 72-foot rear projection screen to "celebrate the American spirit."

The Disney Decade will bring about several changes at EPCOT, beginning in 1992 when six of the eight Future World pavilions— excluding Living Seas and the newest member of the group, Wonders of Life—will be added to or enhanced. Premiering by 1994 will be a new 3-D musical movie from George Lucas and Walt Disney Studios; the end product should be reminiscent of the popular *Captain EO*, starring Michael Jackson, which you and your kids should see when you visit Journey into Imagination. And sometime during the 1990s, Future World will welcome its ninth pavilion, Journeys in Space, which will provide visitors with the ultimate thrill ride: an outer space travel experience.

The big news at the World Showcase is that a new Soviet Union pavilion is expected sometime during the 1990s. There will also be a new Switzerland pavilion and along with it, a second World Showcase ride kids will love: a Matterhorn bobsled ride.

Be advised that the promenade which extends around the EPCOT lagoon measures 1.3 miles, so you may want to catch a ride on a double-decker bus or take an air-conditioned water taxi across the lagoon— which is the size of 85 football fields. But do it to save energy; unless you happen upon one that has space and is about to depart, they won't save you time.

Disney research shows that, on the average, EPCOT visitors can count on seeing five pavilions per day; to improve on that stat, tour as much of Future World as you can before 11 a.m. and again in the evening, keeping in mind that the most popular pavilions are Spaceship Earth and the World of Energy. Your best chance to beat the crowds may be at the World of Motion. When Future World is bursting with people, we switch to the World Showcase where China is usually the most popular pavilion. The movie lines at France and Canada are generally manageable, and you can always peruse the shops at any of the 11 pavilions.

ABOUT THE RIDES/ATTRACTIONS
Thrills and Chills
Body Wars
Located in Future World, this Wonders of Life pavilion ride utilizes flight-simulator technology to make you feel as though you're part of a miniaturized medical team which must take a trip inside the body on an emergency mission against infection. What makes the ride such a rollicking good time is that your seat is computer-synchronized to move in concert with the 3-D graphics on a movie screen in front of you. When the medical team's vehicle dives into the lungs, your vehicle feels like it's diving too (although you don't really go anywhere). Restrictions and words of caution: Pregnant women and children under 3 are not allowed to board, children under 7 must be accompanied by an adult and anyone who suffers from motion sickness should avoid this ride.

Maelstrom
This Viking vessel ride, located in the Norway pavilion at the World Showcase, uses miniature sets and terrific special effects to show how dependent Norway is on the sea. The ride is cool, slightly wet and exciting

enough to do several times— particularly just before closing time when the lines are short.

The Most Fun
World of Energy
This Future World pavilion features animatronic dinosaurs which are awe-inspiring—particularly the first time you see them. These prehistoric beasts are breathtakingly large and their surroundings are dank and creepy. Part of the fun is the way the theater comes apart in sections and transforms itself into moveable cars.

Captain EO
Michael Jackson plays an outer-space hero in this Journey into Imagination film in Future World. His assignment: revive a planet rendered lifeless by an evil sorceress (played by Academy Award winner Angelica Huston). The Gloved One performs this herculean feat through music and dance. The plot may sound hokey, but the 3-D effects put the action right in your lap.

Best Bets for the Younger Set
Journey into Imagination
This Future World pavilion explores how our imagination works, and does it in a way which is both fanciful and appropriately difficult to describe. Your guide is Dreamfinder, a red-bearded professor of imagination who is assisted by a purple dragon named Figment. Your journey is 100 percent fun and so is the Image Works, an interactive play area where your kids can easily spend another 30 minutes.

Wonders of Life
This $100 million Future World pavilion offers an assortment of unique activities and attractions for kids. Right outside the theater where *The Making of Me* is playing (see "Added Attractions"), you'll find a physical fitness area where kids can peddle Wondercycles which, according to the video screen in front of them, seem to be taking them through a crowded street scene at either Disneyland or the Tournament of Roses parade. There's also a "Coaches' Corner" where kids can take a whack at a baseball, golf ball or tennis ball. Then, through a little Disney magic, the appropriate sports expert—Gary Carter, Nancy Lopez or Chris Evert—appears on an overhead monitor to analyze the young athlete's technique and tell them what they need to work on to get better. Don't leave without seeing *Cranium Command*, a humorous film about a day in the life of a 12-year-old boy—as seen from inside his head and body. That's Charles

Grodin as "logic," Bobcat Goldthwaite as "adrenalin" and George Wendt (Norm on "Cheers") as—what else?—the boy's stomach.

ADDED ATTRACTIONS

A mini-controversy surrounded the opening of *The Making of Me* at the Wonders of Life pavilion; some people felt it was improper for a "sex education" film to be offered at a Disney theme park. But be assured that this is an extremely tame and tender approach to the birds and the bees. The plot line focuses on the generational aspect of families—how kids grow up to be parents, who then have kids of their own.

Actor Martin Short's witty narration is obviously intended to keep both parents and their kids at ease during the semi-frank discussion and subtle depiction of how babies are made. For the record, the most we see is a mom and a dad (wearing a nightgown and pajamas) embracing in bed, at which point the film cuts back to Short—who is sitting on the roof of his mom and dad's house on the night he's conceived. As for the actual act of conception, Short describes it as a "great, grand secret that we share as human beings." Mixing elements of *Back to the Future* and *It's a Wonderful Life*, *The Making of Me* is warm-hearted and well-intentioned. Helpful hint: Take kleenex.

If you can avoid it, don't leave EPCOT early; if you do, you'll miss "IllumiNations," the music, laser-graphics and fireworks show which brings down the house every night at closing time (10 p.m. is the usual hour, but be sure to check.) The proper strategy here is to stake out a place to sit at the edge of the EPCOT lagoon well ahead of time. "IllumiNations" begins with the exterior lights of all 11 international pavilions going dark. Then, one by one, they light up again as a superb outdoor stereo system provides music indigenous to that country—for example, the "1812 Overture" for France, "Rhapsody in Blue" for the U.S. After every pavilion is lit, rooftop lasers go nuts, fireworks erupt and the music soars. Watching IllumiNations creates a feeling similar to what you feel when you watch the closing ceremonies of the Olympics: Why can't the world be this joyous?

WHERE TO EAT

EPCOT offers almost too many choices of where to eat—at all prices and all levels of food and service.

Future World (*All ages*)

Dining in Future World is well-suited to families because it's all American food, the quality is consistent and both of the full-service restaurants have things for kids to look at which will help keep them amused. Future World's fast-food spots are all above average: Sunrise Terrace (CommuniCore West), Farmer's Market (The Land), Odyssey (Future World/World Showcase intersection, near the Mexican pavilion) and Stargate (CommuniCore East). For full-service dinners, try the Land Grille Room (The Land) or the Coral Reef Restaurant (Living Seas). The Land Grille is a handsome, wood-trimmed restaurant which revolves, providing customers with a nice view of the "Listen to the Land" boat ride below. The Coral Reef is constructed on several different tiers so all diners have a panoramic view of the coral reef aquarium, which is protected by eight-inch-thick glass.

World Showcase *(With kids)*

Our favorite IllumiNations perch is a lagoon-side table at Cantina de San Angel, a fast-Mex eatery outside the Mexican pavilion. The food (soft tortillas, tostados, refried beans) is just average, but it tastes pretty good after a long day of hoofing it around the park. There's also Dos Equis on tap, plus the flan and the churros (a sugared Mexican doughnut) make delicious desserts. World Showcase has two more ethnic fast-food spots: Yakitori House (Japan) and Lotus Blossom Cafe (China), plus the Liberty Inn (U.S.) which most American kids will favor because it serves burgers, hot dogs, chili and fries. LeCellier (Canada) offers Canadian-style food in a cafeteria setting. Kringla Bakeri og Kafe (Norway) serves open-faced sandwiches topped with smoked salmon, beef or ham.

If you want to take your kids to one of the 11 World Showcase full-service restaurants, we recommend the Mitsukoshi Restaurant (Japan), a Benihana-like establishment where the entire family can enjoy watching the meal prepared on their tableside grill. Depending on your kids' taste in food and their ability to sit still while you wait a considerable length of time for your food, the L'Originale Alfredo di Roma Ristorante (Italy) is a possibility for lunch. The speciality here—as it is at the restaurant of the same name in Rome—is fettucine Alfredo, and the portions are so huge and rich that two people can easily share one order.

(Adults only)

The problem with taking kids to eat in the World Showcase is that it's mostly ethnic food, which they probably won't be enthusiastic about. So why not try for at least one adults-only dinner while you're at EPCOT? We suggest you make it French. The Chefs de France (France) seems like a logical choice because the continental menu is so varied. But some parents bring tired kids to this haute cuisine restaurant; late in the meal, those tired kids become unhappy kids. As a result, Chefs de France can be a bit loud (the EPCOT brochure calls it "bustling") and not nearly as intimate as it needs to be, given the day you've had and the tab you're about to pay. As an alternative, consider the Bistro de Paris upstairs. The traditional bistro menu (filet of grouper, chicken breast in puff pastry, braised beef) is created by the same trio of award-winning chefs responsible for the food downstairs, and the atmosphere is more intimate.

Please note: To eat lunch or dinner at any of Epcot's full-service restaurants, you must make reservations first thing that morning. To do so, you need to speak to a reservation attendant, whose face will appear on one of the WorldKey Information System screens at the Disney Earth Station near Spaceship Earth. Preferred seating times for dinner (5:30 to 7:30 p.m.) are usually booked by 10 a.m., so get to EPCOT when the park opens (9 a.m., ordinarily) so you have a shot at your first or second choice. Guests staying at Disney-owned hotels or at hotels in Disney Village Plaza have an advantage in that they can make reservations two days in advance by simply picking up their room phone.

NEARBY FUN

Universal Studios, Sea World and **Wet 'n Wild** are all nearby. For more information on Orlando attractions, see the CITIES and WATER-PARKS chapters.

WHERE TO STAY

For information on Disney hotels, see "Where to Stay" in the Magic Kingdom section of this chapter. For more information on Orlando lodging, see "Where to Stay" in the CITIES chapter.

WHEN TO GO

EPCOT Center is open 365 days a year. Specials include annual passes. For information on what days of the week and times of the year are the busiest/least crowded, see "When to Go" in the Magic Kingdom section of this chapter.

FOR MORE INFORMATION

Contact:
 Walt Disney World
 PO Box 10,040, Lake Buena Vista, Fla., 32830-0040
 (407-824-4321)

WALT DISNEY WORLD MGM STUDIOS

The Disney-MGM Studios is located 20 miles southwest of Orlando, Fla., off I-4 and U.S. 192.

ABOUT THE PARK

MGM Studios occupies 135 acres, one-third the size of its cross-town competitor, Universal Studios. And with a price tag of $300 million, MGM cost less than half to build. And that, in a nutshell, is the difference between the two movie theme parks. MGM, which opened in May 1989, started much smaller than Universal. But the Disney Decade of the 1990s will change that.

If all goes according to plan, MGM will have 16 new shows and attractions in place by 1995, thereby doubling the park's offerings. The shows will include a revival of the TV game show, "Let's Make A Deal," a pair of Muppets shows, a Dick Tracy musical revue and Disney Channel Auditions, where the best singer, dancer and actor selected from the audience that day will be shown performing (on tape) on cable TV's Disney Channel.

Star Tours, a sensational flight-simulator ride, premiered in January 1990. Other attractions expected by 1995 include: a *Honey, I Shrunk the Kids* adventure (Christmas 1990), a Muppets 3-D experience (1991) and a nighttime musical spectacular from the creative genius of Andrew Lloyd Webber (1992). New attractions for which no completion date has been set include a Muppets movie ride and an entire new MGM area, Sunset Boulevard, which will be home to Roger Rabbit and Dick Tracy adventures.

When these future attractions are in place, MGM will be too much park to do comfortably in one day—just as Universal is now. As is, MGM is still a full day of fun. The park is divided into five areas: Hollywood Boulevard, Lakeside Circle, Backstage Annex, Backstage Studio Tour and Studio Courtyard.

MGM has a twin focus: to make you laugh and to supply a generous dose of movie-buff nostalgia. Unfortunately, most kids aren't old enough to appreciate what they're seeing. For example, after we got off the Great Movie Ride, our daughter said to her grandmother, "You should've seen this man [Gene Kelly] singing in the rain!"

And that will continue to be a problem because until attractions like *Honey I Shrunk the Kids* are operational, there won't be anything at MGM which is specifically designed for kids. Teens face a similar situation:

MGM has only two attractions— Star Tours (Backlot Annex) and Catastrophe Canyon (Backstage Studio Tour)—which will quicken their pulse.

ABOUT THE RIDES/ATTRACTIONS
Thrills and Chills
Star Tours

    Drawing on the imagination and wizardry of George Lucas, Industrial Light & Magic and Disney Imagineers, this flight- simulator ride doesn't need tracks, wheels or rocket engines to convince you that you're piloting a StarSpeeder bound for the moon of Endor. As a matter of fact, you don't even make it out of the space hangar before your equilibrium goes and you begin feeling the physical effects of flight. How did Lucas & Co. do it? By synchronizing the helter-skelter movements of your 40-passenger ship (which, in reality, never goes anywhere) with the computer-generated 3-D space scenario being played out in front of you on a movie screen. Adding to the mystique of this ride is the "Star Wars" giant walker out front and the talking droids you encounter while waiting in line. Best moments: When you get to make the same Death Star bombing run that Luke Skywalker made in the movie. Restrictions and words of caution: See "Body Wars" in the EPCOT section of this chapter.

The Most Fun
The Great Movie Ride

    If this ride went on all day, it would still be too short. You board a tour boat in Hollywood and are transported back in time to some of the most famous moments in motion picture history —with terrific sets and animatronic robots impersonating the real stars with remarkable success. You're there when the Munchkins sing their opening song from *The Wizard of Oz*, when Bogie makes his classic farewell speech to Ingrid Bergman at the airport in *Casablanca* and (Prepare young children!) when the creature from *Alien* descends from the innards of Sigourney Weaver's spaceship. Even if they're not familiar with *Singing in the Rain*, kids will like the special effects that MGM has built into this ride, including a dynamite Western gun battle— and you're caught in the middle! Due to the popularity of this ride, do it first thing in the morning before the hour-long lines form or try it again when the lines have disappeared shortly before closing.

Backstage Studio Tour

    This two-part tour takes about two hours to complete, but the second half is at your own pace. You start out on a tram looking at the costume and scene shops used in MGM's TV and movie productions. You visit a make-believe residential street where the "Golden Girls" home exteriors are shot and you look at famous movie props along the way. Oh, yes, there is that stop at Catastrophe Canyon (Prepare young children!), where a natural disaster seemingly puts your lives in jeopardy. But only for a minute or two. Then it recedes and all signs that it happened disappear. Who's pulling the strings? Your guide will explain it all to you, including the part where 70,000 gallons of water are recycled in 3 1/2 minutes. Next comes the walking phase of the tour, which includes a look at how ocean disasters are filmed and something young children will really like: a demonstration (using two kids from the audience) of how optical effects were used to create those memorable illusions of kids riding a giant bee across the backyard in *Honey, I Shrunk the Kids*.

Best Bet for the Younger Set
Indiana Jones Epic Stunt Spectacular
This attraction begins with a re-creation of the opening scene from *Raiders of the Lost Ark* with an Indiana Jones lookalike trying to escape being squashed by a giant boulder. From there, the action proceeds through other stunt-laden moments from Raiders, including a fiery sequence involving a real airplane. Exciting? You bet. There's even a stuntwoman who keeps up with Indy at every turn. If possible, see this show at night—it's even more dramatic then. If you do it during the day, buy ice cream or a cold drink before getting in line because it's usually a long wait and there's no protection from the sun.

ADDED ATTRACTIONS
"Superstar Television" and "The Monster Sound Show" use audience volunteers and both are totally silly fun. "Superstar Television" puts kids and adults in appropriate costumes and then combines TV-show footage with live camera shots, so the volunteer appears to be impersonating Gilligan on "Gilligan's Island" or playing opposite Lucille Ball in that famous conveyor belt scene from "I Love Lucy." The sound show utilizes a film clip from a mock-horror movie starring Chevy Chase to show how studio-produced sound effects (howling wind, ominous footsteps, broken glass) can enhance a visual image—or spoil it, which is what generally happens when volunteers from the audience try to add the sound effects themselves.

If you're interested in attending a taping/filming of a TV show or movie, call or visit the Production Information Window at the main entrance to MGM. We did, and our kids got to be in the audience for a taping of "The Mickey Mouse Club," which, believe it or not, took four hours.

WHERE TO EAT

We found the Backlot Express (Backlot Annex) next to Indiana Jones to be a convenient stop for lunch. The food (burgers, chef salad, fruit cup) was decent, the portions were sizable and you can eat indoors or out. For a late afternoon snack, we stopped at the Catwalk Bar (Studio Courtyard) on the mezzanine level above the Plaza Hotel set of Big Business. The appetizers were just so-so, but the specialty fruit drinks (which you can order with or without alcohol) were refreshing. And it's a peaceful, out-of-the-way spot. If you're looking for a unique dinner experience, try the 50's Prime Time Cafe (Lakeside Circle) or at least stop by for a laugh. Every table is situated in a tacky, plastic-laminated kitchen of the Fifties. To enhance the effect, every seat has a clear view of a black-and-white TV with a Fifties sitcom (each episode is related to food) on the screen. The menu is also appropriately themed, featuring alphabet soup, meat loaf and chicken pot pie. MGM's fancy sit-down restaurant is the Hollywood Brown Derby (Hollywood Boulevard), which features steaks, seafood and pasta. The Brown Derby's specialty is Cobb salad, a mixture of salad greens, bacon, tomato, turkey, egg, bleu cheese, avocado and your choice of shrimp or lobster. Unfortunately, this concoction is so finely chopped that it's difficult to find either the shrimp or the lobster. A better choice at half the price is the barbecued pork sandwich with avocado and mushroom salad. You can get sandwiches, snacks, ice cream and soft drinks at snack bars throughout the park. The popcorn stands are particularly hard to pass up.

NEARBY FUN

Universal Studios, Sea World and **Wet 'n Wild** are all nearby. For more information on Orlando attractions, see the CITIES and WATER-PARKS chapters.

WHERE TO STAY

For information on Disney hotels, see "Where to Stay" in the Magic Kingdom section of this chapter. For more information on Orlando lodging, see the CITIES chapter.

WHEN TO GO

The Disney-MGM Studio Tour is open 365 days a year. Specials include annual passes. For information on what days of the week and times of the year are the busiest/least crowded, see "When to Go" in the Magic Kingdom section of this chapter.

FOR MORE INFORMATION

Contact:

Walt Disney World
PO Box 10,040, Lake Buena Vista, FL 32830-0040
(407-824-4321)

UNIVERSAL STUDIOS

Universal Studios is located 10 miles southwest of Orlando, Fla., near the intersection of I-4 and the Florida Turnpike (exit 30-B off I-4).

ABOUT THE PARK

It's about time a new mega-theme park came along to give Disney a run for America's entertainment dollars, and while Universal Studios Florida isn't about to challenge Walt Disney World for the top spot in national theme park attendance (see note), at least there's another choice out there—and a mighty good one.

Universal Studios Florida covers 444 acres and cost $630 million to build. It features five movie-themed attractions and eight live shows, plus the Universal backlot, which is home to the largest motion picture studio outside Hollywood.

Universal got off to an inauspicious start at its official opening on June 7, 1990, when two of its heavyweight attractions (Jaws, Earthquake) were unable to answer the opening bell. A third, Kongfrontation, was shown only to the media and celebrities such as Bill Cosby. All three attractions suffered significant down time due to malfunctions over the first several months. Kongfrontation's problems were in its computer network, and technical problems got so bad on Jaws and Earthquake that Universal sued the California company that built the rides. By the fall of 1990, Kongfrontation and Earthquake were working, but Jaws was shut down for re-engineering. Universal weathered the PR storm by handing out free return passes to anyone who bought a full-price ticket when the park wasn't biting, quaking and pounding its chest the way it should have been.

NOTE

Industry attendance figures show Disney World with a huge lead over its competitors in the amusement/theme park business. WDW drew roughly 30 million people in 1989, with Disneyland finishing second at 14.4 million. Universal Studios Hollywood was a distant third (5 million) and initial projections say Universal Studios Florida will perform similarly at the box office. Two Southeast attractions, Sea World of Florida (3.96 million) and Busch Gardens/The Dark Continent (3.5 million) also made the top 10.

Even with those problems, our family really went for Universal in a big way—especially our kids, who loved the rides/attractions and were thrilled to be able to attend a taping of one of their favorite cable TV shows, "Family Double Dare," part of the Nickelodeon network which is in production 365 days a year on Universal's backlot (see "Added Attractions" in this section).

Universal is divided into six areas (Front Lot, Now Shooting, Production Central, Hollywood, On Location and Cinemagic Center) and it's so new and so popular that even experienced park-goers like us couldn't figure out a way to avoid the problem of long lines. Even the usual trick of waiting until near-closing time to try the most popular attractions didn't work; the lines at "Alfred Hitchcock: The Art of Making Movies" remained long round the clock.

The park could use some kind of ground transportation to help people get around because Universal is a BIG place. It took us 13 hours to tour this park, and that's not including Jaws, Earthquake and Kongfrontation, none of which was working the first time we visited.

Families with younger children currently face the same problem at Universal that they do at MGM: With the exception of the Animal Actors Stage (Cinemagic Center), nothing is specifically geared toward them. But the E.T. Adventure (Cinemagic Center) is an all-ages attraction, and Back to the Future—scheduled to open sometime in 1991—will be, too. Because it mixes humor with the supernatural, Ghostbusters (Production Central) may also be suitable for some little ones. The Funtastic World of Hanna-Barbera (Now Shooting) has a marvelous indoor play area, but you can't get to it without standing in long lines for the ultra-exciting H-B flight- simulator ride.

Families with teenagers can't go wrong at Universal no matter what they do. Assuming they're working, Kongfrontation (Production Central), Earthquake and Jaws (On Location) should be the highest priorities, but don't even think about missing Hanna-Barbera.

Universal has a few other attractions which need improving besides The Big Three:

The *Ghostbusters'* set is well-done and so are the holographic effects which cause a gaggle of ectoplasmic ghouls to appear out of nowhere and do battle with the Who-ya-gonna-call? crew. But the mikes weren't working at our show, the woman who played the She-Devil was unconvincing and the guys who portrayed the Ghostbusters were just going through the motions—as though the special effects were enough to dazzle us tourists. (Bill Murray upstaged by special effects? No way.) Until Universal's actors put more comic swagger into their roles, this attraction won't be as good as it should be.

"Murder She Wrote" (Now Shooting) sounded promising in the Universal brochure—lots of audience participation in the post- production process of a top-rated TV show. And some of "Murder" is fun. But for the most part, it seemed superficial and rushed.

When Universal opened, there was no production/backlot tour —a place where MGM really shines—except for a brief look at Nickelodeon. But Universal plans to offer one.

ABOUT THE RIDES/ATTRACTIONS
Thrills and Chills
Kongfrontation
The King Kong soundstage is the world's largest, and it needs most of those 71,000 square feet to accommodate the wrath of a six-ton ape with a 54-foot arm span who wants to snack on a New York tramway car filled with people—one of whom is you! Kong is the largest computer anima-tron ever built and he performs 46 terrifying acts of violence. Most of it looks all too real (those helicopters he swats away like flies are molded from full-size National Guard OH6 copters). Without giving too much away, we thought you'd like to know that the tramway car falls vertically at 12 feet per second with 1.75 g's of acceleration.

Earthquake, The Big One
You have been cast as an extra in an earthquake disaster film. Your acting assignment is to ride a subway train under San Francisco Bay to the Embarcadero station. But as the train pulls into the station, the rumbling and the shaking begins...slowly at first, but then seemingly too violent to be the product of a special-effects team. San Francisco is in the throes of a killer earthquake which will register 8.3 on the Richter scale—and you're trapped in an underground tunnel with San Francisco Bay only a few feet above you! If you want to know what happens next, get in line.

Jaws
Is this picturesque New England fishing village really as sleepy as it looks? And what's that ominous shape off to the side of your inflatable tour boat? Could it have anything to do with that news broadcast about some mysterious disappearances and the sighting of a monster shark? Better hold tight to your loved ones while you're on this ride (assuming it's working) because there could be trouble—about 24 feet and three tons of it! But before it's over, you're going to have a bloody good time, if you know what we mean. We're not going to tell you how many times your boat is placed in jeopardy, only that it would be a mistake to relax too soon.

Alfred Hitchcock: The Art of Making Movies
Question: Why show the shower scene from *Psycho* on a giant screen—and make a point of saying it was based on a real case —when there are children in the audience? That's our gripe with this otherwise

outstanding attraction, which is located in the Now Shooting area. Granted, Universal issues a warning in its park brochure, saying, "Due to the intense nature of the attraction, parental discretion is recommended for children under age 13." But it's our feeling that a lot of unknowing parents will miss or ignore that warning, thinking they'd never see something this brutal and depressing at a theme park. The rest of this attraction is superb: a 3-D surprise during the movie segment, and an interactive phase at the end where you learn how Hitchcock filmed his Statue of Liberty scene from *Saboteur*. You can also pretend you're Jimmy Stewart peering through binoculars at an incredibly realistic, miniature set from *Rear Window*. Our kids have been talking about Hitchcock movies ever since.

The Most Fun
E.T. *Adventure*
Even Steven Spielberg must have shuddered at the task of designing a theme park attraction good enough to wear the name of his heart-warming science fiction masterpiece. Spielberg, who is a creative consultant at Universal, spent $36 million on the E.T. Adventure (more than it cost to build the Houston Astrodome) and the result of his labors is about two-thirds genius and one-third disappointing. The large waiting-in-line area, an indoor rendering of the moonlit forest where E.T. first appears on earth, is beautifully done, with cool, dank air contributing to the illusion that you are there on the night E.T. leaves Earth to return home to the Green Planet. (It also beats standing out in the heat!) But thematic problems crop up if you don't listen carefully to E.T.'s mentor, Botanicus, who appears in the mist to explain that E.T.'s fellow creatures are dying back home and to enlist your aid in helping him return to save them. It's an important message, but unfortunately some people are in the wrong place in line to hear it.

Eventually, you and a group of fellow adventurers board a covey of dirt bikes (E.T.'s along too, if you look closely) for a daredevil escape from a forest which is suddenly crawling with G-Men who want to turn E.T. into a science experiment. The lift-off to safety—with walkie-talkies blaring, city lights twinkling below and John Williams' marvelous musical score pounding at your heart—is vintage Spielberg. Alas, it's downhill from there, as your journey continues on to the Green Planet where baby E.T.s and lots of little green relatives dance and play. From that point on, E.T.'s Adventure looks and sounds like something that might be called "It's a Small World in Outer Space."

Two important footnotes: Tell your kids to listen carefully when E.T. bids you goodbye at the end of the ride. Also, pregnant women and anyone who prefers not to ride a dirt bike can board a cable car-like spaceship instead.

Funtastic World of Hanna-Barbera

An absolute delight, even for those adults who stopped liking Saturday morning cartoons a long time ago. The fun is a product of flight-simulator technology which makes even this high-speed romp through cartoon land seem realistic. The Hanna-Barbera team took some of its most popular characters—Yogi Bear, The Jetsons, The Flintstones and Scooby Doo—and put them in a 3-D movie story which involves little Elroy Jetson being kidnapped by that diabolical cartoon villain, Dastardly. Who can save him? Yogi Bear, his sidekick, Boo Boo—and you! What ensues is a high-speed chase through downtown Bedrock and in and out of a haunted mansion before the hijinks come to an end at The Jetsons' spaceport home. Restrictions and words of caution: If you're young or pregnant or prone to motion sickness, Universal has provided seats up front that don't move—enabling you to enjoy the visual effects without the jostling.

Phantom of the Opera Horror Makeup Show

This show contains one humongous early scare which cannot even be hinted at here without ruining the effect—although you have to be standing in the correct spot or looking in that direction to fall victim. But the overall attraction has been toned down considerably since the park opened because parents of frightened children complained that it was simply too gruesome. So, unlike Alfred Hitchcock, this attraction is actually less scary than you would guess from the brochure language. There's a lot of humor, and we wished it had lasted longer.

Best Bet for the Younger Set
Animal Actors Stage

This 20-minute show is a winner from the opening stunt, in which a dog yanks on a rope that lifts a basket that contains a cat that scares a huge flock of doves that fly out over the audience. And those are just the bit players; the real stars here are descendants of Lassie, Benji and Mr. Ed. This is nice, down-to-earth fun—particularly if you've just been next door at E.T. And again, it could've run longer. Interesting footnote which will make you feel good: Most of Universal's cats and dogs are "discovered" at the pound, which proves you don't need a pedigree to be a star.

ADDED ATTRACTIONS

Nickelodeon, a children's entertainment network, is in production 10 hours a day, 365 days a year, and you and your kids can audition to be contestants on shows like "Family Double Dare" and "Think Fast." If you don't make it as contestants, you can still be members of the studio audience, although some shows are for kids only. If you think they're old enough, you can leave your kids at the studio while you and your spouse enjoy the park on your own. Just be sure they're patient enough to stay in their seats for a couple of hours—which is how long it took to tape the 30-minute segment of "Family Double Dare" that our kids attended. Also make sure your kids are clear about where to meet you when the show ends—and don't assume the Universal guides know when that will be. When we returned to meet our kids at the audition area at the agreed-upon time, they weren't there. We sought help from a guide who told us that the show they attended had ended 20 minutes ago. We started to panic. But before running all over the park, we talked our way into the soundstage area where taping takes place—and sure enough, there were our kids still hootin' and hollerin' at "Family Double Dare," which was running especially long that day.

The Universal lagoon (On Location) is home to a Miami Vice-type boat and thrill show which is heavy on explosions, so make sure you get a good vantage point on either the Central Park or Fisherman's Wharf side of the lagoon. You also need to take a tour of Universal's street sets—from Sunset Boulevard to New York's Lower East Side. (Can you spot where Paul Newman got his signal in "The Sting"?)

WHERE TO EAT

Our kids liked Animal Crackers (Cinemagic Center) for lunch because they could eat quickly and get frozen yogurt. The adults preferred to get out of the sun, so we went around the corner to Cafe LaBamba (Hollywood), which is buffet-style Mex but not too bad. Okay, so the chimichangas were a little tough, but you can wash them down with a Corona or a frozen margarita.

We planned to eat dinner at the Hard Rock Cafe (Cinemagic Center) which, as Universal is quick to point out, is the largest Hard Rock Cafe in the U.S. Unfortunately for this pair of frazzled parents, it is also the loudest Hard Rock Cafe in the U.S. How loud is it? Even the Beatles sound like Bon Jovi. Instead, we headed for Mel's Drive-In (Hollywood) where the juke box sounds of the Beach Boys were much mellower. Universal scrapped the carhops on rollerskates, but everything else is straight out of American Graffiti. Even Milner's hot rod; it's parked out front. The cheeseburgers and fries were just like you'd want 'em, but the shakes weren't hand-dipped.

If you feel like you have too much money in your wallet, you can lighten it significantly by dining at Lombard's Landing (On Location), which is located on the Fisherman's Wharf set. Universal bills it as the only restaurant in Florida with a view of the Pacific. Lombard's specializes in steak, pasta and—of course—seafood. Slightly less expensive is the Universal Studios Commissary (Now Shooting), which features grilled seafood, chicken and salads. This is also a good star-gazing area because many of the actors, directors and producers working on the Universal backlot eat here.

Other sit-down restaurants, plus numerous snack shops and refreshment stands are sprinkled throughout the park.

NEARBY FUN
Walt Disney World, Sea World and **Wet 'n Wild** are all nearby. For more information on Orlando attractions, see the CITIES and WATER-PARKS chapters.

WHERE TO STAY
Howard Johnson-Florida Center (5905 Kirkman Rd., Orlando, FL 32819, 407-351-3333) is located right across the street from Universal. Also extremely close is the Delta Orlando Resort (formerly Delta Court of Flags), where we spent two nights. For more information on the Delta Orlando and other area accommodations, see "Where to Stay" in the Orlando section of the CITIES chapter.

WHEN TO GO
Universal Studios is open 365 days a year. Specials include two-day and annual passes. Universal's business should parallel Disney's, so for information on what days of the week and times of the year are the busiest/least crowded, see "When to Go" in the Magic Kingdom section of this chapter.

FOR MORE INFORMATION
Contact:
Universal Studios/Florida
1000 Universal Studios Plaza, Orlando, FL 32819-7610
(407-363-8000)

SEA WORLD

Sea World is located in Orlando, Fla., at the juncture of I-4 and State Road 528. The 135-acre park features 15 shows and exhibits.

ABOUT THE PARK

A delightfully low-key theme park—and yet you're never bored here, thanks to the remarkable diversity of the world's marine life and the delightful shows which bring out their beauty and personality. Sea World is home to killer whales, beluga whales, dolphins and manatee. But those are just the high- visibility stars. The supporting actors include walruses, seals, sea lions, otters and a couple hundred comical penguins, which waddle around the icy "Penguin Encounter" pavilion.

The penguins are located in Ocean Friends, one of four different areas at Sea World. The other three are Beneath the Sea, Sea Lions/Sharks! and Shamu Stadium/Atlantis. The best way to tour these areas is to take note of the various show times and plan accordingly. Sea World is small enough that you shouldn't get overly tired walking around, plus you'll be seated during all the shows.

As you might guess, humans occupy only a small portion of the spotlight here—at the USO Water Ski Show, which is always a crowd favorite.

ABOUT THE ATTRACTIONS

Thrills and Chills

Sharks!

Located in Sea Lions/Sharks! this is the one attraction at Sea World which should make you gasp. To give you the feeling of what it's like to be swimming in shark-infested waters, Sea World constructed a thick acrylic tunnel which runs across the floor of the shark lagoon. As you proceed across the lagoon on a moving conveyor belt, you can spot nearly three dozen nurse, brown, bull, sand tiger and lemon sharks around and above you.

Tropical Reef

If you want to see octopus, eels and other creepy-looking denizens of the deep, the Tropical Reef aquarium in the Beaneath the Sea area is where to look.

The Most Fun
Shamu: New Visions

Sea World's No. 1 attraction is its killer whale show, which plays at numerous times during the day in the park's $18 million, 5,200-seat aquatic amphitheater. The show stars Shamu, the 8,000-pound killer whale with the heart of gold (he gives his trainer a ride and lets a child from the audience sit on his back). He is ably assisted by Baby Shamu, the "little" female who weighed 350 pounds when she came into this world in November 1988—only the second killer whale ever born in captivity; and Baby Namu, another female who was born in July 1989 and was still being nursed by her mother when she joined the act. Working as a team, these three black-and-white beauties do aerial acrobatics high above their five-million-gallon tank. And the audience can now get a better look at the amazing things they do, thanks to the addition of a 15-by-20-foot, high-resolution video screen (similar to the type you see at Major League baseball stadiums, except this one's waterproof). Four live cameras follow the killer whales both underwater and above the surface, enabling the audience to see these remarkable animals close up.

Sea Lion and Otter Show

We thought this comedy act was almost as good as Shamu & Co. It stars two silly sea lions—Clyde and Seamore—plus a wonderful supporting cast of otters, walruses and Sea World trainers.

Best Bets for the Younger Set
Feeding Pools

At Sea World's version of the petting zoo, kids can interact with friendly sea creatures by reaching into community pools and actually "shaking flippers" with a dolphin (Beneath the Sea). Your kids can even feed them if they want to. There are also community pools in the Ocean Friends area, where your kids can get a close look at seals and sea lions. It's even safe to touch the stingrays because their stingers have been removed.

Cap'n Kid's Fun Ship

Your kids will probably get a bit wet at this interactive play area which is built around a 60-foot pirate ship. They can shoot each other with water cannons (large squirt guns) or skip through an extremely shallow area beneath the rope traverse. The monkey bars are good for releasing pent-up energy, and so is the ball crawl.

WHERE TO EAT

Sea World has a variety of restaurants, snack bars and refreshment stands to keep you from getting hungry. The park's best sit-down restaurant is as unique as its name: Al E. Gator's Key West Eatery, which is located in the Beneath the Sea area at the edge of the Sea World lagoon. You can order almost anything here, from sandwiches to full meals, salads to desserts. You can even sample alligator tail. (Don't worry; the gator is no longer an endangered species.) The menu also includes such exotic delights as Jamaica jerk pork, Bermuda Triangle salad and mango muffins. Seafood offerings include conch chowder and crab quiche.

Beneath the Sea is also the site of a nightly Polynesian luau, complete with hula girls and male dancers with fiery torches in their mouths. Seating is limited and reservations are required (407-351-3600, ext. 195 or, Florida toll-free, 800-227-8048).

NEARBY FUN

Walt Disney World, Universal Studios and **Wet 'n Wild** are all nearby. For more information on Orlando attractions, see the CITIES and WATERPARKS chapters.

WHERE TO STAY

Directly across the street from Sea World is the Stouffer Orlando Resort. If your room overlooks the park, as ours did, you'll have a great view of the Sea World fireworks, which are a regular nightly feature during the summer and holidays. For more information on Stouffers and other lodging choices, see "Where to Stay" in the Orlando section of CITIES.

WHEN TO GO

Sea World is open 365 days a year. Specials include a week-long pass, which costs just a few dollars more than single-day admission, as well as annual passes. Sea World crowds follow the same fluctuations as other Orlando attractions.

FOR MORE INFORMATION

Contact:
Sea World
7007 Sea Harbor Dr., Orlando, FL 32821
(407-351-3600, 800-327-2424 or, inside Florida, 800-432-1178)

Busch Gardens
The Dark Continent

Busch Gardens/The Dark Continent is located in Tampa, Fla., between I-75 and I-275 at the corner of Busch Boulevard and 40th Street.

ABOUT THE PARK

Busch Gardens/The Dark Continent celebrated its 30th birthday in 1989, but the park is so clean and contemporary you'd never know it. In fact, if you can't have fun here, you might as well stay home and watch TV because Busch Gardens is like four parks in one: theme park, zoo, amusement park and yes, it even has a Sea World-type dolphin show. But everything revolves around the African motif with rides and attractions organized by cities and regions of that continent: Morocco, Crown Colony, Nairobi, Serengeti Plain, Timbuktu, the Congo and Stanleyville.

An eighth area, Bird Gardens/Brewery, features bird shows, an on-stage musical variety show, an adorable children's village and a tour of the Busch Brewery. But don't bother with the tour if your principal motivation is a free sample of beer; the tour isn't much, in our estimation, and there's no beer at the end. To get a free sample on tap, visit the Hospitality House adjacent to the brewery.

As you enter the park, skip right on through Morocco; it's primarily for shopping and eating. And since it's located immediately inside the main entrance, you may be able to catch Morocco's main attraction—the ice skating theater—as you make your way back to the entrance late in the day.

Families with young children should start with Nairobi, stopping briefly at the alligator/crocodile pits and then going on to the petting zoo. If you don't mind long lines, your kids can even ride an elephant. Next, board the train at the Nairobi station and ogle the animals that roam the Serengeti Plain (zebras, chimps, giraffes, antelope). Get off at the Congo station, do the bumper cars and assorted mini-rides and then break for lunch. After you eat, go next door to Timbuktu and see the dolphin show and ride the carousel. Depending on your energy level and kids' enthusiasm, you may want to take in some of the more exciting rides—the Congo River Rapids are located just across the railroad tracks from the bumper cars—before pushing on to the Dwarf Village activity area. Parents can rest there while kids enjoy this park within a park.

Teenagers will probably want to spend most of their time in Timbuktu (The Scorpion), the Congo (The Python/Congo River Rapids) and Stanleyville (Stanley Falls/Tanganyika Tidal Wave).

To save wear and tear on your feet, keep in mind that the Trans-Veldt Railroad makes stops in Nairobi and Stanleyville; you can disembark in the Congo, but boarding is not permitted there. The Skyride will take you from Crown Colony to the Congo; it's a beautiful view from up there, as long as you're not afraid of heights.

ABOUT THE RIDES/ATTRACTIONS

Thrills and Chills

The Python/The Scorpion
Is being upside-down in a roller coaster your idea of a good time? If so, these nasty-named attractions are for you. Major difference between the two: The Scorpion goes higher but the Python makes two loops, The Scorpion only one.

Tanganyika Tidal Wave
Don't be deceived into thinking this is just a log flume with a jazzy name; log flumes don't move this fast and they're closer to the ground when they make their final plunge to the splash pool. (If this is a little too much ride for your kids, go next door and try the Stanleyville Falls. It's a typical log flume with a less-scary finish.)

The Most Fun

Congo River Rapids
First of all, the lines are long. And you're gonna get wet! But this whitewater raft ride is guaranteed to raise a smile on most everyone's face. The course is a bit rough in spots, but children of all ages seem to enjoy themselves.

Dolphin Theater
These Atlantic bottle-nosed dolphins dive to the bottom of the pool, then explode from the water and rise to a height of 21 feet to snatch fish from their trainers' mouths. If you're seated close to the front, they'll splash a lot of water your way. And at the end of the show (which comes too quickly), they even pose for pictures.

Best Bets for the Younger Set

Petting Zoo
Special not only because the animal babies are so cute—even the Vietnamese pot-bellied pig!—but also because there's an animal nursery where your kids can look through glass and see just-born or extremely young macaws, wallabys and deer.

Dwarf Village and Activity Area
A don't-miss destination for kids four feet tall and under. The mini-attractions include a tree that talks, a tiny log flume ride, a huge inflated jumping pit flanked by a ball bath, a tree house, a climbing maze and little cars which drive themselves.

WHERE TO EAT
The Crown Colony House offers full-service dining: chicken dinners and fresh seafood, as well as sandwiches. Das Festhaus, a 1,200-seat dining hall in Timbuktu, serves corned beef sandwiches and German specialties, and has Anheuser-Busch beers on tap. We were in the Congo when we got hungry, so we ordered deli-style sandwiches and fried chicken at the Storehouse (both tasty) and ate them at picnic tables where we could watch the magnificent white tigers roam Claw Island.

NEARBY FUN
Probably you will have had your fill of wild animals by the time you leave Busch Gardens. But if you're on an extended stay and the kids get restless—particularly real little ones—check out the **Lowry Park Zoo,** which is in the proces of doubling in size. You'll find the usual animal exhibits—primate world, Asian domain, aviary—and something different: a storybook park with life-sized characters from Little Red Riding Hood and Snow White. Lowry Park's newest attraction is a manatee rehabilitation center (N. Boulevard and W. Sligh Ave., 813-935-8814).

Adventure Island waterpark, a sister property of Busch Gardens, is only a mile away on Bougainvillea Avenue. If you plan to cool off here, don't leave Busch Gardens without discount coupons. For more information on Adventure Island, see the "Best of the Rest" section in the WATERPARKS chapter.

Tampa's **Museum of Science & Industry** is a showcase for physical and natural sciences. It's also the home of a **Challenger Learning Center,** which serves as both a memorial to the seven space shuttle astronauts who died in 1986 and a simulated space station where students in grades 5-12 learn the basic skills of space exploration by applying the educational properties of math, science and technology. The general public can also take part in these simulated space missions, but reservations must be made two weeks in advance (4801 E. Fowler Ave., 813-985-5531).

Great Explorations! is an interactive museum in nearby St. Petersburg, which features mind games and puzzles, a music synthesizer kids can play and a 90-foot-long, pitch-black maze (1120 4th St. S., 813-821-8885).

For information on Tampa area sporting events, see "Shopping/ Nearby Fun" in the Saddlebrook section of the RESORTS chapter.

WHERE TO STAY

Holiday Inn Busch Gardens has the usual HI amentities, plus a shuttle to the park (2701 E. Fowler Ave., 813-971-4710).

We spent two nights at Saddlebrook golf and tennis resort, 15 miles north of Tampa. For more information, see the RESORTS chapter.

Guest Quarters, a favorite of ours in the all-suite hotel genre, is located midway between Tampa International Airport and the downtown area (555 N. Westshore Blvd., 813-875-1555).

WHEN TO GO

Busch Gardens is open 365 days a year. Specials include annual passes. And if you plan to visit Sea World, which is another Anheuser-Busch property, buy your tickets ahead of time at Busch Gardens and save a few bucks on admission. If your travel plans are uncertain, pick up a discount coupon for future use.

FOR MORE INFORMATION

Contact:

Busch Gardens/The Dark Continent
3000 Busch Blvd., Tampa, FL 33612
(813-988-5171; for recorded information, 813-987-5082)

BUSCH GARDENS
THE OLD COUNTRY

Busch Gardens/The Old Country is located in Williamsburg, Va., just off I-64. The park features more than 30 rides on 360 acres of rolling, wooded hills.

ABOUT THE PARK

Seventeenth-century Europe is the theme of this Busch property, which opened in 1975. The park features nine authentically detailed European hamlets: Banbury Cross and Hastings (England), Aquitaine (France), Rhinefeld and Oktoberfest (Germany), Heatherdowns (Scotland), San Marco and Festa Italia (Italy) and New France. Each hamlet has shops, restaurants and architecture indigenous to that region, and, of course, each hamlet has special rides and attractions.

Families with young children will like the Royal Preserve petting zoo (Banbury Cross), the Clydesdale horses (Heatherdowns), the Grimm's Hollow play area (Rhinefeld) and the "Enchanted Laboratory" (Hastings).

Families with teenagers will like Busch Gardens' flight-simulator ride, Questor (Hastings), the Loch Ness Monster/Big Bad Wolf rollercoasters (Heatherdowns/Oktoberfest), LeMans Raceway (Aquitaine) and Roman Rapids whitewater raft adventure (Festa Italia).

To save wear and tear on your feet, keep in mind that the park has two steam locomotives, the Balmoral Castle and Die Hochbiengen, which can help you tour the park. So can the Aeronaut Skyride.

ABOUT THE RIDES/ATTRACTIONS
Thrills and Chills
Loch Ness Monster/Big Bad Wolf

At first glance, Nessie looks like a huge piece of modern art, something Calder might've designed. Then it dawns on you. This thing is a rollercoaster! People ride on it! Before you do, consider the following: Nessie reaches 70 mph, carries its passengers to a heart-stopping height of 13 stories, then plunges 114 feet, skirting a lake before whipping through two interlocking loops.

And Nessie isn't even the scariest coaster at Busch Gardens. Paul Ruben, editor of *Rollercoaster!* magazine, ranks the Big Bad Wolf, a "suspended" roller coaster located in Oktoberfest, as one of the top 10 steel coasters in the U.S. "Suspended" refers to the fact that your four-passenger car hangs below the steel track—with nothing underneath you but air!

The Most Fun
Questor

This attraction opened in 1990, and like the other three flight-simulator rides we've discussed in this chapter, Questor is a white-knuckled good time. You sit in a 59-passenger "ship" and your riding companion is the aforementioned Questor, a gnome-like creature whose air-borne adventures are played out on a 70mm motion picture screen in front of you. Computer technology moves your ship in perfect sync with the objects flying by in front of you on the screen. End result: You'll swear you're flying. This ride may be too intense for very young children or anyone prone to motion sickness, but most kids (and adults) will be nuts about it.

Best Bet for the Younger Set
The Enchanted Laboratory

Special effects and audio-animatronics help recount the antics of Northrup, an alchemist's young apprentice who takes magic into his own hands while his master is away.

ADDED ATTRACTIONS

The 5,200-seat Royal Palace Concert Theatre is a regular tour stop for some of America's best-loved country and western singers. Those who have performed here include: the Judds, Tanya Tucker, George Strait and Barbara Mandrell. And here's the best part: Since you've already paid to get into Busch Gardens, the concert ticket is yours for a nominal fee.

WHERE TO EAT

Ethnic food is a specialty of The Old Country: barbecued ribs at the Three Rivers Smokehouse (New France), Italian cuisine at the multi-tiered Ristorante della Piazza (San Marco), and salads galore at Tournament Tables (Hastings) and authentic German food at Das Festhaus (Oktoberfest). Or grab a quick bite of good ol' American food at one of the snack bars located throughout the park.

NEARBY FUN

Colonial Williamsburg, Jamestown Festival Park and **Yorktown Victory Center** are just a few miles away (see the HISTORY PLACES chapter). If you need to cool off, visit **Water Country USA** (see the "Best of the Rest" section in the WATERPARKS chapter).

WHERE TO STAY

Kingsmill Resort, a 2,900-acre resort and residential community developed by Anheuser-Busch, features one- to three-bedroom suites, plus packages with tickets to the park and complimentary shuttle service. Children stay free (1010 Kingsmill Rd., 804-253-1703 or 800-832-5665).

Two other nearby choices are the Hilton and the Quality Inn at Kingsmill. The Hilton has a heated indoor/outdoor pool and Busch Gardens packages. Children stay free (50 Kingsmill Rd., 804-220-2500). The Quality Inn has a game room and free continental breakfast (U.S. 60 and State Rd. 199, 804-220-1100).

For more lodging information, see the Williamsburg section in the HISTORY PLACES chapter.

WHEN TO GO

Busch Gardens/The Old Country is open on weekends only from April to early May, daily from early May through Labor Day, and daily (except Wednesday/Thursday) in September and October. Specials include two-day tickets and reduced admission for twilight entrance.

FOR MORE INFORMATION

Contact:
Busch Gardens/The Old Country
One Busch Gardens Blvd., Williamsburg, VA 23187-8785
(804-253-3350)

CAROWINDS

Carowinds is located 10 miles south of Charlotte, N.C., on I-77 (exit 90). The 325-acre park has an 83-acre entertainment area (including a six-acre waterpark) and a 60-acre campground adjacent to the park.

ABOUT THE PARK

Carowinds is a beautiful, tree-shaded park which literally straddles the North Carolina/South Carolina border, with the boundary line dividing the park neatly in half. Thus, it figures that Carowinds would have a split personality; it's been an amusement park since it opened in 1973, and in 1989 it added a $2.35 million waterpark area, RipTide Reef. The park has topped the million mark in attendance every year since 1977.

To sample the wet-and-wild pleasures of RipTide Reef, you should bring a bathing suit with you—even though you can enjoy some of the waterpark rides in regular clothes. Carowinds makes that possible by using one- and two-person sleds which keep you from getting soaked on the five-story speed slides and enclosed- tube rides. But on a sizzling day, you'll want to get soaked, and you can do that by jumping into the park's wave pool—so pack a bathing suit. There's even a special kids' waterpark area (Waterworks). Lockers, dressing room and shower facilities are provided next to the enclosed-tube rides in RipTide Reef.

Carowinds has nine other themed areas and swim wear is prohibited in those areas, so wearing a bathing suit all day is not an option. Those nine areas are (clockwise from main entrance): Plantation Square, Old World Marketplace, Hanna Barbera Land, Carolina RFD, County Fair, Pirate Island, Blue Ridge Junction and Carolina Showplace, with Smurf's Island located at the center of the park.

Families with young children should plan to visit Smurf Island, Hanna Barbera Land and the County Fair area. The easiest way to do that is to enter Carowinds at the Carolina RFD entrance, which is much closer to where you park your car than the main entrance. It's also convenient to RipTide Reef. Use the main entrance if you're interested in seeing the Charleston harbor motif, in eating/shopping, or in trying one of the four rides and attractions in that area: Carolina Sternwheeler (boat ride), Carolina Skytower (340-foot revolving observation tower), Rip Roarin' Rapids (whitewater raft ride), Powder Keg Flume (log flume ride).

Families with teenagers will find plenty to satisfy them anywhere in the park, with the exception of Hanna Barbera Land and Smurf Island.

ABOUT THE RIDES/ATTRACTIONS

Thrills and Chills

Carolina Cyclone/Thunder Road/Frenzoid/Gauntlet

These four rides are all hair-raising. The Cyclone (Blue Ridge Junction) is a dizzying, new-age rollercoaster which sends riders through consecutive 360-degree loops followed by a 450-degree spiral. Thunder Road (County Fair) is a double-tracked, wooden coaster which reaches speeds of 60 mph. Frenzoid (County Fair) is a giant Viking ship which swings backwards and forwards, higher and higher, until the ride actually rotates through a series of 360-degree loops with riders hanging upside-down at the top. Gauntlet, introduced in 1990, imitates Frenzoid, but uses a different scare tactic: The riders' platform stays horizontal at the top, but what follows is a six-story free-fall.

The Most Fun

Carolina Goldrusher

The Goldrusher (Blue Ridge Junction) is similar to the Dahlonega Mine Train at Six Flags and it's one of Carowinds' most popular attractions; roughly one million people ride it annually. (If this is too much rollercoaster for your kids, your best bet is the Scooby Doo Roller Coaster in Hanna Barbera Land.)

White Water Falls/Rip Roarin' Rapids

If getting wet is your goal and you didn't bring a bathing suit for RipTide Reef, here's your chance. White Water Falls puts riders in 20-passenger boats and sends them down a 45-foot waterfall (which is pretty scary!) to an incredibly wet splashdown. Rip Roarin' Rapids is a 2,100-foot raft ride which includes waterfalls, rapids, whirlpool and cavern. Beware of long lines at both.

Best Bets for the Younger Set

Smurf Island/Hanna Barbera Land/County Fair

Smurf Island is a wooded, 1.3-acre area which features a giant rope climb, two ball-crawls, trails, slides and a hidden Smurf village. To get there, you have to go by excursion boat from Carolina RFD, so you might want to enter at that gate and do it first thing. In any event, keep an eye on the time because this kiddie paradise closes at 6 p.m. (an hour later on summer Saturdays). Hanna Barbera Land is an amusement park for little tykes. All nine rides are extremely tame, with the possible exception of the Scooby Doo Roller Coaster, which is much longer and a wee bit more exciting than most kiddie coasters. County Fair has four carnival-type rides, plus an arcade and games area with ring toss, basketball, etc.

ADDED ATTRACTIONS

The Palladium Amphitheater was enlarged and refurbished in 1989, then expanded again for 1991, to the tune of $4 million. The result is a stand-alone concert facility which seats more than 13,000 and requires a separate admission; 5,000 of those seats have a roof overhead and the old bleacher seats have been replaced by chair-back seats with arm rests. As a result, outdoor seating capacity was nearly doubled to 8,200. Expect ticket prices to range from $15to $20.. For concert information, call 704-588-2619.

WHERE TO EAT

Carowinds' main eatery, the newly remodeled Casey's Grill, features half-pound burgers, barbecue, grilled chicken sandwiches, salad and dessert. The Country Kitchen, a cafeteria, serves fried chicken, barbecue, baked beans, cole slaw and french fries. Sprinkled throughout the park are 50 food and beverage locations offering Mexican, German, Italian and, of course, American food.

NEARBY FUN

The **Charlotte Nature Museum and Planetarium** is interesting and inexpensive, and your kids can enjoy a puppet show and a nature walk while you're there (1658 Sterling Rd., 704-372-6261).

The other half of the combined Science Museums of Charlotte, Inc., is the **Discovery Place Science and Technology Center,** which has eight major exhibit areas, including an aquarium and a tropical rain forest (301 N. Tryon St., 704-372-6261).

WHERE TO STAY

With Charlotte just 10 miles away, you have a wide variety of hotel/motel choices. For information, contact: Charlotte Convention & Visitors Bureau, 229 N. Church St., Charlotte, NC 28232 (704-334-2282 or 800-231-4636), or the York County Convention & Visitors Bureau (201 E. Main St., PO Box 11377, Rock Hill, SC 29731, 803-329-5200, or 800-866-5200).

If you want to stay close to Carowinds, both Holiday Inn (803-548-2400 or 704-334-4450) and Comfort Inn (803-548-5200) are located within sight of the park (I-77 at Carowinds Blvd.). Another alternative is Carowinds' own 60-acre campground.

WHEN TO GO

Carowinds is open on weekends only from March through early June and again from late August through early October. Daily operation runs from June to late August, but remember this scheduling quirk: with rare exceptions, the park is closed on Fridays. Specials include a two-day ticket, season pass and family season pass.

FOR MORE INFORMATION

Contact:

Carowinds
PO Box 410289, Charlotte, NC 28241-0289
(704-588-2606, or 800-822-4428)

DOLLYWOOD

Dollywood is located 30 miles southeast of Knoxville, Tenn., off U.S. 441 in Pigeon Forge, Tenn. The 100-acre park features 20 rides and attractions, plus a number of music/variety shows.

ABOUT THE PARK

Dollywood opened in 1986, and was so successful in its first season—drawing 1.3 million visitors—that its famous part-owner, Dolly Parton, immediately instituted a $6 million expansion program. The park has continued to grow in popularity, while proudly proclaiming that it is not a haven for those who like "big, scary rides." Dollywood is primarily a celebration of the old-fashioned, mountain way of life that Ms. Parton knew as a girl growing up in this area of Appalachia. The park does have rides, but they're all fairly tame and they play a secondary role to the live music and entertainment, the craft shows and the mountain village which gives Dollywood its rustic atmosphere and down-home identity. Music is everywhere, both onstage and in the air, thanks to the piped-in sounds of such Dolly hits as "Jolene," "Here You Come Again" and, of course, "9 to 5." Crafts people make everything from blown glass to dulcimers. The park also features a working, hand-built gristmill and a replica of the home in which Dolly and 11 other Parton children grew up.

Dollywood is divided into five areas: Daydream Ridge, Rivertown Junction, Craftsmen's Valley, The Village and Fun Country. A new eagle complex which will showcase both bald and golden eagles is scheduled to open in 1991. The complex will include an aviary dedicated to rehabilitating injured eagles and hatching young ones to be released in the wild. The aviary will also serve as a home for eagles deemed "unreleasable" by the U.S. Fish and Wildlife Service because they would be unable to survive in the wild.

Families with young children will find that Dollywood was designed with them in mind. No double-loop roller coasters here, just good, wholesome entertainment which families can enjoy together—as long as the kids aren't too young. We say that because Dollywood is extremely protective of its young visitors; mimimum height restrictions of 36-42 inches will confine small ones to the Critter Creek playground (Daydream Ridge) or the Fun Country kiddie area.

Dollywood is small enough to be seen comfortably on foot. But from a sightseeing standpoint, it's fun to ride the Dollywood Express, a coal-burning steam locomotive, which takes you on a five-mile tour of this beautiful mountain hideaway.

ABOUT THE RIDES/ATTRACTIONS

Thrills and Chills

Thunder Express

By Dollywood standards, this zippy little mountain train-coaster is as scary as it gets. Height restriction: 42 inches.

Blazing Fury

This fast-paced, indoor coaster ride through a burning town provides some surprises along the way, plus a cool finish. Height restriction: 42 inches.

The Most Fun

Mountain Slidewinder

This water toboggan ride, located in Daydream Ridge, will send a little spray your way. And it's rambunctious enough that kids must be at least 39 inches tall to climb on board.

Smoky Mountain Rampage

Most major amusement parks have a whitewater raft ride that's designed and engineered like this one, which you'll find in Rivertown Junction. But few, if any, can match the mountain scenery which embraces Dollywood's version. Kids must be 36 inches tall to ride.

Best Bets for the Younger Set

Critter Creek

This playground area is chock full of slides, rope mazes, towers and bridges—a real mecca for energetic youngsters. Nearby is the Critter Creek toy factory where kids can watch craftsmen make toys by hand.

Fun Country

Kids can ride cars, trucks, planes, balloons, little swings, big swings and bumper cars (the latter pair carry a height restriction of 42 inches).

Dentzel Carousel

This turn-of-the-century merry-go-round is a hand-carved work of art; this particular design is known as a "full menagerie" because kids get to ride lots of different animals—rooster, lion, giraffe, ostrich, etc.—besides 34 beautiful horses.

ADDED ATTRACTIONS

Dollywood's Celebrity Theatre (Daydream Ridge) presents a Memorial Day-Labor Day concert schedule which features some of the biggest names in country music, including the Charlie Daniels Band, Crystal Gayle and Mickey Gilley. Each artist or group performs at 2 p.m. and again at 7 p.m., and you need a separate ticket to get in.

The new Gaslight Theatre (The Village) is home to a pair of shows, one starring country singer James Rogers and the other an original musical production.

The Parton Back Porch Theatre (Rivertown Junction) features Dolly's kinfolk, family and friends in a tribute to her special kind of music.

Dollywood also features both gospel and bluegrass sounds in a new 350-seat open-air theater in Craftsmen's Valley, and an original musical production in Fun Country's Barnwood Theatre.

WHERE TO EAT

Dollywood prides itself on its country cooking, which includes an "all you care to eat" breakfast buffet (Aunt Granny's Dixie Fixins in Rivertown Junction), "honey-stung" chicken (Miss Lillian's Chicken House in Craftsmen's Valley) and hand-pulled barbecued pork sandwiches (Miss Lillian's Barbeque Pit in Craftsmen's Valley). Dollywood restaurants also serve up steak, hamburgers and yummy desserts like funnel cakes and strawberries/peaches and cream.

NEARBY FUN

Dollywood is nestled in the foothills of **Great Smoky Mountains National Park,** the most visited national park in the U.S. For more information, see the NATIONAL PARKS chapter.

WHERE TO STAY

There are nearly 18,000 hotel/motel rooms and 4,000 campsites available in Pigeon Forge, Gatlinburg and Sevierville, plus more than 1,000 campsites and public accommodations in Great Smoky Mountains National Park. For further details, see the NATIONAL PARKS chapter.

WHEN TO GO

Dollywood is open daily from late April until the last weekend in October. But call ahead if you plan to visit on Thursdays because that's sometimes an off-day. The park reopens briefly at Thanksgiving time and again—though at odd times—in December. Specials include free second-day admission if you purchase a full-price ticket after 3 p.m., and season passes which are priced less than a pair of one-day tickets.

FOR MORE INFORMATION

Contact:

Dollywood
700 Dollywood Ln., Pigeon Forge, TN 37863-4101
(615-428-9488)

KINGS DOMINION

Kings Dominion is located 20 miles north of Richmond, Va., on I-95 (exit 40) in Doswell, Va. The 400-acre park features more than 100 rides, shows and attractions.

ABOUT THE PARK

This $50 million park opened in 1975 and it has drawn more than two million people annually since 1986. Those attendance figures are a reflection of Kings Dominion's varied entertainment menu, which includes a stand-up rollercoaster (Shockwave), a sea lion show, a monorail ride which takes you on a wild animal safari and three rides which provide waterpark thrills without getting you soaked.

Kings Dominion is divided into five themed areas: International Street, Old Virginia, Candy Apple Grove, Hanna-Barbera Land and Safari Village.

Families with young children will appreciate the 1990 expansion of Hanna-Barbera Land, which now has five new kids' rides, more Hanna-Barbera characters, new live shows and new games.

Families with teenagers will find a lot to like in Candy Apple Grove, which is home to two roller coasters, Shockwave and Rebel Yell, plus the popular Sky Pilot ride. They will also enjoy Old Virginia, home of the Grizzly roller coaster, the White Water Canyon raft ride and the Shenandoah log flume.

To save wear and tear on your feet, keep in mind that the Sky Ride runs from the intersection of Safari Village and Hanna-Barbera Land out to the edge of Candy Apple Grove, next to the funnel cake stand and the Rebel Yell.

ABOUT THE RIDES/ATTRACTIONS

Thrills and Chills

Shockwave/Rebel Yell/Sky Pilot/Grizzly/Berserker

Shockwave, Rebel Yell and Sky Pilot (Candy Apple Grove) all supply high-altitude thrills. Shockwave, the East Coast's first stand-up roller coaster, uses shoulder restraints to keep you from flying off into space. Rebel Yell is a two-track rollercoaster which climbs to 85 feet and reaches 60 mph. Sky Pilot is a flight trainer ride which you control from the cockpit; your aircraft will dip, soar or do barrel rolls according to your commands. Grizzly (Old Virginia) is a wooden roller coaster which has been ranked among the best in that category. Berserker (International Street) is a forerunner of Frenzoid, the Viking ship ride at Carowinds that turns passengers upside-down.

The Most Fun
White Water Canyon/Diamond Falls/Racing Rivers
These three water attractions can be ridden without changing into bathing suits. White Water is a raft ride which makes its way through geysers and canyons. Diamond Falls boats float to the top of a 50-foot dropoff, then plunge over a waterfall into a mysterious diamond mine. Racing Rivers contains three different water slides which are ridden via a raft, a tube and a sled.

Avalanche Bobsled Ride
A simulated bobsled run in a rubber-wheeled train, which runs freely through a twisting, 2,000-foot banked trough.

Best Bets for the Younger Set
Wild Animal Safari Monorail
The Kings Dominion game preserve is stocked with more than 200 exotic birds and beasts from Africa and Asia. You'll see giraffes, elephants, lions, tigers, zebras, rhinos and cape buffalo.

Jabber Jaws Saltwater Circus
This is the sea lion show, and you'll find it in Candy Apple Grove— between Shockwave and the park's landmark, a 335-foot replica of the Eiffel Tower.

Hanna-Barbera Land
Five new rides have been added to this 30-acre area, including Captain Caveman's Clipper, a pint-sized version of the Berserker, plus a sea planes ride, a miniature driving course, a Grand Prix ride and a boat ride. The Scooby Doo kiddie coaster is also a perennial favorite.

ADDED ATTRACTIONS
Showplace, Kings Dominion's 8,000-seat outdoor amphitheater, features top entertainers such as the Beach Boys, Dolly Parton and New Kids on the Block. Park admission is required in addition to a concert ticket. For concert information, write the park or call the concert information line: 804-876-5000.

WHERE TO EAT
Kings Dominion has the usual array of sandwich shops and snack stands, plus five sit-down restaurants: Restaurante Mexicana (International Street), Country Kitchen (Old Virginia), Victoria Pizza (Candy Apple Grove), Livingston's and Hungry Hippo (Safari Village).

NEARBY FUN

The Science Museum of Virginia in nearby Richmond allows kids to participate in the sciences through hands-on models and, better still in their eyes, computer games. There's also a **planetarium** (2500 W. Broad St., 804-25-STARS). At the **Children's Museum,** the 12-and-under crowd can listen to storytellers, sculpt, fingerpaint and even play career roles in the "When I Grow Up" exhibit (740 N. 6th St., 804-643-KIDO).

WHERE TO STAY

Free shuttle service connects the park to the Best Western Kings Quarters (804-876-3321) and the Kings Dominion Campground (804-876-5355), both of which are located at I-95 and Route 30. The Kings Quarters has a 24-hour recreation area, including a swimming pool, lighted tennis courts, putting green, ping-pong, shuffleboard and a playground. The 225-site campground offers modern hookups, a swimming pool and a complete camp store. Also nearby is the Holiday Inn/Ashland (I-95 and exit 39, 804-798-4231).

WHEN TO GO

Kings Dominion is open on weekends only from late March through May and again from September through early October. Daily operation runs from Memorial Day to Labor Day. Specials include two-day admissions and season passes.

FOR MORE INFORMATION

Contact:
Kings Dominion
PO Box 2000, Doswell, VA 23047
(804-876-5000)

OPRYLAND

Opryland is located nine miles northeast of Nashville, Tenn., between I-40 and I-65 (exit 11 off Briley Parkway). The 120-acre park features 21 rides and attractions and more than a dozen live shows.

ABOUT THE PARK

Opryland opened in 1972, and it's just one segment of the 406-acre Opryland USA music and entertainment complex, which includes the Grand Ole Opry, mecca of country music and home of the nation's longest continuous radio show (first broadcast: 1924), plus the Opryland Hotel, the Nashville Network and the *General Jackson* showboat.

The park has nine areas: Hill Country, New Orleans, Riverside, American West, State Fair, Lakeside, Big G Kid Stuff, Do Wah Diddy City and Grizzly Country.

Families with younger children should concentrate on the petting zoo (State Fair area) and two special children's play areas (Big G Kid Stuff/ Lakeside).

Families with teenagers are in luck because Opryland is chock full of exciting rides and attractions from one corner to the other.

To save wear and tear on your feet, keep in mind that you can catch the Opryland Railroad at the Hill Country station, just to the left of the admission gate. The train makes only one other stop: at the El Paso Station between the American West and Lakeside areas. The Sky Ride will take you from the New Orleans area to Do Wah Diddy City.

As much fun as the rides are at Opryland, what really makes this place special is its music (see "Added Attractions").

ABOUT THE RIDES/ATTRACTIONS

Thrills and Chills

Chaos

Not since Disney World's Space Mountain has anyone created a "concept coaster" like this one, which uses motion picture special effects and state-of-the-art audio to enhance the traditional roller coaster experience. Developed with the help of the film producers of Predator and Alien, Chaos (Grizzly Country) is housed inside a dark, mysterious, eight-story building. It cost $7 million to build and it's a gas to ride.

Wabash C'ball/R&R Coaster/Screamin' Delta Demon/Barnstormer

If you're tired of looking at the world right-side-up, try the Wabash Cannonball (State Fair), a double-loop roller coaster which turns things upside-down. Less intense, but still plenty exciting is the Rock 'n Roller Coaster, which races through the treetops of Do Wah Diddy City. The Screamin' Delta Demon (between New Orleans and Hill Country) coasts down a trackless, bobsled-type chute on rubber wheels. The Barnstormer (State Fair) is a sky-high biplane ride where riders circle a flight tower that's 100 feet off the ground.

The Most Fun
Grizzly River Rampage/Old Mill Scream
The Grizzly (Grizzly Country) is a whitewater raft ride complete with a cavern and, yes, a grizzly! The Old Mill Scream (middle of Eagle Lake) is a 60-foot-high log flume. Wet alert on both.

Best Bet for the Younger Set
Big G Kid Stuff
This kids' activity area features a mini space needle, a boat ride and a gigantic playhouse.

ADDED ATTRACTIONS
Who else would have the resources to spend $12 million on a paddlewheel showboat but Opryland? The 300-foot *General Jackson* is named after the first steamboat to operate on the Cumberland River, which is where it's docked (at the rear of the Opryland parking lot). The *General Jackson* has four decks, its hull is 274 feet long and its most important feature is the Victorian Theater, which seats 1,000 people for concerts or musical theater productions. The *General Jackson* is fully operational and makes as many as five Cumberland River cruises per day during the summer. The daytime cruises last two hours; the dinner cruise is longer and both feature a live show. Tickets must be purchased separately.

Back on land, Opryland has the capability to stage a dozen shows simultaneously—and every one of them uses live musicians and/or a pit orchestra. No canned music and lip-synched vocals here. And while Opryland offers the best country music anywhere in the world, park shows cover the entire spectrum of American music from the 1880s to the present, with special emphasis on Hollywood, Broadway and, of course, Nashville. The trick is how to keep the youngsters happy because—let's face it—if they're not, Mom and Dad aren't. But Opryland has done a good job of updating these selections with young faces, strong voices, imaginative choreography and, whenever possible, special effects. Shows targeted at teen audiences include a rock 'n roll revue (Do Wah Diddy

City) and musical groups which sing current country chart-toppers. Helpful hints for indoor shows: If you want to sit down front, get in line at least 30 minutes before show time. And make sure you're at the right theater.

NOTE

Would you like to see Barbara Mandrell in person? Well, you might be lucky enough to see stars like these if you attend one of the tapings of "Nashville Now" or one of the other shows on The Nashville Network (TNN), the cable channel which is to country music what MTV is to rock 'n roll. To find out about taping schedules ("Nashville Now" tapes weeknights in the Nashville Network Studio), call the Opryland Information Center (615-889-6611) or TNN Information Services (615-883-7000) to see what shows will be in production and which stars will be appearing when you're visiting Nashville. To get tickets, inquire at Opryland's Passport and Guest Relations Center in the Plaza Area.

WHERE TO EAT

Opryland has eight full-service restaurants, including the Cafe Mardi Gras and the Gaslight Beef Room, plus lots of refreshment stands where you can get popcorn, nachos and ice cream.

If you hanker for an old-fashioned picnic, you need to do it off-property. But Opryland has set up picnic tables outside the park next to the Cumberland River. If you want to return to the park, remember to get your hand stamped on the way out.

NEARBY FUN

For information on **Nashville** attractions, see the CITIES chapter.

WHERE TO STAY

The obvious choice, if money is no object, is the on-site Opryland Hotel (615-889-1000), a massive colonial-style complex which is an attraction in itself. The Opryland became the nation's 12th-largest hotel when it grew to 1,891 rooms in 1988.

For more lodging information, see the Nashville section of the CITIES chapter.

WHEN TO GO

Opryland is open on weekends only from late March through April and again from early October through the end of the month. The park is open Friday-Sunday from May until Memorial Day and again from September until the end of the month. Daily operation runs from Memorial Day to Labor Day. Specials include extra-days tickets and season passes. Buy a three-day Opryland USA passport and save 20 percent off regular park admission.

FOR MORE INFORMATION

Contact:

Opryland
2802 Opryland Dr., Room 9003, Nashville, TN 37214
(615-889-6700)

SIX FLAGS OVER GEORGIA

Six Flags Over Georgia is located 12 miles west of Atlanta, just off I-20. This 331-acre park features more than 100 rides, shows and attractions.

ABOUT THE PARK

Six Flags has been around since 1967, but thanks to a steady stream of new rides and attractions, it never seems to lose its appeal. Annual attendance has topped two million every year since 1973, and the Georgia Cyclone—a 100-foot-high roller coaster introduced in 1990—should help Six Flags continue its tradition as one of the top amusement parks in the Southeast.

The park is divided into eight different areas: British, Confederate, Cotton States, French, Georgia, Lick Skillet, Modern and Bugs Bunny Land.

Families with young children should enjoy Bugs Bunny Land, which is located between the diving pool (French Area) and Splashwater Falls (Lick Skillet Area).

Families with teenagers will have no problems finding exciting things to do because the entire park is a thrill-seeker's heaven.

Because it boasts a pair of wooden rollercoasters, Six Flags has something of a Sixties carnival look. But the park offers visitors great variety—from a 20-story parachute ride (Great Gasp) which is the only one in the Southeast, to a Disneyesque Monster Plantation, an animatronics ride which takes place in a flooded antebellum mansion.

To save wear and tear on your feet, you can ride the Sky Bucket from the Confederate Area near the front of the park to the Cotton States picnic area at the rear of the park. Or hop aboard the Six Flags Railroad, which circles the park with stops in the Confederate and French areas.

ABOUT THE RIDES/ATTRACTIONS

Thrills and Chills

Georgia Cyclone/Mind Bender/Scream Machine/Z Force/Free Fall

Six Flags specializes in scaring the wits out of you, and any of these five rides can do it. The Georgia Cyclone is bigger and faster than the ride it was patterned after: New York's legendary wooden roller coaster, the Coney Island Cyclone. The first drop starts at 78 feet up and hurtles you downward at a nerve-shattering 53 degrees. There are 10 more drops along this half-mile-plus run. Maximum speed: 50 mph. "Like flying without the airplane!" said *RollerCoaster!* magazine's editor, Paul Ruben, after a test ride. Mind Bender is a triple-loop roller coaster (two vertical, one horizontal) which was king of the hill here until the Cyclone. And you can't ignore the park's No. 3 coaster, The Great American Scream Machine, which rises 105 feet in the sky and covers nearly three-quarters of a mile per run. Z Force is a difficult-to-describe, one-of-a-kind ride which makes corkscrew dives and changes speeds like a roller coaster with a mind of its own. Free Fall simulates the feeling of being in an elevator that suddenly falls 10 stories. A few years ago, a group of stuntmen commissioned by the makers of an anti-nausea drug traveled the country rating thrill rides. First prize went to Free Fall.

The Most Fun
Dahlonega Mine Train
If your kids have never ridden a real roller coaster and they think it's time, why not break them in here? The mine train never gets very far off the ground, but it has an Indiana Jones-type excitement to it that all but small children should like. The ride roars through a wooded area of the park, zipping into valleys, climbing through holes in the tree cover and eventually diving into a darkened mine shaft. You may scream, but chances are you'll be smiling, too.

Best Bet for the Younger Set
Bugs Bunny Land
A kids-only area. The Yosemite Sam Play Port features a slide, a cave and Bugs Bunny's home in the carrot patch, where kids can meet their favorite Looney Tunes characters. You can also ride with your kids in the air-borne Yosemite Sam Buccaneer Boats. When Six Flags updated this area in 1989, three new rides were added: Road Runner's Convoy, a circular, tractor-trailer ride; Tweety's Swing, a Maypole-type, double-motion ride; and The Flying Tasmanian Devils, a smallish air-racer ride.

ADDED ATTRACTIONS
Seating in the Southern Star Amphitheatre was increased to more than 8,000 in 1989 to attract more people to the series of approximately 25 concerts that Six Flags puts on every season. Musical styles represented in the series range from rock to country to contemporary Christian. For most concerts, tickets are free with the price of admission. When big-name talent is performing, you'll probably have to pay a few dollars per ticket in addition to the price of admission.

WHERE TO EAT

Six Flags has seven sit-down restaurants, four of which are completely enclosed: Contemporary Kitchen (Modern Area), Plantation House and Dixie Belles (Confederate Area) and Tondee's Tavern (British Area). There are also more than 40 portable snack stands and 20 food and beverage locations, so nobody goes hungry here.

NEARBY FUN

White Water is nearby; for information, see the WATERPARKS chapter. For more information on **Atlanta** attractions, see the CITIES chapter.

WHERE TO STAY

For Atlanta lodging information, see the CITIES chapter.

WHEN TO GO

Six Flags is open on weekends only from early March to Memorial Day, but daily for a one- to two-week period during spring break in early April. Regular daily operation runs from Memorial Day until school reconvenes in late August. The park is open on weekends only in September and October, closed during November except for Thanksgiving break, open on weekends and during Christmas break in December. Specials include two-day (non-consecutive) passes, season passes and family season passes.

FOR MORE INFORMATION

Contact:
Six Flags Over Georgia
PO Box 43187, Atlanta, GA 30378
(404-739-3400)

WATERPARKS

❣ WET 'N WILD

❣ WHITE WATER

❣ TYPHOON LAGOON

❣ BEST OF THE REST

WATERPARKS

Wet 'n Wild, America's first waterpark, opened in Orlando, Fla., in March of 1977. It was the brainchild of George Millay, who also created Sea World.

Today, more than 75 major waterparks are in operation in the U.S., with national attendance topping the 30 million mark. And because of the region's favorable weather and heavy tourist trade, the Southeast has the greatest concentration of waterparks in the country.

What's so appealing about waterparks is that they do for summer what skiing does for winter: They tip the elements in your favor. Because all the rides put you in the water, it's easy to stay cool on the hottest day. On a typical ride, you climb to the top of a long, curving fiberglass tube, shove off on a torrent of water and slip-slide your way to the bottom. The fun stems from being gleefully out of control and knowing that a splash pool dunking awaits you at the end of the ride.

Another thing we like about waterparks is that they make it relatively easy to keep families together because, for the most part, school-age children and adults can enjoy almost every ride in the park together—sometimes in the same raft. And they can do it without the kids being terrified or the adults bored to tears. Obviously, this depends on the nature of the ride and how daring you and your kids are. But our niece tried most of the rides at Atlanta's White Water when she was a preschooler.

If your children are still toddlers and can't swim yet, that's no problem because any first-rate waterpark will have a separate children's area where little ones can enjoy a down-sized version of the big park, complete with things like mini-slides, a gentle tube ride, water cannons (big squirt guns) and stuff to climb on.

Another nice thing about waterparks is that they're not as crowded as conventional amusement parks. White Water, one of the top parks in attendance, averages 700,000 customers a year compared to 2.5 million at Six Flags Over Georgia.

Of course, you're still going to be swimming with thousands of strangers, but the waterpark industry is bullish about proper filtration rates, good water chemistry and the highest lifeguard-safety standards. Major waterparks use tons of chlorine every week to keep the water clean and on an average summer day, a park like White Water will have 100 lifeguards and ride attendants on duty. And every one of those lifeguards is Red Cross-certified.

TRAVEL TIP

Waterparks do for summer what skiing does for winter — they tip the elements in your favor:

❏ Because all the rides put you in the water, it's easy to stay cool on the hottest day.

❏ On a typical ride, you climb to the top of a long, curving fiberglass tube, shove off on a torrent of water and slip-slide your way to the bottom.

❏ The fun stems from being gleefully out of control and knowing that a splash pool dunking awaits you at the end of the ride.

If you want to avoid the biggest crowds, here are two suggestions which will help: Stay away on weekends and holidays, and don't enter the park until late afternoon when a lot of people are leaving.

As for admission prices, the most expensive waterpark in the Southeast—and in the U.S.—is Disney's Typhoon Lagoon (1991 rates: $19.61 for adults, $15.63 for children). Both White Water and Typhoon Lagoon's chief competitor, Wet 'n Wild, are a few dollars cheaper—and as you'll read in this chapter, they give you a little more for your money. If you're looking for economy, adults can get into some of the smaller waterparks listed at the end of this chapter for less than $10. Very young children are usually free, and most parks offer reduced admission if you arrive late in the afternoon.

RULES OF THUMB

You can wear your bathing suit to the park or change into it when you get there. Locker rooms with showers are located inside the main gate. But we strongly recommend that you wear your suit because changing clothes in a slippery-floored public locker room is a hassle you only want to go through once, when you're leaving the park. But be sure to take a change of clothing so you won't have to ride home or back to the motel in a wet suit.

You can't wear cutoffs or t-shirts on the rides because ragged threads could catch in a fiberglass seam and cause an accident. Two-piece bathing suits can be risky business; women have been known to lose the top half in some of the splash pools.

Don't take anything inside the gates that can't be compressed into a small locker. Besides your bathing suit and a change of clothing, the essentials include towels, suntan lotion and sandals, plus a wallet or small purse. If you don't want to leave with wet towels or worry about losing them, some parks rent them. But some don't, so call ahead and check, particularly if you're traveling without towels from home.

Don't take anything with you once you lock your locker except your locker key. No, not even towels. The object of being at a waterpark is to stay wet. And unless it's a chilly day or it's gotten cool after sundown, you'll be having too much fun to get cold.

When you want to take a break for food/refreshments, open your locker, towel off, put on a t-shirt (optional), get out your money and relock the locker. To do so, you may have to put more quarters in the slot unless you're at a park where you pay a flat fee for locker use. Lockers may seem like a nuisance, but keep in mind how little money you're spending for the freedom of not having to worry about having your valuables stolen or lost.

The park provides inner tubes/rafts for every ride where you need one, but sometimes you have to wait for people to get out of the splash pool and hand you the one they just used before you can get in line for the ride. To avoid waiting, you can rent inner tubes/rafts at the park. The down side is having to lug them everywhere you go, plus having to stash them somewhere if you want to ride the body flumes. Question: Will your tube or raft be there when you come back? Our suggestion: Don't rent.

Life vests are free for the asking. Children should leave their waterwings and other swim aids at home.

> **TIP**
>
> Before you let little ones go on a ride, make sure you've familiarized them with the splash pool where they'll end up— and how/where to get out of it. The depth should be marked, and they may have to swim to the side. You also need to emphasize that they can't linger in the splash pool because another person — perhaps a lot bigger than they are—will be landing there soon after they do.

RIDES/TERMINOLOGY

How do you know what to expect from the various rides? Granted, the names/terminology can be confusing, but basically it's simple. Here's what you need to know:

Most waterpark rides are made from fiberglass, which is molded into conventional slides, U-shaped body flumes and speed slides or encapsulated tubes. Fiberglass is surprisingly smooth and remarkably slippery when thousands of gallons of water are pumped through it every minute.

A **splash pool** is literally where you splash down at the end of a ride.

Speed slides are, obviously, fast—particularly the kind which are a straight shot to the bottom. You generally lie on your back, but you may also use an inner tube, ride a rubber toboggan or share an oversized raft with others.

Flumes are a bit slower, and they curve all over the place. Again, you may lie or sit, or use an inner tube.

A **wave pool** creates its own waves from submerged machinery at the deep end of the pool. This attraction can be dangerous for non-swimmers, who must wear a life preserver. Best advice: Keep little ones in the shallow end where you can control how much of the waves they sample. The wave pool can also be stressful for parents of kids who are old enough to like this ride, but still young enough to need supervision. It's not easy for parents to provide that supervision while they're negotiating four-foot swells themselves and ricocheting off other surfers. So use caution. But keep in mind that the place is crawling with lifeguards.

A **lazy river ride** is just that: You float, swim or ride an inner tube on a gentle current that encircles all or part of the park. This ride is so soothing, it's not unusual to see somebody float by who's fallen asleep in an inner tube. But it is possible for a family to get separated here. The problem has to do with the current and the fact that most lazy river rides have several entry/exit points. So make sure you and your kids agree ahead of time on when/where you're getting out.

PARTING SHOTS

If you're not sure about a ride, ask a park attendant or lifeguard. They'll be glad to tell you what it's like before you or your children try it. Or stand at the bottom of a ride and check out the faces of the kids getting out of the splash pool. Do they have grins on their faces or a dazed look?

There are also height guidelines to help you decide whether your child is old enough to enjoy a particular ride.

WET 'N WILD

Wet 'n Wild is located in Orlando, Fla. (take the 435 South exit off I-4). This 25-acre park features 20 adult rides and attractions plus a special children's area.

ABOUT THE PARK

Wet 'n Wild bills itself as the industry leader in high-tech thrills, and we can't argue with that.

Der Stuka is the King of the Speed Slides. Mach 5 has the best set of body flumes we've ever ridden. The Black Hole has a Space Mountain-type feel to it. And the knee ski ride is a special feature you won't find at most waterparks.

But for people with even mild cases of vertigo, the scariest or most thrilling aspect of some of the rides is the mere act of climbing to the top.

The reason the climbs are so scary is that Wet 'n Wild sits on extremely flat land. So as you climb to the top of Der Stuka, which towers 76 feet above the ground, there's nothing but air around you—meaning you're going to feel a bit like an Olympic ski jumper when you get to the takeoff platform. Those palm trees which loomed so high above as you started up the spiral staircase are now quite a ways below.

But this isn't a park just for daredevils. There's lots of easy-going fun to be had, plus splash pools which are so huge they double as swimming pools. At Mach 5, for example, the Beta Level splash pool is a perfect spot for a parent to swim or just sit and cool off while waiting for a young child to finish the ride.

In fact, Wet 'n Wild gets high marks for all its spectator areas, which offer respite for tired kids, parents who want to relax for a few minutes, and anyone who wants to bypass a ride but not lose contact with family members. Wet 'n Wild's spectator areas are well-positioned, there's usually plenty of shade and you rarely have to hunt for a deck chair.

The park's one weakness is a factor of its mid-Seventies design scheme: There's just too much exposed concrete; better landscaping would help. Nevertheless, this park was the industry's attendance leader until Disney World's Typhoon Lagoon came along. And it should continue to prosper despite TL's popularity and the birth of a new waterpark in nearby Kissimmee —both of which are covered later in this chapter.

ABOUT THE RIDES
Thrills and Chills
Der Stuka

Touted as the highest/fastest speed slide in the world. If you're not sure whether you and your kids want to brave Der Stuka's 70-degree, "free fall" slide, you can get a close look at what the ride's really like from the top of its six-story next-door neighbor, the Blue Niagra, a pair of spaghetti-like tubes which are fast enough to flatten your eyelids.

But Blue Niagra is nothing compared to Der Stuka, where it's possible to hit 35 miles per hour coming down. That's fast enough to send a rooster-tail of water into the air as your feet hit the deceleration chute at the end of the ride.

> **NOTE**
>
> **The Knee Ski** uses the same principle as water skiing, but without a boat. You kneel on a boogie board and an automated ski line pulls you around a man-made lake. Key to not wiping out: Remember to lean right as soon as the ski line jerks you off the takeoff platform. That takes up the slack in the line and allows you to sit back and enjoy the ride instead of fighting to hang on. You must wear a lifejacket and helmet, and there's a height restriction (48 inches). But this is still no ride for inexperienced swimmers/neophyte skiers. If you wipe out, it's not an easy swim to the surrounding dock and you can't just tread water because you're right in the path of the next skier.

The Most Fun
Mach 5

This serpentine-like structure anchors the Wet 'n Wild property at the corner of International Drive and Republic Drive. You pass through a half-dozen platforms on the way to the top of the seven-story tower, and along the way you can choose from two shorter runs which begin part way up (Alpha Level) or three longer runs which start at the top (Beta Level). You ride the shorter runs in an inner tube and the longer ones on a small mat. Mach 5 lines are usually long, but management claims it can handle up to 1,000 people per hour. The three runs at the top are well worth the wait—and one has an extra dip you won't expect!

The Black Hole

This black-and-chrome monstrosity snorts and blows steam like a giant spaceship that's about to take off, and the departure deck uses fiber optics and great sound effects to enhance the illusion. In reality, you descend into the bowels of the ship on one of two completely enclosed tubes that take you on a 500-foot, can't-see-the-nose-in-front-of-your-face ride. The Black Hole uses two-person rafts, so you and one of your kids can go together. If they're even mildly adventuresome, they should love it.

Kiddie Area

Be a Pepper Park

Wet 'n Wild's kiddie area isn't as shiny and modern as those at some of the newer parks; it actually looks more like a conventional school playground after a hard rain. But this one-acre area is very user-friendly. It has the usual array of small flumes, water cannons, play forts and a playground with water just inches deep.

NOTE

The Bubble Up is so simple, you can't even call it a ride; it's a giant inflated, red-white-and-blue bubble with a fountain on top. Kids who are 48 inches tall and under can haul themselves up via ropes, then slide down into a moat. Meanwhile, parents or older brothers/sisters can "shoot" them with water cannons.

WHERE TO EAT

Concession stands feature taco salad and subs, plus burgers, hot dogs and pizza. Ice cream and frozen yogurt are served in regular cones or as sidewalk sundaes. You can also bring a picnic with you. Coolers are permitted, as long as they don't contain glass or alcohol.

NEARBY FUN

Walt Disney World, Universal Studios and **Sea World** are all nearby. For information, see the THEME PARKS/AMUSEMENT PARKS chapter. Other Orlando attractions are covered in the CITIES chapter.

WHERE TO STAY

International Drive is teeming with motels, restaurants and night-spots. For more information, see "Where to Stay" in the Orlando section of the CITIES chapter.

WHEN TO GO

Wet 'n Wild is closed from January through mid-February (see the Typhoon Lagoon section in this chapter for Orlando weather information). Specials include half-price tickets for afternoon and evening admission. The park also offers two-day tickets and annual passes.

FOR MORE INFORMATION

Contact:

Wet 'n Wild
6200 International Dr., Orlando, FL 32819
(800-992-WILD or 407-351-WILD)

WHITE WATER

White Water is located on North Cobb Parkway in Marietta, Ga., eight miles northwest of the Atlanta city limits. Take exit 113 off I-75. The park features 40 rides and attractions on 35 acres.

ABOUT THE PARK

All things considered, White Water is our favorite waterpark in the Southeast. The fact that it's near the top of the industry's national attendance figures every year shows that others agree with us. White Water is also one of the most beautiful waterparks in the country.

The park gets its distinctive appearance from its location in a hilly, wooded area of suburban Atlanta. Unlike the vast majority of American waterparks, which are constructed on barren tracts of land, White Water's rides are built into those hills. So as you climb to the top of the rides, you're shaded by the trees, plus you have almost no sensation of height because the natural slope of the hills adds support and a nice design quality. As a result, White Water's flumes and slides don't look like exposed plumbing.

ABOUT THE RIDES

Thrills and Chills

Dragon's Tail Falls

A long, tall speed slide with three mini-dropoffs. You have to be 48 inches tall to ride the Dragon's Tail, and your back takes a pounding as you hit top speed. But it's not as dangerous as it looks, and most kids emerge from the splash pool with smiles on their faces.

The Most Fun

The Bermuda Triangle

A two-person raft ride which takes you on a 500-foot descent into a high-banked, darkened tunnel. How do you know which way to lean when everything's black? Pin-points of light outline the curve ahead. But the dips come without warning.

White Water Rapids

Start from the lower takeoff platform (the upper one is more flume than rapids) and get ready for a super silly ride which could be renamed "bumper tubes" due to all the crashing-into- each-other which goes on in this series of slides and swirling pools. This ride is especially good late in the day when fatigue is setting in and you're getting slap-happy.

Kiddie Area
Little Squirt's Island

In a word, "perfect." A miniature version of White Water, with 25 special attractions for children up to 48 inches tall, including mini-slides, ultra-tame body flumes and, of course, water cannons. The climbing fort, which White Water calls a "playport," is particularly ingenious.

WHERE TO EAT

White Water's burgers are tasty, and the pizza and hot dogs aren't bad either. Or is it just that we're always so famished by the time we drag ourselves away from the rides long enough to eat? Dessert lovers go for WW's funnel cakes and the park has just opened a new deli.

NEARBY FUN

White Water also owns and operates **American Adventures,** a small-fry's amusement park located on 10 acres of land between the parking lot and the main gate at White Water. AA attractions include a balloon ride, Formula K go-karts, both indoor and outdoor miniature golf and a mini-rollercoaster. But it's also a marketing come-on to get you to try White Water. If you buy a ticket to White Water and add $5, you get unlimited rides at AA (with the exception of the go-karts). Without that deal, you can drop a bundle at little AA. When we were there in the summer of 1990, the rollercoaster cost $1.20 (and the ride was over before you knew it). Nine holes of miniature golf on concrete cost $2.40. The go-karts were $4. Bottom line: We took four kids to AA and they used up $28 worth of tickets in one hour. You can control the damage slightly by purchasing admission tickets in large quantitites. But if you're smart, you'll go for the package deal. Getting all the White Water and all the American Adventures you want for less than $20 is a steal.

For information on other Atlanta attractions, see "Things to Do" in the Atlanta section of the CITIES chapter.

WHERE TO STAY

See "Where to Stay" in the Atlanta section of the CITIES chapter.

WHEN TO GO

White Water's season starts in May (weekends only), and daily operation runs from Memorial Day to Labor Day. Specials include reduced admission after 4 p.m.

FOR MORE INFORMATION

Contact:
White Water
250 N. Cobb Parkway, Marietta, GA 30062
(404-424-9283)

TYPHOON LAGOON

Typhoon Lagoon is located in Orlando, Fla., just off I-4 and midway between two other Disney attractions, MGM Studios and Pleasure Island. This 56-acre park features a dozen rides and attractions.

ABOUT THE PARK

Disney's mammoth new waterpark opened in 1989—13 years after WDW's first water attraction, River Country. And, in many ways, it was worth the wait. Typhoon Lagoon is four times the size of River Country, and it has a resort-like feeling that no other waterpark in the Southeast has. Disney accomplishes this in a variety of ways:

▲ Tropical design scheme.
   100-foot-high Mt. Mayday is a terrific backdrop, and the main swimming/wave pool area is surrounded by palm trees and white sand.

▲ Heavily-themed incidentals.
   The bleached-out wooden refreshment shacks look authentically sea-worn, and there's flotsam floating in the lazy river.

▲ Adult amenities.
   Unlike most waterparks in the U.S., Typhoon Lagoon serves alcoholic drinks.

On the negative side, Typhoon Lagoon needs more rides or additional runs to accommodate the tremendous number of people brought in by the Disney name. It took us approximately two hours to sample Typhoon Lagoon's three whitewater raft rides: Mayday Falls, Keelhall Falls and Gangplank Falls. The wait was 35-40 minutes for each. Part of the slowdown: Having to wait for riders to finish the run so they could hand us their rafts. Simple solution: Provide more rafts.

Please note: Walt Disney World passports won't do you any good at Typhoon Lagoon, which requires a separate admission.

ABOUT THE RIDES

Thrills and Chills

Humunga Kowabunga

Riders reach a speed of 30 mph on this 214-foot speed slide, which has a vertical drop of 51 feet and an added wrinkle: You roar through a darkened cave on the way down. If you're concerned about whether your kids should go on this ride, keep in mind that pregnant women aren't allowed to—a prohibition which holds true on most of the rides at TL. You'll also see signs which advise that riders be free of back trouble, heart conditions and other physical limitations.

The Most Fun
Wave Pool
Every 90 seconds, Typhoon Lagoon sends out a four-foot "tidal wave" that's perfect for body and inflatable raft surfing. Drawback: Who wants to wait that long between waves?

Kiddie Area
Ketchakiddie Creek
The kids' area is okay—but not the wonderland you expect from Disney. It includes a short raft ride, two small water slides (one shaped like a whale) and some mini-geysers.

NOTE

Shark Reef, the saltwater snorkeling area, was a bit of a disappointment to us. For one thing, it's time-consuming just renting and getting checked out in your gear (flippers, mask and snorkel). Then there's the wait for one group to finish so you can have your turn looking at snapper, angelfish, groupers and parrot fish. Best advice: If you really want to go snorkeling, go to Biscayne (Fla.) National Park, where you'll see gobs of tropical fish in a gorgeous natural environment. For more information, see the NATIONAL PARKS chapter.

WHERE TO EAT
Philly cheese sandwiches and foot-long hot dogs make the bill of fare here a cut above the competition. Plus, Disney bartenders will fix you a pina colada or reach into a mound of ice and grab you a wine cooler or an ice-cold can of beer. Now that's something you can't get at the Magic Kingdom.

NEARBY FUN
Disney's theme parks, plus **Universal Studios** and **Sea World** are all nearby. For more information on these Orlando attractions, see the THEME PARKS/AMUSEMENT PARKS chapter. For information on other attractions, see "Things to Do" in the Orlando section of the CITIES chapter.

WHERE TO STAY
For lodging information, see "Where to Stay" in both the Orlando

section of the CITIES chapter and the Magic Kingdom section of the THEME PARKS/AMUSEMENT PARKS chapter.

WHEN TO GO

Typhoon Lagoon is open from February through December (9 a.m.- 5 p.m.), but keep in mind that Orlando is not Miami. The average high temperature—72 in February and 72 in December—may be too cool for some would-be waterparkers. March and November, both with average highs of 76, are the only other months when daytime temps don't reach the 80-90 degree range. Specials include both two-day and annual passes.

FOR MORE INFORMATION

Contact:

Typhoon Lagoon
Walt Disney World, Lake Buena Vista, FL 32830-1000
(407-824-4321)

BEST OF THE REST

If your travel plans don't include Orlando or Atlanta, you're still in luck when it comes to waterparks because they've sprung up all over the Southeast. Here's a state-by-state sample in alphabetical order (by state):

Waterville USA, Gulf Shores, Ala.

Located less than a mile from the Gulf of Mexico, this 17-acre layout has seven waterslides, a wave pool and a lazy river ride. There's also mini golf and go-karts (Hwy. 59, 205-948-2106).

Water Mania, Kissimmee, Fla.

Located 1.5 miles east of Walt Disney World, Water Mania has a full complement of rides, including The Double Berserker, a pair of identical, side-by-side speed slides where family members can race each other to the bottom (6073 W. Hwy. 192, 407-396-2626 or 800-527-3092).

Atlantis, The Water Kingdom, Hollywood, Fla.

The first park in the region to mix conventional amusement park rides (roller coasters, etc.) with water attractions. Don't miss The Slidewinder, which has eight different slides emanating from its seven-story tower. Adults can have a cocktail or just relax at the Oasis Spa, where huge jacuzzis hold 10-20 people (2700 Stirling Rd., 305-926-1000).

Shipwreck Island, Panama City Beach, Fla.

Located in the same complex as the Miracle Strip Amusement Park, this tiny seven-acre park is beautifully landscaped and packed with water fun. There's a 35-mph speed slide, a 370-foot tube ride, plus a wave pool, a lazy river and Tadpole Hole, a special area for kids (12000 W. Hwy. 98-A, 904-234-0368).

Adventure Island, Tampa, Fla.

This 22-acre sister property of Busch Gardens specializes in slides—the Everglides high-speed sensation, the twists and turns of the Water Moccasin or the 450-foot Barratuba tube ride. If you visit Busch Gardens first, you can get discount coupons for Adventure Island (4545 Bougainvillea Ave., 813-971-7978).

Summer Waves, Jekyll Island, Ga.

A smallish park (11 acres), but one with a lot of nice features: wave pool, lazy river ride, two triple-drop speed slides, a pair of serpentine slides and a kids' area. Plus, it's near the beach (375 Riverview Dr., 912-635-2074, 800-841-6586 or, in Georgia, 800-342-1042).

RipTide Reef, Charlotte, N.C.

For information on this six-acre waterpark, see "About the Park" in the Carowinds section of the THEME PARKS/AMUSEMENT PARKS chapter.

Myrtle Waves, Myrtle Beach, S.C.

The largest waterpark on the east coast, and the place to go if you want to combine waterparking and the beach. Excitement revolves around a pair of inner tube slides, King Cobra and Python, which make 360-degrees turns along their 200-foot run (U.S. Hwy. 17 Bypass at 10th Ave. N., 803-448-1026).

Ogle's Water Park, Pigeon Forge, Tenn.

Located near Dollywood in the foothills of the Smokies, Ogle's features one giant figure-eight-shaped waterslide called Suicide and another one called Twin Twister, which has four 360-degree turns on its 284-foot route (Hwy. 441 N., 615-453-8741).

Water Country USA, Williamsburg, Va.

Nestled in a hilly, hardwood forest, everything is fun here —from the Sea Lion show to appearances by the U.S. High Diving Team. But don't miss the Double Rampage, where you ride a rubber sled down a 75-foot chute and 120 feet across the top of the splash pool before you come to a stop. Water Country also offers a unique sneak-a-peek tour: Sample the park for 30 minutes; if you don't like it, you get your money back. But refund requests are few and far between (Rte. 199, just off I-64 at exit 57-B, 804-229-9300).

APPENDIX 1: *Quick Guide to Airports in the Southeast*

HARTSFIELD-ATLANTA INTERNATIONAL AIRPORT

Atlanta, GA (404-530-6600)

This very big, very busy airport is located nine miles south of Atlanta.

Getting around—Two terminals, North and South, are joined by connecting "bridges." The terminals each feed four domestic concourses (A is the closest; D the furthest). A subway and a moving sidewalk connect concourses and terminals.

Information/assistance—A Georgia Welcome Station is located at the escalator exit in the terminal complex. Traveler's Aid is in the North terminal.

Restaurants/snack bars—Concourses A, B and C have cafeteria-style snack bars and gourmet ice cream shops. Concourse D has a frozen yogurt stand. A full-service restaurant is located on the eastern bridge of the terminal complex. Snack shops are everywhere.

Killing time—A game room/video arcade is located in the terminal complex.

CHARLOTTE/DOUGLAS INTERNATIONAL AIRPORT

Charlotte, NC (704-359-4013)

A major hub of USAir, this airport has experienced tremendous growth since deregulation. Expect construction to be underway for some time to come.

Getting around—The terminal is a two-level complex with four concourses radiating outward. Most passenger traffic is concentrated in B and C concourses.

Information/assistance—An information booth—open around-the-clock—is located on the upper level of the main terminal.

Restaurants/snack bars—Pizza Strada (open daily 7 a.m.-9 p.m.) is in the main terminal. Stand-up snack bars are located throughout the complex.

Nursery/changing rooms—Adjacent to the restrooms in the ground floor area.

Killing time—Video game room (open 24 hours) is on the upper level.

MEMPHIS INTERNATIONAL AIRPORT

Memphis, TN (901-922-8000)

Located nine miles southeast of Memphis, this airport is known as "Mid-America's Gateway to the World." Its geographic location makes it a natural multi-regional center.

Getting around—Memphis International has three terminals (A, B, C), with B considered the main terminal. Each terminal has a concourse and gates are numbered respectively.

Information/assistance—The Tele-Trip booth in the terminal B ticket lobby functions as an information reference point.

Restaurants/snack bars—There are 22 eating places throughout the airport, ranging from casual snack bars to a Polynesian restaurant (open daily 11 a.m.-9 p.m.).

Nursery/changing room—Located on the west end of terminal B ticket lobby.

Killing time—The Aviation Historical Room in the terminal B ticket lobby is free and open 24 hours a day. Photos, memorabilia and models highlighting Memphis aviation are displayed.

MIAMI INTERNATIONAL AIRPORT

Miami, FL (305-876-7000)

This is the site of the first passenger complex as we know airports today, built by Pan Am in 1929. The old terminal was demolished in the early Sixties to make way for the present facilities. Today, Miami International handles more international travelers than any other U.S. airport except JFK.

Getting around—A U-shaped terminal feeds passengers onto seven concourses (B-H). Moving sidewalks, called Skyriders, on the third level connect the parking garages to the terminal and provide easy transport between concourses. The focal point of activity is concourse E.

Information/assistance—A 24-hour multilingual booth is centrally located at the entrance of concourse E. Information assistance phones are located on pillars throughout the complex.

Restaurants/snack bars—Delis, seafood bars, buffeterias and food kiosks/carts abound. The snack bar at concourse F is open 24 hours; most others close around 9 p.m. The rooftop restaurant, Top of the Port, is expensive. There's an ice cream parlor in concourse H.

Nursery/changing rooms—Located in concourse E and in the International Terminal.

Killing time—Ride out to the International Terminal and go to the fourth level sundeck to watch flight operations. The Concorde lands here three times a week. There's also an historical aviation exhibit at the entrance of concourse E and a video game room in concourse H.

ORLANDO INTERNATIONAL AIRPORT
Orlando, FL (407-825-2001)

What once was McCoy Air Force Base has now become the second largest airport in the nation (behind Dallas-Ft. Worth). With lots of greenery and huge skylights above the Great Hall of the main terminal, the facility has a nice airy feel. The first simultaneous landings of Concordes took place here in 1982, when Disney's EPCOT opened.

Getting around—Three Airside Terminals are joined to the main terminal by automatic shuttle cars. Each Airside has basic amenities, but the main terminal has more complete services, most of which are clustered in the Great Hall on the third level. The newest terminal, leased exclusively by Delta Air Lines, opened in 1990.

Information/assistance—There's a kiosk in the center of the Great Hall (open daily 7 a.m.-11 p.m.). You can also pick up one of the white in-terminal phones located on just about every pillar. Disney World and Sea World have information booths in the Great Hall. And if you need transportation from the airport, check the "rate bank" of fares on level 2.

Restaurants/snack bars—Each Airside has a full-service restaurant/snack bar. At the Orlando Marketplace in the Great Hall you'll find a variety of offerings by concessionaires. At Beauregard's in the mezzanine you can sample gator tail!

Nursery/changing rooms—In Airsides only.

Killing time—The game room in the Great Hall is open 8 a.m.-midnight.

TAMPA INTERNATIONAL AIRPORT
Tampa, FL (813-870-8700)

One of Tampa's claims to fame is that it was the first airport to install the now standard people-mover trainway in 1971. Though its growth has been slowed by its proximity to Orlando International, this airport is popular with travelers for its slick efficiency.

Getting around—The main terminal has three levels: ground transportation and baggage claims are on level 1, ticketing on level 2, shops and restaurants on level 3. Elevated, automatic trains run from level 3 to airside buildings, each of which has basic amenities.

Information/assistance—Guide stations are at the top of each escalator in the main terminal; Travelers Aid is on level 3 (9 a.m.-9 p.m. daily). Over 100 white paging response and emergency phones are located on pillars in key passageways.

Restaurants/snack bars—The main terminal has several sit-down eateries; each airside has a snack bar. The Vintage Confectionary features triple-scoop waffle cones and other goodies.

Nursery/changing room—On level 3 of the main terminal.

Killing time—Tampa International offers two TV lounges, plus some of the best viewing areas at any airport. There's also a full-fledged bookstore (open daily 7 a.m.-10 p.m.).

APPENDIX 2: *Amtrak Routes to Southeast Destinations*

COLONIAL: Between Boston and Williamsburg, Norfolk and Virginia Beach, VA

VIRGINIAN: Between New York and Richmond, VA

These two routes run almost parallel to each other, connecting in New York and again in Richmond. The Colonial goes on to Newport News, Va., via Williamsburg, where the station is within walking distance of the restored colonial area. Thruway bus service can then take you from Newport News through Norfolk to Virginia Beach.

There are no sleeping cars on either route. The Colonial has a combination dining/lounge car where you can get pre-prepared tray meals. The Virginian has a cafe where you can buy sandwiches and snacks.

Hotel packages are offered at Virginia Beach and Williamsburg.

SILVER SERVICE: Between New York and Tampa and Miami, FL

PALMETTO: Between New York and Savannah, GA, and Jacksonville, FL

Both routes run from New York to Jacksonville, with Silver Service making an additional loop through parts of North and South Carolina and also continuing on from Jacksonville through Orlando to West Palm Beach and Miami. Thruway bus service connects just outside the Orlando area and can take you to Gulf Coast beach areas such as St. Petersburg and Sarasota. Also, in Florence, S.C.—a stop on both routes—you can get connecting train service on another carrier to Myrtle Beach.

In addition to coach cars, the Palmetto has a lounge car with tray meal service, while Silver Service (Silver Meteor and Silver Star) offers a buffet-style dining car, a lounge car, and a choice of sleeping cars or slumbercoaches.

Hotel packages are available for Orlando-Kissimmee, Tampa and Miami Beach, as well as Virginia Beach and Williamsburg. In addition, tour packages are offered for Miami Beach and Orlando. Besides hotel accommodations, these include various extras—like a two-hour boat cruise (Miami Beach) and Walt Disney World tickets (Orlando).

AUTO TRAIN: Between Washington, DC, and Florida

The Auto Train will take you, your car, and all the baggage you pack in your car non-stop from Lorton, Va. (just outside of Washington, D.C.) to Sanford, Fla. (near Orlando). Included in the price of your ticket is complimentary dinner in the buffet dining car and continental breakfast the next morning. A feature-length movie is shown after dinner or you can look at the stars from the glass-topped dome car. Sleeping accommodations include two-bedroom suites, which contain four berths. If you want to save money by sleeping in the coach car, blankets and pillows are provided.

One problem with the Auto Train is that you must arrive two hours before departure, which is a lot of time to kill. Plan some pre-boarding activities for the kids or your trip is likely to get off to a bad start.

Hotel packages are available for Orlando-Kissimee, Tampa and Miami Beach.

CARDINAL: Between New York and Chicago, through Washington, DC, with stops in Virginia

This route offers spectacular scenery through Blue Ridge Mountain country. To appreciate it, however, you need to be traveling from west to east. In the other direction, you go through the area at night. Among the stops along this route is Staunton, Va., where you'll find the Museum of American Frontier Culture (see HISTORY PLACES chapter).

The Cardinal has sleeping cars and slumbercoaches, plus a full-service dining car and a lounge car.

CRESCENT: Between New York and New Orleans through Atlanta

GULF BREEZE: Between Birmingham and Mobile, AL, with through service to New York

Gulf Breeze, one of Amtrak's newest routes, is an extension of the Crescent and takes you through Alabama to the Gulf Coast city of Mobile. The Crescent stops in six Southeastern states before reaching New Orleans.

Sleeping cars and slumbercoaches are available. Full-service dining is offered on the Crescent, tray-meal service on the Gulf Breeze.

Hotel packages are available for Atlanta, Mobile and New Orleans. A number of tour packages are offered on this route, but they are not particularly well-suited for children.

CITY OF NEW ORLEANS: Between Chicago and New Orleans through Memphis and Jackson, MS

The City of New Orleans follows the Mississippi River Basin. It passes through the western end of Kentucky and Tennessee, then bisects Mississippi on the way to New Orleans.

Features on this route include a dome coach, sleeping cars, a lounge car and tray-meal service.

A three-day tour package is offered for Memphis.

For details on schedules and fares, which are subject to change, call Amtrak at 1-800-USA-RAIL.

APPENDIX 3: *State Tourism Offices*

You may want to contact the following state agencies before setting off on your vacation. Most will provide enticing full-color travel guides for their respective states and such other freebies as highway maps and calendars of events. The direct phone numbers listed are answered during business hours; you can call the 800 numbers any time.

ALABAMA
Bureau of Tourism & Travel
532 South Perry St.
Montgomery, AL 36104
205-242-4169
800-ALABAMA

FLORIDA
Division of Tourism
126 Van Buren St.
Tallahassee, FL 32399
904-487-1462

GEORGIA
Tourism Division
PO Box 1776
Atlanta, GA 30301
404-656-3590
800-847-4842

KENTUCKY
Department of Travel
Development
Capital Plaza Tower
Frankfort, KY 40601
502-564-4930
800-225-TRIP

NORTH CAROLINA
Division of Travel and
Tourism
430 N. Salisbury St.
Raleigh, NC 27611
919-733-4171
800-VISITNC

SOUTH CAROLINA
Division of Tourism
PO Box 71
Columbia, SC 29202
803-734-0235

TENNESSEE
Tourist Development
PO Box 23170
Nashville, TN 37204-3170
615-741-2158

VIRGINIA
Division of Tourism
1021 East Cary St.
Richmond, VA 23219
804-786-4484
800-847-4882

APPENDIX 4: *Hotel/Motel Toll-free Numbers*

You can use the 800-numbers listed below to save yourself a phone charge when making reservations with any of these hotel/motel chains. All have properties in the Southeast. You can also use these numbers to request a free directory. Dial "1" before each number.

Best Western
800-528-1234

Budgetel Inns
800-4-BUDGET

Clarion Hotels and Resorts
800-CLARION

Comfort Inns and Suites
800-228-5150

Compri Hotels
800-4-COMPRI

Courtyards by Marriott
800-321-2211

Days Inns, Hotels, Suites
and Daystops
800-325-2525

Doubletree
800-528-0444

Econo Lodges of America
800-446-6900

Economy Inns of America
800-826-0778 (except
FL)
800-423-3018 (FL)

Embassy Suites
800-EMBASSY

Fairfield Inn
800-228-2800

Friendship Inns of America
800-453-4511

Guest Quarters
800-424-2900

Hampton Inn
800-HAMPTON

Harley Hotels
800-321-2323

Hawthorne Suites
800-527-2360

Hilton Hotels
800-HILTONS

Holiday Inns
800-HOLIDAY

Howard Johnson
800-654-2000

Hyatt
800-228-9000

La Quinta Motor Inns
800-531-5900

Marriott Hotels, Resorts
and Suites
800-228-9290

Master Hosts Inn
800-251-1962

Omni Hotels
800-843-6664

Park Inns
800-437-PARK

Quality Inns, Hotels and
Suites
800-228-5151

Radisson
800-333-3333

Ramada Inns
800-2-RAMADA

Red Carpet/Scottish Inns
800-251-1962

Red Roof Inns
800-843-7663

Regal 8 Inn
800-851-8888

Residence Inns by
Marriott
800-331-3131

Ritz-Carlton
800-241-3333

Rodeway Inns International
800-228-2000

Sheraton Hotels, Suites
and Inns
800-325-3535

Sleep Inn
800-62-SLEEP

Sonesta Hotels
800-343-7170

Stouffer Hotels and
Resorts
800-HOTELS-1

Super 8 Motels
800-843-1991

Travelodge / Viscount Hotels
800-255-3050

Treadway Inns
800-873-2392

Westin Hotels
800-228-3000

Wyndham Hotels
800-822-4200

INDEX